# The Jihad Factory
## Pakistan's Islamic Revolution

# THE JIHAD FACTORY

## PAKISTAN's ISLAMIC REVOLUTION

Dr. (Prof.) Anil K. Saxena

GAURAV BOOK CENTRE PVT LTD

DELHI

*Publisher*
**GAURAV BOOK CENTRE PVT LTD**
4832/24,Prahlad Lane,S-207 Ansari
Road, Daryaganj, Delhi-110002
Ph.: 43570976, 23278261
Email: gauravbookcentre@gmail.com

**Edition:** 2015



**ISBN:** 978-93-83316-15-1

Laser Typesetting
**JEE-VEE Graphics,** Delhi

**Price:** 1195/-

*Printed*
Vikas Computers, Delhi

# Contents

# Preface

Pakistan's jihad factories - mixed with some of the usual mainstream media twaddle, but still containing some useful information. The beginnings of Jihad are traced back to the words and actions of Muhammad and the Quran.

Jihad means "to struggle in the way of Allah". *Jihad* appears 41 times in the Quran and frequently in the idiomatic expression "striving in the way of God *(al-jihad fi sabilAllah)*". A person engaged in jihad is called a *mujahid;* the plural is mujahideen. Jihad is an important religious duty for Muslims. A minority among the Sunni scholars sometimes refer to this duty as the sixth pillar of Islam, though it occupies no such official status. In Twelver Shi'a Islam, however, Jihad is one of the 10 Practices of the Religion. Ahmadi Muslims consider only defensive jihad to be permissible while rejecting offensive jihad.

Pakistan is situated in a region where fundamentalism has been posed, of late, as one of the most threatening questions. The process initiated by the Islamic revolution in Iran has even been internationalised by the Taliban's victory in Afghanistan. At the same time, the rise of Hindu radicalism in India has further complicated the situation in Pakistan. Recently Islamic fundamentalism has risen as an alternative political phenomenon not only in Pakistan but also in the entire Muslim world. Islamic fundamentalism in Pakistan is partly a link of this international phenomenon and partly caused by specific local reasons. When analysing Islamic fundamentalism, one must understand that the religion of Islam and Islamic fundamentalism are not one and the same thing. Islamic fundamentalism is a reactionary, non-scientific movement aimed at returning society to a centuries-old social set-up, defying all material and historical factors. It is an attempt to roll back the wheel of history.

Pakistan's rule as the epicenter of jihad or Islamic terrorism around the world, is open to charges of bias, dubious information, non-credible sources, or mouthing handouts given by intelligence agencies like RAW or CIA. The state-sponsored jihadist culture provided them a safe haven in Pakistan.

*—Editor*

# 1

# Introduction to Jihad

Jihad, an Islamic term, is a religious duty of Muslims. In Arabic, the word *jihâd* translates as a noun meaning "struggle". The word jihad appears in 23 Quranic verses. Within the context of the classical Islam, particularly the Shiahs beliefs, it refers to struggle against those who do not believe in the Abrahamic God (Allah). However, the word has even wider implications.

Jihad means "to struggle in the way of Allah". *Jihad* appears 41 times in the Quran and frequently in the idiomatic expression "striving in the way of God *(al-jihad fi sabilAllah)*". A person engaged in jihad is called a *mujahid;* the plural is mujahideen. Jihad is an important religious duty for Muslims. A minority among the Sunni scholars sometimes refer to this duty as the sixth pillar of Islam, though it occupies no such official status. In Twelver Shi'a Islam, however, Jihad is one of the 10 Practices of the Religion. Ahmadi Muslims consider only defensive jihad to be permissible while rejecting offensive jihad.

There are two commonly accepted meanings of jihad: an inner spiritual struggle and an outer physical struggle. The "greater jihad" is the inner struggle by a believer to fulfil his religious duties. This non-violent meaning is stressed by both Muslim and non-Muslim authors. However, there is consensus amongst Islamic scholars that the concept of jihad will always include armed struggle against persecution and oppression.

The "lesser jihad" is the physical struggle against the enemies of Islam. This physical struggle can take a violent form or a non-violent form. The proponents of the violent form translate jihad as "holy war", although some Islamic studies scholars disagree. The *Dictionary of Islam* and British-American orientalist Bernard Lewis both argue jihad has a military meaning in the large majority of cases. Some scholars maintain non-violent ways to struggle against the enemies of Islam. An example of this is written debate, often characterized as "jihad of the pen".

According to the BBC, a third meaning of jihad is the struggle to build a good society. In a commentary of the hadith Sahih Muslim, entitled al-Minhaj, the medieval Islamicscholar Yahya ibn Sharaf al-Nawawi stated that "one of the collective duties of the community as a whole (fard kifaya) is to lodge a valid protest, to solve problems of religion, to have knowledge of Divine Law, to command what is right and forbid wrong conduct".

## ORIGINS

The beginnings of Jihad are traced back to the words and actions of Muhammad and the Quran. This encourages the use of Jihad against non-Muslims. The Quran, however, never uses the term Jihad for fighting and combat in the name of Allah; qital is used to mean "fighting." Jihad in the Quran was originally intended for the nearby neighbors of the Muslims, but as time passed and more enemies arose, the Quranic statements supporting Jihad were updated for the new adversaries. The first documentation of the law of Jihad was written by 'Abd al-Rahman al-Awza'i and Muhammad ibn al-Hasan al-Shaybani. The document grew out of debates that had surfaced ever since Muhammad's death.

### *Usage of the Term*

In Modern Standard Arabic, *jihad* is one of the correct terms for a struggle for any cause, violent or not, religious or secular. The terminology is also applied to the fight for women's liberation.

The term 'jihad' has accrued both violent and non-violent meanings. It can simply mean striving to live a moral and virtuous life, spreading and defending Islam as well as fighting injustice and oppression, among other things. The relative importance of these two forms of jihad is a matter of controversy. A poll by

Gallup showed that a "significant majority" of Muslim Indonesians define the term to mean "sacrificing one's life for the sake of Islam/ God/a just cause" or "fighting against the opponents of Islam".

In Lebanon, Kuwait, Jordan, and Morocco, the majority used the term to mean "duty toward God", a "divine duty", or a "worship of God", with no militaristic connotations. Other responses referenced, in descending order of prevalence:

- "A commitment to hard work" and "achieving one's goals in life"
- "Struggling to achieve a noble cause"
- "Promoting peace, harmony or cooperation, and assisting others"
- "Living the principles of Islam"

## Distinction of "Greater" and "Lesser" Jihad

In his work, *The History of Baghdad*, Al-Khatib al-Baghdadi, an 11th-century Islamic scholar, referenced a statement by the companion of Muhammad Jabir ibn Abd-Allah.

The reference stated that Jabir said, "The Prophet... returned from one of his battles, and thereupon told us, 'You have arrived with an excellent arrival, you have come from the Lesser Jihad to the Greater Jihad—the striving of a servant (of Allah) against his desires (holy war)."

This reference gave rise to the distinguishing of two forms of jihad: "greater" and "lesser". Some Islamic scholars dispute the authenticity of this reference and consider the meaning of jihad as a holy war to be more important.

According to the Muslim Jurist Ibn Hajar al-Asqalani, the quote in which Muhammad is reported to have said that greater Jihad is the inner struggle, is from an unreliable source:

"This saying is widespread and it is a saying by Ibrahim ibn Ablah according to Nisa'i in al-Kuna. Ghazali mentions it in the Ihya' and al-`Iraqi said that Bayhaqi related it on the authority of Jabir and said: There is weakness in its chain of transmission." Hajar al Asqalani, Tasdid al-qaws, see also Kashf al-Khafaa'.

### The best of Jihad

During the Arab Spring, many peaceful demonstrations in the Arab world faced violence and gunfire by their government's regime. The gunfire encouraged the protesters and led them to revolutions, based on their strong faith in what is called "the best of jihad". The best of jihad was encouraged by their prophet, Muhammad, saying:

"The best Jihad is the word of Justice in front of the oppressive Sultan [ruler]." In a battlefield context, when *jihad* is used to denote warfare, Ibn Núhaas cited the following hadith to explain the meaning of the "best Jihad":

Ibn Habbaan narrates: The Messenger of Allah was asked about the best jihad. He said: "The best jihad is the one in which your horse is slain and your blood is spilled." In a similarly worded Hadith to the one above, Ibn Nuhaas cited a hadith from Musnad Ahmad ibn Hanbal, where it states that the highest kind of Jihad, is "The person who is killed whilst spilling the last of his blood."(Ahmed 4/144)

It has also been reported that Muhammad considered performing hajj to be the best jihad for Muslim women.

### Spiritual Struggle

Muslim scholar Mahmoud Ayoub states that "The goal of true *jihad* is to attain a harmony between *islam* (submission), *iman* (faith), and *ihsan* (righteous living)." In modern times, Pakistani scholar and professor Fazlur Rahman Malik has used the term to describe the struggle to establish "just moral-social order", while President Habib Bourguiba of Tunisia has used it to describe the struggle for economic development in that country.

### Warfare (Jihad bil Saif)

Within classical Islamic jurisprudence—the development of which is to be dated into the first few centuries after the prophet's death —jihad is the only form of warfare permissible under Islamic law, and may consist in wars against unbelievers, apostates, rebels, highway robbers and dissenters renouncing the authority of Islam. The primary aim of jihad as warfare is not the conversion of non-

Muslims to Islam by force, but rather the expansion and defense of the Islamic state. In later centuries, especially in the course of the colonization of large parts of the Muslim world, emphasis has been put on non-militant aspects of the jihad. Today, some Muslim authors only recognize wars with the aim of territorial defense as well as the defense of religious freedom as legitimate.

Whether the Quran sanctions defensive warfare only or commands an all out war against non-Muslims depends on the interpretation of the relevant passages. This is because it does not explicitly state the aims of the war Muslims are obliged to wage; the passages concerning *jihad* rather aim at promoting fighters for the Islamic cause and do not discuss military ethics.

In the classical manuals of Islamic jurisprudence, the rules associated with armed warfare are covered at great length. Such rules include not killing women, children and non-combatants, as well as not damaging cultivated or residential areas.

More recently, modern Muslims have tried to re-interpret the Islamic sources, stressing that Jihad is essentially defensive warfare aimed at protecting Muslims and Islam.

Although some Islamic scholars have differed on the implementation of Jihad, there is consensus amongst them that the concept of jihad will always include armed struggle against persecution and oppression.

## Debate

Controversy has arisen over whether the usage of the term *jihad* without further explanation refers to military combat, and whether some have used confusion over the definition of the term to their advantage.

Middle East historian Bernard Lewis argues that "the overwhelming majority of classical theologians, jurists, and traditionalists (specialists in the hadith) understood the obligation of jihad in a military sense." Furthermore, Lewis maintains that for most of the recorded history of Islam, from the lifetime of the Prophet Muhammadonward, the word jihad was used in a primarily military sense.

### *Resistance against Globalization*

Benjamin R. Barber used the term Jihad to point out the resistant movement against globalization (which he refers to as 'McWorld') as well as the modern-institutionalization of nation states. The forces of 'Jihad' come from fundamentalist ethnic groups who want to protect their traditions, heritage and identity from modernization and universalized markets. The resistance has led to fragmented, small-scale violent conflicts between cultures, peoples and tribes. Although 'Jihad' strengthens the solidarity within the resisting group, it obeys to hierarchy and cannot tolerate foreign influence, which discourages democracy.

## AN IN-DEPTH ANALYSIS OF JIHADISM

Jihad is an Arabic word that literally means "combat" or "striving" and jihad is sometimes regarded along with allegiance to the Iman as the violent Sixth Pillar of Islam, although orthodox Islam only recognizes Five Pillars. The idea of jihad being the violent Sixth Pillar comes from the Khawarij sect, which was part of the fundamentalist Islamism movement that started in the early 20th Century.

The Khawarij sect is named after Dhul-Khuwaysarah, a man that Muhammad prophesied would have an overprotective love of religion. The Khawariji interpretation of the role of excommunication is completely the opposite of the Salafist interpretation of excommunication (*takfir*). Salafism is rather restricted about who should be declared an infidel and therefore excommunicated. Followers of the Khawariji interpretation, or Jihadists, see few if any restrictions on who can be declared an infidel, and therefore justify unrestricted warfare or terrorism against infidels. Even traditional Qur'anic interpretations hold that those who reject Islam reject God, and one of the principal characteristics of rejecting God (*kufr*) is the inclination toward violence and oppression, encapsulated by the broad concept *zulm*, which means transgression against one's own soul or human nature. Now, many if not most Muslims reject the duty to propagate Islam by force and limit jihad to self-defence (Hashmi 2006), but then again, there is no such thing as a pacifist movement in Islam, and most Muslims respect the necessity of a continuous tension between incessant warfare and peace.

There is some controversy in Islamic thought as to whether jihad can be declared before or after an enemy attacks, or in other words, in a pre-emptive strike or in self-defence. A strict and literal reading of the Qur'an says self-defence only, but Islamic law has always justified a first-strike position. Just saying that women ought to have a right to vote is a crime of violence against all of Islam, and this can trigger a Jihadist reaction against not only the person who said that, but against whomever they got that idea from — a kind of scorched earth policy or nipping things in the bud. The basis for most anti-Americanism among Muslim extremists is part of the notion that any country that would give women the right to vote, or all minorities equal rights, is probably a country populated by infidels who are attacking Islam with crimes of violence. It may be important to note the quite popular opinion in the Muslim world that it was under attack by America first. Jihad is also part of the name in at least two terrorist groups that make up the shadowy umbrella group called Islamic Jihad, which has millions of supporters throughout the Islamic world because these supporters agree with militaristic interpretations of jihad. The two main groups are the Egyptian Islamic Jihad and the Palestinian Islamic Jihad, both formed in the mid-1970s with origins going back to the 1928 Muslim Brotherhood.

Suicide bombings (a tactic that came into popularity around 1983) are a trademark of jihadists. The religious element involved is that believers think they will attain a heavenly reward for their sacrifice. The political element involved is that it sends a message of how desperate and passionate the believers are. Expert opinion is mixed on the effectiveness of suicide bombing as a strategy of asymmetric warfare. Experts also agree that it is difficult if not impossible to profile a suicide bomber. Some say it ultimately backfires by turning public opinion against the bombers and those who support them. Support often comes in the form of charitable donations to the family of suicide bombers. Many poor parents in the Arab world may be inclined to encourage their children to become suicide bombers. For its photogenic value in a globalized world of mass communication, suicide bombing is a weapon of genius.

### The Guarantee of Heaven for Islamic Martyrs

Suicide, under orthodox Islam, is a sin. However, Jihadists consider the circumstances to cleanse the sin, making it the act of a holy martyr, not a suicide. The actual percentage of Muslims who agree with this interpretation is hotly disputed, as is the concept of martyrdom. A martyr is technically someone who dies for their religious faith, but the outcome also matters, in terms of who gets to write history. Martyrdom, therefore, is intimately tied up with Islamic arrogance that their goal of religious domination will be victorious in the end. The study of all things in the end is known by the religious term *eschatology,* and Islam contains strong elements of Zoroastrianism, the world's first religion to have a full-blown eschatology. Many experts believe that Zoroastrianism, a religion that existed from 1500 BC to 700 AD in Persia and still popular in parts of Iran and India, had a significant impact on Islam. In a nutshell, the basic idea that Zoraster had is that earth is a battlefield between good and evil, and that good is destined to win out over evil, and anyone who allies themselves with good is guaranteed to be part of this destiny. What Mohammed took from this is the idea that whoever martyrs themselves for the sake of good goes directly to a special place in heaven, or in a worst case scenario, goes to hell for a short time and then goes to heaven. Satan, as the embodiment of evil, also plays a big role, as a real entity who tempts people to renounce their faith, and the martyr with the most guarantee of a special place in heaven is the one who fights Satan.

Demonizing America as the "Great Satan" makes it a fitting opponent in the predestined war between good and evil. Heaven is more than a transcendental place to Muslims. Orthodox Islamic eschatology holds that the afterlife is physical; people are said to have bodies, and they will experience material pleasures, including unlimited food, drink and sex. Heaven is known to some Muslims as the Gardens of Paradise where unimaginable spiritual and sensual pleasures await. To other Muslims, the rewards are quite imaginable, such as the 72 virgins waiting to have sex with each martyr every day (their hymens miraculously regrow the next day). This account was popularized by the media in 2001 when a CBS reporter interviewed a Hamas recruiter who talked about it. According to one translation, the Koran 78:31 reads *"As for the righteous, they shall surely triumph. Theirs shall be gardens and vineyards, and high-bosomed virgins for companions."* Some Islamic scholars argue this is a false translation, and that passages like that are referring to angels or heavenly beings. Other Islamic scholars argue it's only 70 virgins instead of 72, and that your wife is always one of them. Yet other Islamic scholars say the whole thing is intended to be taken in a transcendental way, the pleasures of heaven being so great it's like having an eternal erection or first-time sex all the time.

## THE MEANING OF THE CONCEPT OF "JIHAD"

Another concept that deserves clarification due in the context of our discussion is that of "jihad". The exact meaning of "Jihad" is "effort". Thus, in Islam, "to carry out jihad" is "to show effort, to struggle". The Prophet Muhammad explained that "the greatest jihad is the one a person carries out against his lower soul". What is meant by "lower soul" here is selfish desires and ambitions.

Assessed from the Qur'anic point of view, the word "jihad" can also mean a struggle carried out on intellectual grounds against those who oppress people, treat them unjustly, subject them to torture and cruelty and violate legitimate human rights. The purpose of this struggle is to bring about justice, peace and equality. Apart from these ideological and spiritual meanings, struggle in the physical sense is also considered as "jihad". However, as explained above, this has to be a struggle carried out solely for defensive purposes. The use of the concept of "jihad" for acts of aggression against innocent people, that is for terror, would be unjust and a great distortion of the true meaning of the term.

### *Killing Oneself, In Other Words Committing Suicide, is Forbidden in the Qur'an*

Another important matter that arose in the wake of the latest terrorist assaults against the United States is that of suicide attacks.

Some people who are ill-informed on Islam have made utterly erroneous statements to the effect that this religion of peace allows suicide attacks, whereas in Islam killing oneself and killing other people are both prohibited. In the words, "Do not kill yourselves." (Qur'an, 4:29) God has declared suicide to be a sin. In Islam it is forbidden for anyone to kill himself or herself, for no matter what reason.

The Prophet reveals suicide to be a sin in a parable, when he says that those who commit suicide will be punished:

> *Indeed, whoever (intentionally) kills himself, then certainly he will be punished in the Fire of Hell, wherein he shall dwell forever.*

As this makes clear, committing suicide, and thus carrying out suicide attacks, and causing the deaths of thousands of innocent people while doing so, is a total violation of Islamic morality. God says in the Qur'an that it is a sin to put an end to one's own life. For that reason, it is quite impossible for someone who believes in God and says he abides by the Qur'an to do such a thing. The only people who can do such things are those who have a very mistaken perception of religion, have no idea of true Qur'anic morality, fail to use their reason and conscience, are under the influence of atheist ideologies, and who have been brainwashed with feelings of hatred and revenge. Everybody must oppose such actions.

## *Compassion, Tolerance and Humanity in the History of Islam*

To sum up the facts we have seen so far, we can say that the political doctrine of Islam (in other words, Islamic rules and principles regarding political matters) is exceedingly moderate and peace-loving. This truth is accepted by many non-Muslim historians and theologians. One of these is the British historian Karen Armstrong, a former nun and an expert on Middle East history. In her book Holy War, which examines the history of the three divine religions, she makes the following comments:

> *... The word 'Islam' comes from the same Arabic root as the word 'peace' and the Koran condemns war as an abnormal state of*

*affairs opposed to God's will... Islam does not justify a total aggressive war of extermination... Islam recognises that war is inevitable and sometimes a positive duty in order to end oppression and suffering. The Koran teaches that war must be limited and be conducted in as humane a way as possible. Mohammad had to fight not only the Meccans but also the Jewish tribes in the area and Christian tribes in Syria who planned on offensive against him in alliance with the Jews. Yet this did not make Mohammed denounce the People of the Book. His Muslims were forced to defend themselves but they were not fighting a 'holy war' against the religion of their enemies. When Mohammad sent his freedman Zaid against the Christians at the head of a Muslim army, he told them to fight in the cause of God bravely but humanely. They must not molest priests, monks and nuns nor the weak and helpless people who were unable to fight. There must be no massacre of civilians nor should they cut down a single tree nor pull down any building.*

After the death of the Prophet, the Caliphs who succeeded him were also very sensitive in exercising justice. In conquered countries, both the indigenous people and the newcomers led their lives in peace and security. Abu Bakr, the first Caliph, demanded his people adopt just and tolerant attitudes in these lands. All these attitudes were in compliance with the values of the Qur'an. Abu Bakr gave the following command to his army before the first Syrian expedition:

*Stop, O people that I may give you ten rules to keep by heart: Do not commit treachery, nor depart from the right path. You must not mutilate, neither kill a child or aged man or woman. Do not destroy a palm tree, nor burn it with fire and do not cut any fruitful tree. You msut not slay any of the flock or herds or the camels, save for your subsistence. You are likely to pass by people who have devoted their lives to monastic services; leave them to that to which they have devoted their lives. You are likely, likewise, to find people who will present to you meals of many kinds. You may eat; but do no forget to mention the name of Allah.*

Umar ibn al-Khattab, who succeeded Abu Bakr, was famous for the way he exercised justice and made contracts with the indigenous people of the conquered countries. Each one of these contracts proved to be an example of tolerance and justice. For instance, in his declaration granting protection to Christians in Jerusalem and Lod, he ensured that churches would not be demolished and guaranteed that Muslims would not worship in churches in groups. Umar granted the same conditions to the Christians of Bethlehem. During the conquest of Medain, the declaration of protection given to the Nestorian Patriarch Yeshuyab III (650 - 660 AD) again guaranteed that churches would not be demolished and that no building would be converted into a house or a mosque. The letter written by the patriarch to the bishop of Fars (Persia) after the conquest is most striking, in the sense that it depicts the tolerance and compassion shown by Muslim rulers to the Book of People in the words of a Christian:

> *They [Abbasids] have not attacked the Christian religion, but rather they have commended our faith, honored our priests... and conferred benefits on churches and monasteries.*

All these are very important examples revealing the understanding of justice and tolerance of true believers. In a verse God commands the following:

> *God commands you to return to their owners the things you hold on trust and, when you judge between people, to judge with justice. How excellent is what God exhorts you to do! God is All-Hearing, All-Seeing. (Qur'an, 4:58)*

Canon Taylor, one of the mission leaders of the Anglican Church, expresses the beauty revealed by the Islamic morality in one of his speeches as follows:

> *It [Islam] brought out the fundamental dogmas of religion – the unity and greatness of God, that He is merciful and righteous, that He claims obedience to His will, resignation and faith. It proclaimed the responsibility of man, a future life, a Day of Judgment, and stern retribution to fall upon the wicked; and enforced the duties of prayer, almsgiving, fasting and benevolence. It thrust aside the artificial virtues, the religious frauds and follies, the perverted moral sentiments, and the verbal subtleties of theological disputants... It gave hope to the slave, brotherhood to mankind, and recognition to the fundamental facts of human nature.*

The false assertion that people in conquered countries converted to Islam under threat has also been disproved by Western researchers, and the justice and tolerant attitude of Muslims has been confirmed. L.Browne, a Western researcher, expresses this situation in the following words:

> *Incidentally these well-established facts dispose of the idea so widely fostered in Christian writings that the Muslims, wherever they went, forced people to accept Islam at the point of the sword.*

In his book The Prospects of Islam, Browne goes on to say that the real motive behind the Muslims' conquests was the brotherhood of Islam. The vast majority of Muslim administrators who have reigned over the Muslim lands throughout history continued to treat the members of other religions with the utmost tolerance and respect. Within the borders of all Islamic states, both Jews and Christians lived in safety and enjoyed freedom.

Georgetown University's Professor of Religion and International Relations John L. Esposito describes how Jews and Christians who came under the administration of Muslim states met with enormous tolerance:

> *Muslim armies proved to be formidable conquerors and effective rulers, builders rather than destroyers. They replaced the indigenous rulers and armies of the conquered countries, but preserved much of their government, bureaucracy, and culture. For many in the conquered territories, it was no more than an exchange of masters, one that brought peace to peoples demoralized and disaffected by the casualties and heavy taxation that resulted from the years of Byzantine-Persian warfare. Local communities were free to continue to follow their own way of life in internal, domestic affairs. In many ways, local populations found Muslim rule more flexible and tolerant than that of Byzantium and Persia. Religious communities were free to practise their faith-to worship and be governed by their religious leaders and laws in such areas marriage, divorce, and inheritance. In exchange, they were required to pay tribute, a poll tax (jizya) that entitled them to from Muslim protection from outside aggression and exempted them from military service. They were therefore called the "protected ones" (dhimmmi). In effect, this*

*often meant lower taxes, grater local autonomy, rule by fellow Semites with closer linguistic and cultural ties than the hellenized, Greco-Roman elites of Byzantium, and greater religious freedom for Jews and indigenous Christians. Most of the Christian churches, such as the Nestorians, Monophysites, Jacobites, and Copts, had been persecuted as heretics and schismatics by Christian orthodoxy. For these reasons, some Jewish and Christian communities aided the invading armies, regarding them as less oppressive than their imperial masters. In many ways, the conquests brought a Pax Islamica to an embattled area.*

Another "Pax Islamica" brought by Islam was to women, a segment of society that was tremendously abused in the pre-Islamic times. Professor Bernard Lewis, known to be one of the greatest Western experts on the Middle East, makes the following comment:

*In general, the advent of Islam brought an enormous improvement in the position of women in ancient Arabia, endowing them with property and some other rights, and giving them a measure of protection against ill treatment by their husbands or owners. The killing of female infants, sanctioned by custom in Pagan Arabia, was outlawed by Islam. But the position of women remained poor, and worsened when, in this as in so many other respects, the original message of Islam lost its impetus and was modified under the influence of pre-existing attitudes and customs.*

The reign of the Seljuk Turks and that of the Ottoman Empire were also marked by the just and tolerant outlook of Islam. In his book, *The Spread of Islam in the World*, Sir Thomas Arnold, the British researcher, explains the Christians' willingness to come under Seljuk rule because of this attitude:

*This same sense of security of religious life under Muslim rule led many of the Christians of Asia Minor, also, about the same time, to welcome the advent of the Saljuq Turks as their deliverers... In the reign of Michael VIII (1261-1282), the Turks were often invited to take possession of the smaller towns in the interior of Asia Minor by the inhabitants, that they might escape from the tyranny of the empire; and both rich and poor often emigrated into Turkish dominions.*

Malik Shah, the ruler of the Islamic Seljuk Empire during its brightest age, approached the people in the conquered lands with great tolerance and compassion and thus was remembered with respect and love by them. All objective historians refer to the justice and tolerance of Malik Shah in their works. His tolerance also kindled feelings of love towards him in the hearts of the People of the Book. For this reason, unprecedented in history, many cities came under Malik Shah's rule of their own free will. Sir Thomas Arnold also mentions Odo de Diogilo, a monk of St. Denis, who participated in the Second Crusade as the private chaplain of Louis VII, refers in his memoirs to the justice administered by Muslims regardless of the subjects' religious affiliation. Based on the graphic account of Odo de Diogilo, Sir Thomas Arnold writes:

> *The situation of the survivors would have been utterly hopeless, had not the sight of their misery melted the hearts of the Muhammadans to pity. They tended the sick and relieved the poor and starving with open-handed liberality. Some even bought up the French money which the Greeks had got out of the pilgrims by force or cunning, and lavishly distributed it among the needy. So great was the contrast between the kind treatment the pilgrims received from the unbelievers and the cruelty of their fellow-Christians, the Greeks, who imposed forced labour upon them, beat them, and robbed them of what little they had left, that many of them voluntarily embraced the faith of their deliverers. As the old chronicler [Odo de Diogilo] says: "Avoiding their co-religionists who had been so cruel to them, they went in safety among the infidels who had compassion upon them, and, as we heard, more than three thousand joined themselves to the Turks when they retired."*

These statements by historians reveal that Muslim administrators who truly adopted the morality of the Islam always ruled with tolerance, compassion and justice. Likewise, the history of the Ottoman Empire which ruled lands on three continents for centuries abounds with examples of tolerance.

The way the Jews settled in Ottoman lands during the time of Sultan Beyazid II, after being subjected to massacre and exile in the Catholic kingdoms of Spain and Portugal, is a fine example of the tolerance that Islamic morality brings with it.

The Catholic monarchs who ruled much of Spain at the time brought grave pressure to bear on the Jews who had formerly lived in peace under Muslim rule in Andalusia. While Muslims, Christians and Jews were able to live side by side in peace in Andalusia, the Catholic monarchs tried to force the whole country to become Christian, and declared war on the Muslims while oppressing the Jews. As a result, the last Muslim ruler in the Granada region of southern Spain was overthrown in 1492. Muslims were subjected to terrible slaughter, and those Jews who refused to change their religion were sent into exile.

One group of these Jews without a homeland sought shelter in the Ottoman Empire, and the state allowed them to do so. The Ottoman fleet, under the command of Kemal Reis, brought the exiled Jews, and those Muslims who had survived the slaughter, to the land of the Ottomans.

Sultan Beyazid II has gone down in history as a most pious believer, and in the spring of 1492 he settled these wronged Jews who had been expelled from Spain in certain parts of his empire, around Edirne, and Thessalonica in present-day Greece. Most of the 25,000 Turkish Jews living in Turkey today are the ancestors of those Spanish Jews. They have adapted their religion and customs, which they brought from Spain some 500 years ago, to the conditions in Turkey, and continue to live most comfortably with their own schools, hospitals, old people's homes, cultural associations and newspapers. In the same way that they have traders and businessmen, they also have representatives in numerous professions, from technical subjects to advertising, with increasingly developing intellectual circles. While Jewish communities in many countries in Europe have for centuries been exposed to the fear of anti-Semitic racist attacks, those in Turkey have lived in peace and security. This example alone is enough to demonstrate the tolerance that Islam brings with it and its understanding of justice.

The compassion and tolerance exhibited by Sultan Beyazid II applied to all the Ottoman sultans. When Sultan Mehmet the Conqueror captured Constantinople, he allowed the Christians and the Jews to live freely there. André Miquel, who is known for the valuable works he has written about the just and tolerant practices of Muslims and the world of Islam, says:

> *Christians lived under a very well-administered government which they were unable to find in the time of the Byzantine and Latin states. They at no time saw any systematic oppression. On the contrary, the empire, and Constantinople in particular, became a shelter for those Spanish Jews who had been tortured. There was no forced imposition of Islam anywhere.*

As is clear from these facts, Muslims have at no time in history been oppressive. On the contrary, they have brought peace and security to all nations and beliefs wherever they have gone. They have abided by God's verse which says: "Worship God and do not associate anything with Him. Be good to your parents and relatives and to orphans and the very poor, and to neighbours who are related to you and neighbours who are not related to you, and to companions and travellers and your slaves. God does not love anyone vain or boastful." (Qur'an, 4:36) and have behaved well to all people.

In short, friendship, brotherhood, peace and love are the bases of Qur'anic morality, and it is to these superior virtues that Muslims try to adhere.

## PAKISTANI JIHADISTS AND THE KASHMIR JIHAD

The Islamic Revolution in Iran in 1979, followed by the jihad in Afghanistan (1979-89) against the Soviet occupation soon turned Pakistan into what one commentator termed as 'the original staging ground of Jihad as an international movement'. Large sums of money and huge quantities of arms now began pouring into Pakistan from various sources, particularly from the USA and Saudi Arabia, apprehensive as both of them were of Soviet expansionism and the Iranian-style anti-monarchical and anti-Western Islamic radicalism in the region. From the early 1980s, Pakistan emerged as the major launching pad for numerous militant

Islamist groups fighting in Afghanistan, with large numbers of activists flocking there not only from Afghanistan, but also from the Arab world and from Muslim communities in the West, fired by an irrepressible zeal for the cause of the jihad against the godless Soviets.

Several Pakistani Islamic parties, particularly the Jama'at-i Islami, the Jami'at-i 'Ulama-i-Islam and the Jami'at-i 'Ulama-i-Pakistan were also drawn into the jihad, and set up or sponsored their own militant wings.

Numerous Islamic seminaries (madrasas) sprang up all over the country, lavishly patronized by the Pakistani military dictator Zia ul-Haq and the Saudis, almost all based on sectarian affiliation, to train their students for the jihad. The consequent spread of what has been called the 'gun-culture' in Pakistan was a major consequence of all these factors. Thus, with arms and funds easily available, Pakistan was rapidly faced with widespread internal conflict, which took several forms—ethnic, between Mohajirs and Pathans in Karachi; and sectarian, between Sunnis and minority Shi'as and, among Sunnis themselves, between Deobandis and Barelwis.

Besides the Soviet presence at Pakistan's very doorstep, several internal factors were responsible for Zia's patronage of radical jihadist outfits. Having captured power through a military coup in 1977, and lacking legitimacy for his rule, he sought to win support for his regime through appeals to Islam, introducing cosmetic changes in the law, such as Islamic punishments, in the name of Islamization, for which he won the warm support of Islamist groups such as the Jama'at-i Islami. Linked to the Islamization project that Zia and Pakistani rulers after him sought to pursue at home was Pakistan's Kashmir policy. To begin with, Pakistan is believed to have extended armed support to the JKLF, arranging for training some of its fighters in the wake of the beginning of the armed uprising in Kashmir in 1989. Soon, however, it was clear to the Pakistani establishment that the JKLF, with its agenda of a free, democratic Kashmir, would not only not toe its line but also pose a threat to its own strategic interests. Hence, from the early 1990s began a policy of deliberate marginalization of the Kashmiri nationalists by the Pakistani establishment, alongside with the cultivation of Pakistani Islamists, who had emerged in the years of the Afghan war, to enter the Kashmir jihad, coupled with lavish patronage extended to Kashmiri Islamist groups such as the JIJK and the HM.

As a result of this change in Pakistan's Kashmir policy from the early 1990s onwards, particularly since the mujahidin victory in Afghanistan in 1992, numerous jihadist outfits in Pakistan began turning their attention towards Kashmir. By the late 1990s, these Pakistani jihadists were playing a key role in the fighting in Kashmir, eclipsing even local Kashmiri groups. Thus, a report brought out by the Indian army in 2000 highlighted the fact that almost all the militant groups active in Kashmir were pro-Pakistan or Pakistan-based, and that the JKLF, the only non-Islamist group included in its list, was 'presently on a low profile'. It estimated that there were some 2750 pro-Pakistan Islamist militants active in Kashmir, while it put the number of JKLF militants at only 60. The groups to whom these Islamists belonged groups were actively assisted by the Pakistani establishment, in particular by its ISI.

With increasing Western criticism of the Pakistani state's role in sponsoring what some have termed as 'Islamic terrorism', an increasing 'privitization of jihad' has occurred. Thus, Pakistan-based organizations that claim to be autonomous of the Pakistani establishment, but are, of course, still dependent on it for patronage, have taken up the task of spearheading the jihad. What is particularly striking about most of these groups is the relatively small Kashmiri presence in both the leadership as well as cadre levels, with almost all their leaders being Pakistani and most of their fighters being Pakistani nationals as well as some Afghans, Arabs and others. Apparently, it is felt that Pakistani strategic interests can be secured only if the leadership and even the rank-and-file of the jihadists remain in Pakistani hands. It has also been argued that the failure or the unwillingness of Kashmiri militant groups to engineer large-scale killings of non-Muslims in Jammu and Kashmir so as to reduce the Hindu population has been an important factor in the promotion of Pakistani-based groups, who have little such compunctions, to take over the armed struggle.

## *Jihadist Discourse: The Markaz Da'wat ul-Irshad and the Lashkar-i Tayyeba*

If the JIJK seeks to seriously question the legitimacy of the discursive framework of the Kashmiri nationalists by seeking to present the Kashmiri armed struggle as a jihad between Islam and disbelief, a further radicalization of the jihadist discourse is clearly evident in the writings and statements of the several Pakistan-based Islamist organizations actively involved in fighting in Kashmir. The most prominent of these groups are the Harkat ul-Ansar, also known as the Harkat-ul Jihad-i Islami, al-Badr, Jami'at ul-Mujahidin, al-Jihad and, probably the most influential of them all, the Lashkar-i Tayyeba ('The Army of the Pure'). All these groups share a common Islamist ideology and advocate the merger of Kashmir with Pakistan.

The Pakistan-based Islamist groups actively involved in the Kashmir conflict are thus today central players in the Kashmiri armed struggle. One of the consequences of their emergence and growing influence has been the further radicalization of the terms of discourse within which the JIJK has sought to portray the Kashmiri armed struggle, arguing against the claims of the Kashmiri nationalists and further developing certain themes that are only vaguely touched upon in Gilani's writings. The jihad is no longer limited to liberating Kashmir from India, but goes far beyond, as we shall see. This is strikingly illustrated in the publications and statements of the Lashkar-i Tayyeba, the 'new masters of Kashmir', and said to be 'the largest jihadi organization in Pakistan'.

The Lashkar is the military wing of an organization called the Markaz Da'wat ul- Irshad ('The Centre for Preaching and Guidance'), set up in 1986 by two Pakistani university professors, Hafiz Muhammad Sa'eed and Zafar Iqbal. Its headquarters are located in a sprawling 160-acre campus at Muridke, a small town in the Gujranwala district of Pakistani Punjab, some thirty kilometres from Lahore. The Markaz is affiliated to the Ahl-i Hadith school, known for its fierce opposition to Sufism and to the established schools of Islamic jurisprudence, insisting that Muslims must go back to the original sources of inspiration—the

Qur'an and the Hadith. It seeks to refashion the worldwide Muslim community in the mould of the Companions of the Prophet. It sees itself as the inheritor of the legacy of the first major jihadist movement in modern times in India, the movement launched by Sayyed Ahmad Barelwi and his band of followers, who, in the early nineteenth century, attempted to set up an Islamic state in the Pathan borderlands and launched an abortive jihad against the Sikhs. The Markaz is believed to be closely linked to the Pakistani establishment as well as to the Jama'at-i Islami of Pakistan.

The Markaz, like many other Pakistani Islamist outfits, was originally designed to serve as a training base for Pakistani militants involved in the Afghan jihad against the Soviets. In 1987, a year after its founding, it set up a training centre inside Afghanistan itself, at Jaji in the Patkia province, and then, shortly after, another in the Kunnar province. It claims that the warriors produced at these centres 'performed outstanding operations' against the Russians. In Afghanistan it carried out its jihad in league with an Afghan outfit, the Jama'at al-Da'wat il al-Qur'an. As the Markaz's activities rapidly grew, it was decided to divide its work into two separate but related sections: the educational and the jihadist. Thus, in 1993, the Markaz established its separate 'jihadic and warfare' wing, the Lashkar. The Lashkar later established four training centres in Pakistan and Afghanistan, where, 'thousands of mujahidin from all over the world are being trained'. Markaz authorities claim that militants produced at these centres have played a leading role in the armed struggles in Afghanistan, Bosnia, Chechenya, Kosovo, the southern Philippines, Kashmir and 'in other areas where Muslims are fighting for freedom'. According to one report, in recent years the spread of the Markaz in Pakistan has 'been phenomenal', and today it has some five hundred offices all over the country, most of them in Punjab, which operate as recruitment centres for would-be mujahidin.

At its Muridke headquarters, the Markaz runs an Islamic school and university, most of whose students are local Pakistanis, with some from Pakistan-administered Kashmir, a few Kashmiris from the Indian-ruled part of the state, and several Afghans and Arabs. Besides, the Markaz has established a network of over seventy schools, mainly in Punjab, where Islamic and modern education are imparted. Young boys of the age of eight are taken in and are given a twelve-year training. A strict military atmosphere is enforced, students must wear military uniforms, abide by military discipline and 'properly assimilate the commandments of their theologians and military instructors that their future profession—as mujahidin—will be in great demand in the Muslim world on the threshold of the new millennium'. At its four training centres, would-be mujahidin are given rigorous military training. This is of two kinds. Firstly, a short twenty-one day course, the daura-i 'ama ('general course'). Secondly, a three month intensive course, the daura-i khasa ('special course'), geared to guerrilla warfare, in which trainees learn how to handle small arms as well as survival and ambush techniques. These courses, it is claimed, 'change the course of life' of the trainees completely', and a sign of this is said to be that they 'no longer shave' and 'wear their shalwars above their ankles, as enjoined by the Prophet Muhammad'.

As in the case of the other Pakistan-based militant groups active in Kashmir today, the Markaz's direct participation in the Kashmir conflict dates to the end of the Afghan war in 1992, in which an estimated 1600 of its militants are said to have participated. After the Soviet withdrawal from Afghanistan, it shifted its attention to Kashmir to 'help the oppressed and innocent Kashmiris who were undergoing Indian aggression for the past fifty years'. In this, they were assisted by the Jama'at-i Islami of Pakistan and the Pakistani intelligence agency, the ISI, key players in the Afghan jihad. The Lashkar is said to have first entered Kashmir in 1990, and then to have 'upgraded' its jihad there in 1993, when its militants attacked an Indian army base in Poonch. In 1994 it began sending large numbers of its fighters into Kashmir, most of them non-Kashmiris. From 1995 it claims that its fighters have been 'engaged properly and striving hard' against the Indian forces. 1996 witnessed a major shift in the Lashkar's Kashmir strategy, with greater attention being paid to the border districts of Jammu, particularly Rajouri and Poonch, as well as Doda. Reports suggest that some of the mass killings of Hindu villagers in these areas have been the work of the Lashkar, with the aim of causing an exodus of the Hindu population of these areas so as to make their task easier. By 1998, it was estimated that the Lashkar had some 350 mujahidin present in Indian-controlled Kashmir. Its fighters are considered by the Indian armed forces to be the best trained among all the militant groups in the region.

In mid-1999 India and Pakistan almost came to war after Pakistan-based militants, believed to be backed by the Pakistani army, occupied certain strategic heights in the Kargil sector in the Ladakh province in the remote northern part of Indian-controlled Kashmir. The four principal militant groups taking part in this operation, all Islamist and manned almost entirely by non-Kashmiris, were the Harkat ul-Mujahidin, the Tahrik-i Jihad, al-Badr and the Lashkar. These groups together formed a joint military command to co-ordinate their military operations against the Indian army. The Lashkar contingent consisted, among others, of several students from its college at Muridke, led by one 'Abdur Rahman 'Abid, a graduate of Medina University. They were joined by some two hundred militants from the Nuristan province of Afghanistan, the first time that such a large number of Afghan fighters had entered Kashmir in recent years.

The Pakistani attempt to enter Kashmir through Kargil failed, however, and under pressure from the West, the country's then Prime Minister, Nawaz Sharif, appealed to the militants to withdraw from the heights that they had captured. The militants, on their part, were reluctant to obey, and they saw Sharif's capitulation to the USA as a betrayal of their jihad. Instead of toeing Sharif's line, they announced what they called 'the second stage' of the Kashmir jihad—taking the battle against the Indian army right inside the Kashmir valley itself, in order, as Zaki ur-Rahman Lakhvi, the amir of the Lashkar, put it, 'to avenge' the atrocities of the Indian army. According to the amir of the Markaz, Hafiz Muhammad Sa'eed, in this second phase 'the jihad would spread all across Kashmir. It would spread to every peak, every forest and every path'. As part of this new strategy, the Lashkar came up with a new means of attack—suicide bombers, which it named as Ibn Taimiya Fida'i Missions, in memory of the medieval Arab Islamic scholar who crusaded against what he saw as un-Islamic practices, and to whom the Ahl-i Hadith as well as the Lashkar owe much of their inspiration. So far, the Lashkar has conducted scores of fida'i missions in Kashmir and beyond. In all, the Lashkar claimed that by early 2000, it had killed some 2100 Indian army personnel, including senior officers, and to have lost some 500 of its own men in its Kashmir operations.

In the wake of a Lashkar attack on the Indian army headquarters in Srinagar, the capital of Kashmir, in 1999, the head of the Markaz, Hafiz Muhammad Sa'eed declared before an audience of an estimated three hundred thousand people that his fighters could now 'strike anywhere in India', threatening to target even the Indian prime minister's office if India did not stop its aggression on the Kashmiri Muslims and vacate Kashmir.

The jihad, declared Hafiz, was not limited simply to freeing Kashmir from Indian control. Rather, he stressed, it was aimed at 'liberating' India itself. He revealed that the Lashkar was now planning to extend its activities beyond the borders of Kashmir, deep inside India. 'To set up a mujahidin network across India is our target', said Zaki ur-Rahman Lakhvi, chief of the Lashkar, addressing the same congregation. He claimed that his organization was 'preparing the Muslims of India against India' and that once they were ready, 'it would be the start of the disintegration of India'. Some 50,000 Pakistani youth are said to have responded to this appeal to join the grand anti-India crusade.

## JIHAD VIEWS OF DIFFERENT MUSLIM GROUPS

### *Ahmadiyya*

In Ahmadiyya Islam, jihad is primarily one's personal inner struggle and should not be used violently for political motives. Violence is the last option only to be used to protect religion and one's own life in extreme situations of persecution.

### *Quranist*

Quranists do not believe that the word jihad means holy war. They believe it means to struggle, or to strive. They believe it can incorporate both military and non-military aspects. When it refers to the military aspect, it is understood primarily as defensive warfare.

## Sunni

Jihad has been classified either as *al-jihâd al-akbar* (the greater jihad), the struggle against one's ego or self (*nafs*), or *al-jihâd al-asghar* (the lesser jihad), the external, physical effort, often implying fighting (this is similar to the Shia view of jihad as well).

Gibril Haddad has analyzed the basis for the belief that internal jihad is the "greater jihad", *Jihad al-akbar*. Haddad identifies the primary historical basis for this belief in a pair of similarly worded hadith, in which Mohammed is reported to have told warriors returning home that they had returned from the lesser jihad of struggle against non-Muslims to a greater jihad of struggle against lust.

Although Haddad notes that the authenticity of both hadeeth is questionable, he nevertheless concludes that the underlying principle of the superiority of internal jihad does have a reliable basis in the Quran and other writings.

In contrast, the Hanbali scholar Ibn Qayyim Al-Jawziyya did believe that "internal Jihad" is important but he suggests those hadith as weak which consider "Jihad of the heart/soul" to be more important than "Jihad by the sword". Contemporary Islamic scholar Abdullah Yusuf Azzam has argued the hadith is not just weak but "is in fact a false, fabricated hadith which has no basis. It is only a saying of Ibrahim Ibn Abi `Abalah, one of the Successors, and it contradicts textual evidence and reality."

Muslim jurists explained that there are four kinds of *jihad fi sabilillah* (struggle in the cause of God):

- Jihad of the heart *(jihad bil qalb/nafs)* is concerned with combatting the devil and in the attempt to escape his persuasion to evil. This type of Jihad was regarded as the greater jihad (*al-jihad al-akbar*).
- Jihad by the tongue *(jihad bil lisan)* is concerned with speaking the truth and spreading the word of Islam with one's tongue.

- Jihad by the hand *(jihad bil yad)* refers to choosing to do what is right and to combat injustice and what is wrong with action.
- Jihad by the sword *(jihad bis saif)* refers to *qital fi sabilillah* (armed fighting in the way of God, or holy war), the most common usage by Salafi Muslims and offshoots of the Muslim Brotherhood.

Some contemporary Islamists have succeeded in replacing the greater jihad, the fight against desires, with the lesser jihad, the holy war to establish, defend and extend the Islamic state.

### *Sufic*

The Sufic view classifies "Jihad" into two parts: the "Greater Jihad" and the "Lesser Jihad". Muhammad put the emphasis on the "Greater Jihad" by saying, "Holy is the warrior who is at war with himself". In this sense external wars and strife are seen as but a satanic counterfeit of the true "jihad", which can only be fought and won within. There is no salvation for man without his own efforts being added to the work of self-refinement. In this sense it is the western view of the Holy Grail which comes closest to the Sufic ideal, for to the Sufis, perfection is the Grail, and the Holy Grail is for those who, after they become perfect by giving all they have to the poor then go on to become "Abdal" or "changed ones" like Enoch, who was "taken" by God because he "walked with God" (Genesis:5:24). Here the "Holy Ones" gain the surname "Hadrat" or "The Presence".

## HISTORY

### *Early Muslim Conquests*

Two years after the death of the Islamic prophet Muhammad in 632, Muslims under the leadership of caliph Umar began military campaigns against the Byzantine empire and the Sassanian empire. In the Battle of Yarmukin 636, Muslims defeated the Byzantine army, forcing the empire to withdraw from Syria. The Byzantines surrendered near Cairo in 641. The conquest of Alexandria, then capital of Egypt, took longer. Muslims faced little resistance from the locals as they had suffered under Byzantine rule. In the Battle of al-Qadisiyya in 637 where the Persian army was defeated. In 642, Muslims defeated the Persians at the Battle of Nahâvand, opening up the plateau to Muslim conquest. Within 15 years Iran had been conquered. Muslims later pushed into central Asia.

Often called "the Great conquests", the role of Islam in them is debated. Medieval Arabic authors said that the conquests had been commanded by God. They were presented as orderly and disciplined, under the command of the caliph. Many modern explanations dispute the idea that jihad was a motivating force in the conquests. They hold that Arabs on the eve of the conquests were poor and desertification in the Arabian peninsula had reduced local resources. These explanations cite material causes as opposed to religion as the fundamental cause of the conquests. Some recent explanations cite both material and religious causes in the conquests.

## WARFARE IN MUSLIM SOCIETIES

The major imperial Muslim dynasties of Ottoman Turkey (Sunni) and Persia (Shia) each established systems of authority around traditional Islamic institutions. In the Ottoman empire, the concept of ghaza was promulgated as a sister obligation to jihad. The Ottoman ruler Mehmed II is said to have insisted on the conquest of Constantinople (Christian Byzantium) by justifying *ghaza* as a basic duty.

Later Ottoman rulers would apply *ghaza* to justify military campaigns against the Persian Safavid dynasty. Thus both rival empires established a tradition that a ruler was only considered truly in charge when his armies had been sent into the field in the name of the true faith, usually against *giaurs* or heretics — often meaning each other. The 'missionary' vocation of the Muslim dynasties was prestigious enough to be officially reflected in a formal title as part of a full ruler style: the Ottoman (many also had Ghazi as part of their name) Sultan Murad Khan II Khoja-Ghazi, 6th Sovereign of the House of Osman (1421–1451), literally used Sultan ul-Mujahidin.

The so-called Fulbe jihad states and a few other jihad states in western Africa were established by a series of offensive wars.

The commands inculcated in the Quran (in five suras from the period after Muhammad had established his power) on Muslims to fight those who will neither embrace Islam nor pay a poll-tax (*Jizya*) were not interpreted as a general injunction on all Muslims constantly to make war on the infidels (originally only polytheists who claimed to be monotheists, not "People of the Book", Jesus is seen as the last of the precursors of the Prophet Muhammed; the word infidel had different historical uses, notably used by the Crusaders to refer to the Muslims they were fighting against). It was generally supposed that the order for a general war can only be given by the Caliph (an office that was claimed by the Ottoman sultans), but Muslims who did not acknowledge the spiritual authority of the Caliphate (which is vacant), such as non-Sunnis and non-Ottoman Muslim states, always looked to their own rulers for the proclamation of a jihad; there has been in fact no universal warfare by Muslims on non-believers since the early caliphate. Some proclaimed Jihad by claiming themselves as mahdi, e.g. the Sudanese Mahommed Ahmad in 1882.

### Non-Muslim Opinions

The United States Department of Justice has used its own *ad hoc* definitions of jihad in indictments of individuals involved in terrorist activities:

- "As used in this First Superseding Indictment, 'Jihad' is the Arabic word meaning 'holy war'. In this context, jihad refers to the use of violence, including paramilitary action against persons, governments deemed to be enemies of the fundamentalist version of Islam."
- "As used in this Superseding Indictment, 'violent jihad' or 'jihad' include planning, preparing for, and engaging in, acts of physical violence, including murder, maiming, kidnapping, and hostage-taking." in the indictment against several individuals including José Padilla.

In her book *Muhammad: a Biography of the Prophet*, Karen Armstrong writes:

"Fighting and warfare might sometimes be necessary, but it was only a minor part of the whole jihad or struggle."

Maxime Rodinson, an orientalist, wrote that "Jihad is a propagandistic device which, as need be, resorts to armed struggle – two ingredients common to many ideological movements."

In NATO countries, especially the United States, the term "jihadist" has been used in Western media as a synonym for *mujahid*, and frequently used to describe militant Islamic groups, including but not restricted to Islamic terrorism.

## Non-Muslim Opinions about Muslim Opinions

David Cook, author of *Understanding Jihad*, said "In reading Muslim literature – both contemporary and classical – one can see that the evidence for the primacy of spiritual jihad is negligible. Today it is certain that no Muslim, writing in a non- Western language (such as Arabic, Persian, Urdu), would ever make claims that jihad is primarily nonviolent or has been superseded by the spiritual jihad. Such claims are made solely by Western scholars, primarily those who study Sufism and/or work in interfaith dialogue, and by Muslim apologists who are trying to present Islam in the most innocuous manner possible." Cook argued that "Presentations along these lines are ideological in tone and should be discounted for their bias and deliberate ignorance of the subject" and that "[i]t is no longer acceptable for Western scholars or Muslim apologists writing in non-Muslim languages to make flat, unsupported statements concerning the prevalence – either from a historical point of view or within contemporary Islam – of the spiritual jihad."

# 2

# Jihad: Islamic Holy War

## INTRODUCTION

War is not desirable, and never pleasing to the living almighty God of the Holy Bible. The reality of the darkest horrors of the scourge of war is found in fear, death, destruction, lawlessness and human suffering. It has been estimated that twenty-five million soldiers and twenty-four million civilians were killed in World War II. Technically, war is a function of the state. War is, nevertheless, simply a large scale manifestation of the fallen nature of man (James 4: 1). Alienation between man and God leads to alienation between man and man. War is one manifestation of alienation between man and man. However, God may permit wars, to work out his purpose of judgment and redemption through it.

The analysis herein deals with the doctrine of Jihad (holy war) in Islam to spread the religion of Islam, and force the laws of the god of Islam (Sharia) throughout the earth. The doctrine of forced religion is unique to Islam. No other religion proclaims it. Historical examples of Islamic jihad are presented from late antiquity to modern times. In addition, a brief analysis is provided on the fundamental differences between Islamic jihad on the one hand, and the ancient biblical wars and Christian wars on the other hand. This includes a presentation of the Christian doctrine that some wars are not only just and justifiable, but also virtuous and good moral actions. The Christian crusades of the Middle Ages are discussed with emphasis on its historical milieu.

Islamist apologists, liberal academicians and the media in the West have undertaken to sanitize Islamic jihad by distorting Islamic history and doctrine. The revised polished version of Islam they preach in order to deceive the innocent Westerner is considered heretical Islam in Islamic countries. It is falsification of traditional Islam. The result is to becloud reality, obstructing the possibility of achieving a clear understanding of what the West is confronting, and why? Islamist individuals and organizations usually cloak the truth in moderate public language when referring to jihad in order not to arouse fears and not to isolate themselves. Their talk is pure disinformation, reminiscent of the language of Soviet propagandists in decades past.

Western academicians who avoid or whitewash the primary meaning of jihad in Islamic law and history are motivated by political correctness and the multiculturalist urges to protect non-western civilization from criticism. In addition, some of them do not want to lose the petrodollar funding they get from oil-rich Arab countries for their academic programs.

## HISTORY AND THE HOLY KORAN

In the course of the analysis of Islamist terrorism, we made a basic analytical distinction that needs to be discussed in more detail. On the one hand, we said, there existed the history of societies and political orders informed by Islam, an account of which we called a history of the Islamic community. We assumed here that the status of the history of this community, its *res gestae,* was as unproblematic as the history of the U.S. mail or of gunpowder.

On the other hand we said there existed a paradigmatic Islamic history, which we tentatively described as the account of God and his messengers to humanity. Islamic history, which we also identified as the "Islamic vulgate," by analogy with the Christian Bible given its official form by Saint Jerome in the fourth century, would be discussed "without prejudice." The intention of this terminology was to maintain the frontier between piety and political science; we assumed here that it was possible to study the Islamic story of God and his messengers to humanity without taking a position with respect to the veracity or the literal truth of Islamic history. But this means that it is possible to be neutral before the actual messages that were delivered concretely on specific occasions. We have seen, notwithstanding the Koranic assurance that there can be no compulsion in matters of religion, that this second assumption, even more than the first one concerning the history of Islam, contains or expresses a major problem.

From time to time, in explicating the significance of Islamic history we have imaginatively adopted the perspective of "the pious Muslim." This was, of course, a simplification because (we further assume) there may be a plurality of perspectives that are compatible with Islamic piety. Simplification or not, for one holding to that position of piety, the plurality of perspectives presents an issue that cannot be so easily discussed nor, implicitly, so easily disposed of or dismissed. To put the matter more simply still: one is either pious or not. Muslim living the reality of Islamic history, a pious Jew or a pious Christian *is* a pious Muslim because, within the experienced reality of Islamic history, Islam is the fulfillment of both Judaism and Christianity, to say nothing of paganism.

On the basis of such an understanding of Islamic history, the adjective in the phrase "Islamic piety" is superfluous. Accordingly, the assumptions we have made, or the attitude we have taken, first, with respect to the distinction between the history of Islam and Islamic history and, second, with respect to the veracity of the latter, may be seen (and for the pious, quite properly) as entirely disingenuous, not to say the expression of an impiety. To begin with, a pious (Muslim) individual, one who we said believed in the Muslim vulgate, would never have made the initial distinction. Furthermore, for a pious (Muslim) individual, the veracity of Islamic history is its meaning, much in the same way as God spoke to Moses from the burning bush. Thus, neutrality with respect to that meaning is rebellion against it, and so rebellion against God's revealed message to Moses.

In short, for a pious individual *the* problem of existence is not understanding the word of God but obeying it. Even within Islam, however, matters are not so simple, as the discussion above of the position of the *faylasuf* indicated. There is an equivalent problem within Western history more generally, a history that, for present purposes, can include the Bible and Greek philosophy as well as Islam. We will first present Leo Strauss's version of this question, then Eric Voegelin's, and finally we indicate how recent scholarship, much of it undertaken outside the Islamic lands, has a bearing on the issues of salafism and Islamism raised in the course of this study. In 1967, Strauss delivered a lecture, "Jerusalem and Athens: Some Preliminary Reflections," at the City College of New York.

According to Strauss, "as far as we Western men are concerned" the genesis of what "Western man" became is "indicated by the names of the two cities Jerusalem and Athens." Today, of course, the realities signified by these intelligible analytic terms—the names of the two cities, Athens and Jerusalem—are widely considered to be cultural options. Strauss then questioned the intelligibility of culture and of a cultural understanding of culture, which calls itself a science of culture. His reasoning is straightforward: a science of culture claims to be neutral with respect to the plurality of cultures that actually exist. Accordingly, it fosters a universal tolerance of plurality. But this amounts to an assertion of the rightness of cultural pluralism and so of pluralism as right. That is, the science of culture, far from giving cultures their due, reduces them to elements of something they are not, namely, science. The science of culture does not, therefore, lead to scientific objectivity, as often has been claimed. Indeed, the science of culture, or to be more accurate, a tolerant neutrality with respect to the validity or veracity of the realities expressed by the terms *Athens* and *Jerusalem,* is simply evasive and, *au fond,* unintelligible. The conclusion to be drawn at this point, then, is that there is simply a stand-off between piety and political science.

Strauss did not, however, leave the matter at an impasse. What leads to objectivity, he said on this as on many other occasions, is the attempt to understand the several and various cultures, positions, arguments, philosophies, and so on, as they understood themselves or understand themselves. "Men of ages and climates other than our own did not understand themselves in terms of cultures because they were not concerned with culture in the present-day meaning of the term. What we now call culture is the accidental result of concerns that were not concerns with culture but with other things and above all with the Truth." But this approach, when the object to be understood is the Bible, and so of the biblical exposé of truth—or Truth, as Strauss wrote—presents a major additional problem: it seems to require that the one undertaking the enquiry go beyond the self-understanding of the Bible to say nothing of the Greeks, because it amounts to gaining wisdom, or knowledge of Truth. This consideration leads to a further problem: according to the Bible, "the beginning of wisdom is fear of the Lord; according to the Greek philosophers, the beginning of wisdom is wonder." Can there be two beginnings? But to raise such a question—or any question, for that matter—means that one does not already have the answer, does not already have the knowledge of Truth, or is not wise, however much one may wish to become wise. "We are seekers for wisdom, 'philosophoi,'" said Strauss; but "by saying that we wish to hear first and then to act to decide, we have already decided in favor of Athens against Jerusalem." However, by taking the side of Athens against Jerusalem, one must abandon the attempt to understand Jerusalem on its own or any other terms: for the pious city, the city of righteousness, one must obey and fear the Lord. End of story. To use the imagery of "hearing the word of God," seeking to understand it would already be an act of impiety because (for the pious) God's word demands obedience, not understanding. Indeed, to seek understanding is already to use the imagery of sight, not of hearing: we seek to "*see* what God's word, or any other word, *means,*" quite a different enterprise than hearing and obeying.

On the other hand, Strauss pointed out, if one follows through on the side of Athens against Jerusalem one is compelled to treat the Bible as a text suitable for the same kind of "historical-critical study" as the *Nicomachean Ethics* or the Code of Hammurabi. Strauss then proposed an alternative way of reading the Bible and of grasping the tension between Athens and Jerusalem. Unquestionably, Strauss's position on this point is both complex and controversial. Fortunately, it need not concern us. What counts is that Strauss was very much aware of the general problem that concerns us at present.

So was Eric Voegelin. In "The Gospel and Culture," Voegelin discussed this same question along different but complementary lines. Characteristically, Voegelin began with a brief historical reference to the initial absorption of the "life of reason," or the "culture of the time," namely, Hellenistic philosophy, by the community of the gospel. In this way, Voegelin said, the sectarian community was able to become the Christianity of the church. The gospel was acceptable to the culture of the time, furthermore, because it appeared to answer the questions raised by the philosophers. In the *First Apology* of Justin the Martyr, the author claims that the *Logos* of the gospel is the developing *logos* of philosophy. "Hence, Christianity is not an alternative to philosophy, it is philosophy itself in its state of perfection; the history of the Logos comes to its fulfillment through the incarnation of the Word in Christ." Accordingly, the distinction between philosophy and the gospel is the difference between stages in the history of reason.

A modern way of posing the same question that has a more direct bearing on the issue under analysis is the controversial 1966 *New Catechism,* published by the Dutch bishops of the Roman Catholic Church. The opening chapter is called "Man the Questioner." It asserts that Christians are human beings with "inquiring minds" and are searching for ways to account for their faith. The motivation of the Dutch bishops is a mirror image of the motivation of Justin: he began as an "inquiring mind" and, following the philosophical schools, was led to the gospel; the bishops, in contrast, had somehow to recover a sense of inquiry because it had been lost and, as is true of many contemporary Christians, they remained in a tranquil state of uninquiring faith. Voegelin adds a "supplement" or a "reminder" that "neither Jesus nor his fellowmen to whom he spoke his word did yet know that they were Christians—the gospel held out its promise not to Christians, but to the poor in the spirit, that is, to minds inquiring, even though on a culturally less sophisticated level than Justin's." The conflict that lay behind the assertion of the Dutch bishops and what expressed itself in the ensuing controversy over the *Dutch Catechism,* as it is generally known, was not between the gospel and philosophy "but rather between the gospel and its unenquiring possession as doctrine."

The conflict, that is to say, is between an inquiring mind and a doctrine that prohibits inquiry. Whatever the pragmatic effectiveness of doctrine as a means of ensuring the credal integrity of a community, the price is invariably the suppression of questions that an inquiring mind is apt to ask. Just as Strauss found a way to deal with the tension between Athens and Jerusalem, so did Voegelin find a way to deal with an inquiring mind in the context of Christianity. To put the issue simply: "the question to which, in Hellenistic-Roman culture, the philosopher could understand the gospel as the answer" concerns "the humanity of man," which "is the same today as it ever has been in the past." The emphasis for both Voegelin and Strauss lies on the questions asked, not the more or less adequate answers received, nor on the equally questionable criteria by means of which the more adequate can be distinguished from the less.

These reflections have a bearing on the issue of Islamist terrorism insofar as Islamists have undertaken the "reducing diets" (to recall the image of Meddeb) of an already astringent regimen. In less colorful language, the issue concerns the relationship of an inquiring mind, which is characteristic of the "humanity of man," and uninquiring obedience to the equally unproblematic word of God, the unproblematic status of which is, to the inquiring mind, evidence only of a dogmatic and closed mind.

The literature on this question in the context of Islam far surpasses anything we can discuss here, and the following sketch is intended chiefly to illustrate a political problem rather than analyze or evaluate the underlying religious, interpretive, or spiritual problem—which, as mentioned above, on philological grounds alone far exceeds my competence.

In 1953, Franz Rosenthal began an article with an understated title, "Some Minor Problems of the Qur'an," in this way: "The basic problem involved in the following discussion is whether we are permitted to doubt the traditional understanding of the Qur'an." In light of the explicit direction given in the Koran (2:1), that "this is the Perfect Book, free from all doubt," the answer, within the context of Islamic history or the Muslim vulgate, is obvious: no doubt at all is permitted because there are no genuine "problems" in the Koran, not minor ones and certainly not major ones. The Koran is not to be doubted because it is meant to be heard and obeyed. Likewise, the title of Warraq's recent book, *What the Koran Really Says,* which reproduced Rosenthal's paper, raises for Islamic history a thoroughly inappropriate but implicit question: what does the Koran really say? We are asked, therefore, to see what God's word means, which is a philosophical inquiry rather than an act of obedience.

This is a radical question, an expression of an inquiring mind, because the appropriate answer to the implicit question is: the Koran records God's eloquence. If one is unsure of what God's eloquence means, master the exegetical tradition and find out. The grave problem with this answer, which is the answer of Rosenthal's "traditional understanding," is that an examination of the tradition will tell you what the exegetes took it to mean, not what God's word means nor even, to follow Strauss's formulation, what it meant to the contemporaries of the Prophet, the pious ancestors, nor to the Prophet himself. To answer that question, which is one that eventually the inquiring mind must consider, brings us to a basic fork in the interpretive road: if one rejects "traditional understanding," which in the Islamic context we may call the teachings of the *ulema* (roughly analogous to the teachings and disputes of the pre-Reformation Church), then there is left only independent interpretation, ijtihad, or something like what Strauss called a "historical-critical study."

We have already considered the conflict between the "traditional understanding" and "independent interpretation" and in this context analyzed the writings of men such as Ibn Taymiyya, Qutb, and bin Laden from the perspective of political science or "historical-critical study." The issue here, however, involves a different and more radical one: it is possible to bring to light the pneumopathological attributes of an Asahara or a bin Laden by analyzing their texts in order to understand them on their own terms. However, it is one thing to try to understand an author as the author understood himself or herself, which we may call the principle of Straussian hermeneutics, but when the author of a text is God, something quite different is involved. A historical-critical study of a text, for example, that Islamic history upholds as "uncreated" in the sense that it is the direct Word of God, is a recipe for conflict, even for war. In other words, to examine the text of the Koran as a product of a particular set of historical or cultural or individual experiences is easily seen by those living Islamic history, whether in accord with "traditional understanding" or in terms of some idiosyncratic ijtihad, as an attack on Islam. Mindful of the post-fatwa life of Salman Rushdie, this is why today so many minds inquiring into "problems of the Koran" use pseudonyms. A half century ago Rosenthal could publish in his own name, which speaks to a changed political rather than interpretive climate today.

Today, for Muslims living within Islamic history, matters are made worse when the inquiring minds are also Western and so doubly damned as both infidel and formerly or neo-colonial. For Westerners derailed by dogmatic postcolonial, postmodern sensibilities, things are no better: there can be no serious distinction between scholarship and polemic for postmoderns because there are no inquiring minds. There are only interested minds. Or, as Michel Foucault once put it, there is no knowledge, only power-knowledge. Notwithstanding the unpropitious context for the appearance of a mind inquiring into the text-critical problems of the Koran, or into what the Koran "really says," a good deal of the traditional understanding has been radically revised by the past generation of scholars—inquiring Muslim and non-Muslim minds working in the area of Middle Eastern studies—to give as neutral a designation as possible. Their concerns, to reiterate a point just made, are not with the perverse interpretations of ijtihad nor of the politics of the Ikhwan, though we shall argue that it has political as well as scholarly significance.

Two aspects of the problem concern us. The first deals with recent accounts of the formation of the Islamic community on the basis of what may be termed allegiance to the Islamic vulgate, and second is the textual status of the vulgate documents. The analogous problems in Judaism would consist in the reconciliation of (1) the archeological history of ancient Palestine, which provides a physical record of the gradual historical development of hilltop villagers into a kingdom, which then was conquered and exiled forcibly to Babylon where the "prophets" brought together the theology of the exodus from paganism into monotheism, with (2) the content of this theology, which told the well-known stories of: Yahwe's initial revelation to Moses, the exit from Egypt to Sinai, the episode of the Burning Bush, Yahwe's gift of the Ten Commandments, the wandering in the desert, the conquest of the Promised Land, the Davidic kingdoms, the Babylonian captivity, the revelations of Daniel, and so on.

The Islamic equivalent to the distinction between the history of the tribal villagers of Palestine and their political life, and the theology of the exodus from paganism, has a similar structure: (1) the revelation at Mecca, the creation of the new community in Medina, the early rightly guided caliphs, their conquests, and the creation of the Umayyad Empire, is an equivalent version of (2) the Israelite exodus under different historical circumstances and experiences. Not humiliation, defeat, and exile, but triumphant imperial succession to Rome and Persia furnished the contents of the Muslim story of exodus from paganism to monotheism.

This multidimensional historical/symbolic complex is far more subtle than the Islamic vulgate, which combines the two dimensions into a single story. Voegelin has given the name *historiogenesis* to the creation of the compound story that combines an account of "what happened," the *res gestae,* with a meaning that provides significance to "what happened," in this instance, obedience to the word of God.

The elaboration of what might be termed a secular vulgate or secular historiogenetic account by Montgomery Watt. Watt provided a conventionally Western and secular account of the origins of the history of Islam. For present purposes it provides a useful starting point and a contrast to both the Muslim vulgate and a remarkable study, published in 1977 by Patricia Crone and Michael Cook, *Hagarism: The Making of the Islamic World.* They argued that Islam began as a messianic movement, "Hagarism," the objective of which was to rule the Holy Land in a peculiar kind of alliance with the Jews. The peculiarity, according to Crone and Cook, was that messianic Israelite redemption was conducted by an army with an Ishmaelite genealogy. "There were," they wrote, really only two solutions. On the one hand they [the proto-Muslim "Hagarenes"] could proceed after the manner of the Ethiopian Christians, that is to say by themselves adopting Israelite descent. But in view of the play they had already made of their Ishmaelite ancestry, it is hardly surprising that they should have clung to it throughout their entire doctrinal evolution. On the other hand, if they would not go to the truth, the truth might perhaps be persuaded to come to them. On the foundation of their Ishmaelite genealogy, they had to erect a properly Ishmaelite prophetology. It was a daring move for so religiously parvenu a nation, but it was the only way out.

The tension between Israelite redemption and Ishmaelite genealogy, to say nothing of the transformation of the exodus symbolism from defeat and humiliation to victory and triumph, was extreme. As John Wans-brough remarked in a celebrated review of *Hagarism,* "it seems, indeed, that the problem of identity in Islam is not exclusively a legacy of colonialism; it has been there all the time." Wansbrough himself developed his own systematic analysis of Islamic history about the same time. He explicitly applied to the Koran and the story of the Prophet at Mecca and Medina the techniques of biblical criticism developed over the preceding century and a half by Western scholars. He did so, moreover, on the commonsensical (at least to an inquiring Western scholar) grounds that if the Christian and Jewish revelations could be discussed using "source-critical" or "historical-critical" methods, so could the Islamic.

In addition to a novel approach to Muslim sacred texts, a kind of "critical history" was applied to the early years of the Umayyad Empire. Between the death of the Prophet in 632 and the establishment of an Arab-ruled Islamic empire by the end of the century, the purely pragmatic necessity of establishing the superiority of Islam over the two competing monotheisms, as well as over Zoroastrianism and "paganism" or paganisms, was obvious. At the same time, the three religious communities strongly outnumbered the ruling Muslims. In addition, the Umayyad rulers were faced with the need to unify a wide range of traditional legal customs in order to reduce the instability of the eighth century that had led to dynastic wars of succession. The point of this effort to create a coherent "theologico-political" synthesis was to create a civil theology or a "minimum dogma" (to use a formula that Voegelin applied to Spinoza's efforts under similar circumstances).

Starting around 800, commentators and scholars invented Islamic history, or what we have called the historiogenetic myth of Islam, on the basis of "trustworthy authorities" who were alleged to have transmitted faithfully the oral reports of the Prophet during the previous five or six generations.

Wansbrough argued the Koran was the finalized version of "an extensive corpus of prophetic *logia* drawn from traditional Judaeo-Christian imagery that gained whatever unity the text has by means of a "limited number of rhetorical conventions." In his second book, Wansbrough argued that Muslim practices underwent a similar kind of transformation so that existing ninth-century practices were said to date from the time of the Prophet. These actions by what he called a "clerical elite," that is, the *ulema,* raised Islam above the other sects—Christian, Jewish, and Zoroastrian—by "neutralizing" Christian Trinitarian doctrine into Muslim unity and attacking Jewish scripture as having been abrogated by successive revelation.

These Western analyses of the origins of Islam naturally enough provoked considerable controversy both from Muslim traditionalists and from tradition-minded Western Arabists and Orientalists. The controversy has redoubled in light of a parallel line of philological analysis focused on the textual history of Muslim scripture.

Let us begin our summary of this issue with a reprise of some agreed-upon historical data. The earliest texts from the Koran date from 691, fifty-nine years after the death of the Prophet. They are inscribed inside the Dome of the Rock in Jerusalem and vary slightly from the standard Koran. The third caliph, Uthman ibn Affan (644–656) ordered the hitherto oral text to be set down in writing. This "Uthman recension" was to be authoritative and constitutes the first book in Arabic. It is also widely agreed that the political purpose of the Uthman recension was to ensure that, all over the growing Umayyad Empire, Muslims would make reference to the same text and not quarrel, like the Jews and the Christians, over what the scripture said. At the same time, Uthman ordered all "imperfect" copies of the Koran destroyed.

The original Koranic script, called the *rasm,* in which the text established by Uthman was written, is without diacritical marks, written as dots, that are used to distinguish various letters and vowels. The diacritical points were added around the turn of the eighth century on orders of Hajjaj bin Uusuf, governor of Iraq (694–714). The result essentially transformed an orally transmitted text into a written one.

Apart from the inscriptions inside the Dome of the Rock, the earliest text of the Koran was, until recently, the Mail Manuscript in the British Library, which dated from the late seventh century; two other manuscripts, one in the Library of Tashkent, in Uzbekistan, and another in Istanbul at the Topkapi Museum, are from the eighth century. In 1972, a number of manuscripts were discovered in the Grand Mosque of Sanaa, in Yemen, during repairs to the loft between the inner and outer roofs following a major rainstorm.

They were turned over to Qadhi Ismail al-Akwa, president of the Yemeni Antiquities Authority. A few years later, al-Akwa showed them to Gerd-Rüdiger Puin, a German Arabist and Islamic paleographer at Saarland University. In 1981, Puin and Hans-Caspar Graf von Bothman, an Islamic art historian and colleague at Saarland, and Albrecht Noth, of the University of Hamburg, obtained support from Germany to preserve, clean, and restore some fifteen thousand sheets and fragments. It turned out that the Sanaa materials were older than the Mail Manuscript.

The Yemeni authorities did not publicize the find or the work done by the Germans. The Germans said very little either and went about their work, which now included making photocopies. In 1997, von Bothman returned to Germany with 35,000 pictures, some of which were clearly palimpsests, manuscripts containing faint earlier texts that had been erased in order to reuse the parchment at a later date.

The political reason for their reticence was obvious. As Puin put it, "So many Muslims have this belief that everything between two covers of the *Koran* is just God's unaltered word. They like to quote the textual work that shows that the Bible has a history and did not fall straight out of the sky, but until now the *Koran* has been out of this discussion. The only way to break through this wall is to prove that the *Koran* has a history too. The Sana'a fragments will help us do this."

Another German scholar, the pseudonymous Christoph Luxenberg, has drawn additional implications from the Sanaa discovery and from prior philological work by Günter Lüling. Lüling reopened an argument that had been made in the nineteenth century by Western Orientalists, that a dialect of Aramaic, namely, Syriac, or Syro-Aramaic, had influenced the vocabulary of the Koran.

In the Prophet's time, Syriac was the language of written communication in the Middle East. Equally important, the literature written in Syriac was chiefly Christian. Now, the Koran is filled with biblical references, yet the Prophet was an illiterate merchant. Leaving aside the intervention of Gabriel, this means either that Mecca was home to large numbers of Jews and Christians, and not just pagan Bedouins, as the Islamic tradition maintains, or the Koran was written some place other than Mecca.

Luxenberg continued his interpretation along the same philological lines as Lüling but drew some even more significant (and controversial) conclusions. Not only was the Koran soaked in Christianity and written in a language that used a large number of Syro-Aramaic words, but the very meaning of the term *Koran* derives from a Syriac word, *qery ana,* which is a technical term in Eastern Christianity that means "lectionary," which is to say, a set of liturgical readings taken from the Bible and read aloud at various ritual occasions during the year. The method used by Luxenberg is complex and can best be judged over the long term by philologically competent scholars. The short-term implications, as the discussion of the dark-eyed houris above has indicated, are politically very important.

More than the fantasies of recruits to "martyrdom operations" are involved in the revisions to the Koran that follow from Luxenberg's argument. For those living within Islamic history, that is, for the pious Muslim, the Koran was not only transmitted from God to the Prophet without human intervention, but it was communicated in perfect Arabic, a unity of form and style and language and content that is itself a representation of the perfection and unity of God.

Luxenberg's argument simply destroys this account entirely. Not only is the Koran a Christian lectionary, the text itself put together at Uth-man's command was compiled by people who could not read the language in which parts of it were written, namely, Syro-Aramaic. That is why they misread the passage about the dark-eyed houris as well as several other ones of much greater theological significance.

Even if scholars know that the questions raised by Westerners such as Luxenberg, or by Lüling, Puin, and von Bothman, or by contemporary Muslim scholars have been raised before in the history of Islam, those previous efforts by inquiring minds have long been forgotten.

As a result, the current work is bound to be seen widely as yet another attack by Western scholarship or by apostate Muslim scholars. As with the controversy over the houris, it should come as no surprise that the Lux-enberg thesis was not simply critically examined and analyzed according to the conventions of ordinary scholarship, but the argument has been characterized as a "plot against the Qur'an under the guise of academic study and archive preservation."

Toward the end of her study of the seductive appeals of terrorism, especially of Islamist terrorism, Jessica Stern indicated the challenge to Westerners. Clearly military opposition or a policy change with respect to Israel or Saudi Arabia is not the main issue. Nor is it the simple fact that the cultures and societies and religions of the world provide human beings with many forms of collective identity. "One of our goals," she said, "must be to make the terrorists' purification project seem *less* urgent: to demonstrate the humanity that binds us, rather than allow our adversaries to emphasize and exploit our differences to provide a seemingly clear (but false) identity, at the expense of peace."

A concern for the common humanity of all people is possible only for inquiring minds, minds in search of a common humanity. In terms of the historical and the theological issues raised in this appendix, such a person would see in Revelation, whether Jewish, Christian, or Muslim, a symbolic, not a literal truth. The alternative would be to capitulate not to Islam but to fundamentalists who have no need to inquire about anything because their impulses no less than their acts lead to totalitarian domination and the superfluousness of humanity itself.

## JIHAD: ISLAMIC HOLY WAR

Two variant forms of jihad are distinguished in Islam: a spiritual mode (inner struggle), and a violent mode of striving in holy war to spread Islam and expand the Islamic state domain by force. Only 2% of the Bukhari hadiths that relate to jihad refer to the spiritual mode. The other 98% of the hadiths devoted to jihad claim that the violent mode of jihad is the supreme Islamic religious act. The small marginalized heretical Sufi sect adheres to the first mode of jihad. However, the paramount mainstream understanding and usage of Islamic jihad throughout fourteen centuries of Islamic history has been striving in offensive military conflict to expand the territory of Islam, conquer new populations for Islam, and establish Islamic law (Sharia). This is the classic primary meaning of jihad codified in Islamic law (Sharia) and attested in Islamic history. Contemporary Islamists are striving to impose Sharia globally and restore the totalitarian Islamic caliphate which Kemal Ataturk, the father of modern Turkey, abolished in 1924 in order to modernize Turkey.

There is no doubt from the historical record of Muhammad, the prophet of Islam, and his followers that he meant the jihad verses in the Qur'an to be understood literally, not spiritually (an-Nisa' 4:95; al-Anfal 8:65; etc). In fact, the Islamic scholarly consensus on the definition of jihad as aggressive warfare against non-Muslims was achieved over a thousand years ago. Muhammad was born into a culture of tribal conflict and bloodshed. Instead of improving it, he incorporated it into Islam through the concept of violent jihad. He retained the tribal warring culture as the basis for Islamic survival. Jihad warfare is a central doctrine of Islam. It helped define Islam from its very dawn. Islam was born as an ideology of totalitarian terror.

While wars are the exception to the norm in the history of any civilization, it is the norm in the Islamic civilization in dar-al-harb (the house of war), which is the territory of the non-Muslim populations. Jihad warfare is an Islamic institution, not a mere isolated event in Islamic history. The long bloody history of Islam reflects these teachings. It is rife with continuous harassment, persecution, subjugation and killing of non-Muslim infidels. All the battles of Muhammad were offensive except for the battles of Uhud (625 AD) and the ditch (627 AD) which were defensive.

Although Muhammad proclaimed in the Qur'an, al-Baqarah 2: 256 and al-Kafirun 109: 6 that there is no compulsion in religion, he abrogated that concept in al-Baqarah 2: 193; Al-'Imran 3: 83, 85; an-Nisa' 4: 89, 101-102; al-Anfal 8: 9, 12-13; al-Tawbah 9: 5, 29; Muhammad 47: 4; al-Hashr 59: 7; etc. In fact, the verse of the sword (al-Tawbah 9: 5) commanding Muslims to fight all who choose not to convert to Islam, whether they are inside or outside Arabia, abrogated at least 124 verses in the Qur'an that speak about love, peace, and forgiveness. Muhammad taught and practiced persecution, military conquest, subjugation, coercion and killing of non-Muslims. While Islam prohibits Muslims from paying or charging interest, it permits them to extort money from infidels and suppress them with usury to gain the upper hand.

At the end of his life, Muhammad, the prophet of Islam, said: "... I have been made victorious with terror, and while I was sleeping, the keys of the treasures of the world were brought to me and put in my hand ..." (Bukhari 4.52.220). On his deathbed, he commanded his followers to purge Arabia of non-Muslims (Bukhari 4.52.288; 5.59.716; 4.53.392, 380). He started the process (Muslim 19.4366), and his followers completed it (Bukhari 3.39.531; Muslim 10.3763). In fact, till this day, it is illegal to build a church in Saudi Arabia. In addition, the religious police will raid a house where Christians are gathered to worship, will arrest the leader of the worship service and torture him in prison.

## THE ISLAMIC DOCTRINE OF JIHAD

Islam is not a religion of peace. It provides a recipe for perpetual war. It is the only major religion in the world of today that institutionalizes violence against non-Muslims, which it calls jihad (normally translated "holy war," as it is usually used in that context. The literal translation is "struggle" or "strive"). Many verses in the Qur'an exhort Muslims to wage jihad against those who reject Islam, and against Muslims who do not practice Islam to its fullest. An entire sura 8 is called al-Anfal which means "spoils of war." There is no sura called "peace." Only 56 verses in the entire Qur'an mention peace, and most of them occur in the context of the Islamic greeting of "peace be upon you." Others deal with the peace that occurs after a military battle. The most vivid and repeated themes in the Qur'an are on jihad and the punishment of hell.

The Arabic word "jihad" appears in its various forms about thirty-five times in the Qur'an: nine times in the Meccan chapters (suras), and twenty-six times in the Medinan ones. The Arabic word "qatal," means "kill" (it does not mean inner struggle against vices). It appears in its various forms, meaning "kill" or "fight," about one hundred and twenty-three times in the Qur'an: thirty-four times in the Meccan chapters (suras), and eighty-nine times in the Medinan suras. The increase of these words in the Medinan Qur'an reflects the rise of the military power of the prophet of Islam after he immigrated to Medina, though a few uses of these words are not in a military context. In sura 9, al-Tawbah of the Qur'an, thought to be one of last suras given, each of these two words appear ten times in the context of war. In fact, verses al-Tawbah 9: 111 and an-Nisa' 4: 74 each contains three words rooted in the Arabic word "qatal" (meaning to kill): "God has bought of the believers their lives and their possessions, promising them paradise in return, so they fight (from "qatal") in God's cause, and kill (from "qatal"), and are killed (from "qatal")..." (al-Tawbah 9: 111).

In contrast with that, the Holy Bible (KJV) provides 420 verses on the subject of peace. Man strove for peace since ancient times (Isaiah 52: 7). Deep inner peace is the gift of the living God. Man cannot create his own peace. "The peace of God, which surpasses all understanding, will guard your hearts and minds through Christ Jesus" (Philippians 4: 7); "Now may the Lord of peace Himself give you peace always in every way" (2 Thessalonians 3: 16; James 3: 17-18); "There is no peace," says the LORD, "for the wicked" (Isaiah 48: 22; 57: 20-21; 59: 1-4, 7-11; etc).

In fact, the whole of the Qur'an and Islam support jihad in its various forms: jihad with money, with the written and spoken word and with the sword. The verses that do not refer to jihad directly or indirectly marshal the Muslims into a militant fraternity (ummah) on the basis of a common belief system, a common set of rituals, and a common code of conduct. Jihad in any form can be practiced only when there is an organized and disciplined community to practice it. The Qur'an marshals and motivates the ummah to impose Islam on the rest of mankind by every possible means, including the sword.

The purpose of jihad is the islamization of the conquered populations either by pressuring them to convert to Islam, or by forcing them to submit to Islamic rule. The main purpose of jihad is political, not religious. It is an instrument for both the universalization of the Islamic religion, and the establishment of an imperial world state. Islamic jihad must continue until the whole world is under the rule of Islamic law. All the Sunni and Shia Islamic schools of jurisprudence command waging war against unbelievers in order to establish the rule of Islamic law over them. War is the main vehicle of Islamic religious expansion. Without the sword of Muhammad and his followers after him, Islam will not exist today. Over a thousand years of unprecedented military expansion, the Islamic armies invaded vast territories in the Middle East, North Africa and even Europe. Muslim Arabs and Moors had controlled Spanish territory for eight hundred years, Portugal for six hundred years, Greece and Bulgaria for five hundred years, Romania and Serbia for four hundred years, Sicily for three hundred years, and Hungary for one hundred fifty years.

Authoritative Muslim historians, such as Ahmad ibn Yahya al-Baladhuri (d. 892) and al-Tabari (838-923), attest the fact that Islam was spread by the sword.

### *Jihad in the Qur'an, Hadith and Sharia*

Violent jihad is a central Islamic doctrine. The prophet of Islam repeatedly stressed that there is nothing better and nobler for a Muslim to do than to engage in jihad warfare (Bukhari 1.2.26; Muslim 20.4642). He claimed that engaging in jihad warfare is more meritorious than prayers, fasting, pilgrimage, etc. He warned Muslims who did not participate in jihad warfare of punishment (Abu Dawud 14.2497). He taught that Muslims who fight in jihad would be rewarded with a higher level in the Islamic paradise (an-Nisa' 4: 95; Muslim 20.4645).

Muslims are called upon to proclaim Islam by subduing and conquering non-Muslims, murdering them, destroying their temples, and looting their possessions.

In general, the obligation to participate in violent jihad is a collective one. It becomes a personal imperative one for every Muslim when Muslim lands are invaded by uninvited non-Muslim forces (Reliance of the Traveler, o9.3).

The violent activities of the Muslim zealots are fully supported and encouraged by the Islamic teachings. Muhammad said: "I have been ordered to fight with the people till they say, 'None has the right to be worshipped but Allah ..." (Bukhari 4.52.196; 1.2.25; etc). Jihad is a Muslim religious duty and obligation, like pilgrimage (al-Baqarah 2: 216). Rejecting jihad amounts to rejecting a fundamental Qur'anic dogma. The Qur'an condemns Muslims who refuse to fight in jihad (al-Anfal 8: 20, 47, 49; al-Tawbah 9: 24, 39, 81-82). Some Islamist groups consider Muslims that do not participate in jihad infidels. Those who wage jihad rank highest in Islam.

References to jihad, and killing of infidels who reject Islam and of apostates who leave Islam abound in the Qur'an. It contains about 164 verses that refer to jihad warfare against non-Muslims and distributing the spoils of war. 24% of Medinan Qur'an is devoted to jihad.

"Fight against such of those to whom the Scriptures were given (Christians and Jews) as believe in neither god (the god of Islam) nor the last day, who do not forbid what god and his apostle (Muhammad) have forbidden, and do not embrace the true faith (Islam), until they pay tribute out of hand and are utterly subdued" (al-Tawbah 9: 29)

"When the forbidden months are past, then fight and slay the Pagans wherever you find them, and seize them, beleaguer them, and lie in wait for them in every stratagem; but if they repent, and establish regular prayers and practice regular charity, then open the way for them: for Allah is Oft-Forgiving, Most Merciful" (al-Tawbah 9: 5, 12, 14, 19, 20, 29, 36, 38, 39, 41, 73, 81, 86, 88, 111, 123; al-Baqarah 2: 190, 193, 216, 244; Al-Imran 3: 169; an-Nisa' 4: 47, 74, 76, 77, 84, 89, 95; al-Ma'idah 5: 33, 51; al-Anfal 8: 12-17, 39, 59-60, 65, 67, 74; al-Anbiya' 21: 44; Muhammad 47: 4-6, 35; al-Fath 48: 16; al-Hujurat 49: 15; al-Mumtahanah 60: 1, 11; as-Saff 61: 4; at-Tahrim 66: 9; etc).

The Qur'an urges Muslims to kill, even those willing to surrender (al-Anfal 8: 67). The Qur'an claims that Islam is superior to all other religions (Al-Imran 3: 85; al-Tawbah 9: 33; al-Fath 48: 28; as-Saff 61: 9; etc). The jihad warfare commands for waging offensive, aggressive and unjust wars to Islamize all the non-Muslim populations are open-ended, perpetual, global, and generic in nature. That is what motivates Islamists to terrorize and kill non-Muslims following the example of Muhammad, the architect of Islam.

To read such blood thirsty injunctions in the Qur'an, the holiest book of Islam, is shocking. It grants Muslim jihadis a license to kill in the name of the Islamic god in the Islamic jihad. Extreme hatred and bloody violence against the non-believers are built into the religion of Islam. It is a historical fact that, with the exception of some Indonesian islands, no nation has ever willingly converted to Islam. On the other hand, no nation has ever unwillingly been converted to Christianity in the first three centuries of the Christian era. In addition, the Hadith collections of Sahih al-Bukhari and Sahih Muslim include hundreds of references to jihad warfare. A sampling of the Islamic teaching on violence is provided herein from the Hadith of Sahih al-Bukhari which is second in authority only to the Qur'an in Sunni Islam. It contains about 199 references to jihad in the sense of armed warfare against non-Muslims. Muhammad, the prophet of Islam, said:

"The example of a Mujahid in Allah's Cause— and Allah knows better who really strives in His Cause——is like a person who fasts and prays continuously. Allah guarantees that He will admit the Mujahid in His Cause into Paradise if he is killed, otherwise He will return him to his home safely with rewards and war booty" (Bukhari 4.52.46; 1.2.35);

"Nobody who dies and finds good from Allah (in the Hereafter) would wish to come back to this world even if he were given the whole world and whatever is in it, except the martyr who, on seeing the superiority of martyrdom, would like to come back to the world and get killed again (in Allah's Cause)" (Bukhari 4.52.53);

"There is no migration (after the Conquest of Mecca), but Jihad and good intentions, and when you are called for Jihad, you should immediately respond to the call" (Bukhari 4.52.42; etc).

All the four principal Sunni schools of jurisprudence, the Maliki, Hanbali, Hanafi, and Shafi'i, agree on the importance of jihad. Prominent Islamic scholars of antiquity from each of the four major schools of jurisprudence in historical Islam clearly understood the Qur'anic injunctions of jihad to command holy war. This includes al-Tabari (838-923), al-Biadawi (d. 1286), Ibn Khaldun (1332-1406), Ibn Kathir (1301-1373), Ibn Taymiyya (1263-1328), al-Ghazzali (1058-1111) who was a peaceful Sufi, etc.

Reliance of the Traveler (Undat al-Salik), the Shafi'i manual of Islamic law, devotes three sections o9, o10, o11 (eleven pages) to jihad. Making war on unbelievers is one of the responsibilities of the Muslim nation. The Islamic umma (nation) must exist in a state of perpetual war, interrupted only by temporary truces, with the non-Muslim world in order to compel either conversion to Islam, or subjugation to its rulers. When the Islamist regime is militarily weak, it reaches out for truce and peace simply in order to buy time to build up its strength (Muhammad 47: 35). Those that reject the invitation to convert to Islam are required to pay the poll tax (jizya) in humiliation and subjugation in their homelands. Should they refuse, war is to be declared against them (Muslim 19.4294; etc). In addition, Shia Islam calls for the necessity of jihad. Islam lacks any doctrine of equal coexistence. Islam lacks any doctrine of coexistence with non-Muslims in equality. In fact, peaceful coexistence as equals in a pluralistic society is not an option in Islam.

Islam divides humanity into two classes: a superior class of Muslims (Al-'Imran 3: 110; at-Tawbah 9: 33), and an inferior class of non-Muslims (infidels). There are more than four hundred verses in the Qur'an that describe the torment of hell that the god of Islam has prepared for the infidel. There are approximately seven hundred verses in more than fifty Qur'anic suras that have explicit negative references to the Jews (an-Nisa' 4: 47; al-Ma'idah 5: 13; etc.). The Qur'an dehumanizes and demonizes the non-Muslim infidels and calls them "... the vilest of animals ..." (al-Anfal 8: 55; al-A'raf 7: 179), and the vilest of all creatures (al-Bayyinah 98: 6; al-Mujadilah 58: 20). It claims that Jews were transformed into apes (al-Baqarah 2: 65 and al-A'raf 7: 166), and Jews and Christians into swine (al-Ma'idah 5: 59-60)? It likens Jews to asses (al-Jum'ah 62: 5). It tells Muslims that Jews are cursed because of their unbelief (al-Ma'idah 5: 78). Muhammad claimed that Muslims will eventually exterminate the Jews in a global holocaust. "Allah's Apostle said, The Hour will not be established until you fight with the Jews, and the stone behind which a Jew will be hiding will say, O Muslim! There is a Jew hiding behind me, so kill him" (Bukhari 4.52.177; Muslim 41.6981-5).

The Qur'an goes as far as commanding Muslims to eschew friendships with infidels, including Christians and Jews (Al-'Imran 3: 28, 118; an-Nisa' 4: 89, 101, 144; al-Ma'idah 5: 51, 82), even if they be their fathers, sons, brothers, or kin (al-Tawbah 9: 23; al-Mujadalah 58: 22). Abu Obaida, son of Garah, who was praised by the prophet of Islam, killed his own father who refused Islam. Musaab, son of Omair, never listened for his mother's cries for help and left her to die because she rejected Islam. Abu Bakr, the first guided caliph, told his father he would kill him if he refused Islam.

Traditional orthodox Islam promises the jihadist that if he dies fighting for the god of Muhammad in Islamic jihad, he is guaranteed to be rewarded with the sinful Islamic paradise of sexual promiscuity and gluttony (as-Saff 61: 10-13; ad-Dukhan 44: 51-56; at-Tur 52: 17-29; ar-Rahman 55: 46-78; al-Tawbah 9: 111; Al-Imran 3: 157-8, 169; an-Nisa' 4: 74; al-Fatir 35: 50; Muhammad 47: 6; etc). Muhammad said: "Know that Paradise is under the shades of swords" (Bukhari 4.52.73, 72, 46, 48, 53; 4.53.386). Muhammad promised these fictitious rewards, which are merely a desert mirage, in order to motivate his fighters. Unable to give them a reason to live, he gave them a reason to die.

On the other hand, should the jihadist survive and live, he gets a share from the spoils of war, which enriches him (al-Anfal 8: 41, 60). In addition, he obtains forgiveness of his sins (as-Saff 61: 11-12), and the love of the Islamic god (an-Nisa' 4: 95; al-Anfal 8: 16). According to orthodox Islamic belief, martyrdom in Islamic jihad is the only sure way a Muslim could take to avoid the horrifying torments of the grave and hell, and to get into the Islamic paradise. In fact, when a Muslim dies in jihad, his corpse is not washed or dressed in clean clothes. It goes in his coffin just as he died. The stains of blood on it are a witness for him before the Islamic god. It is a sign of honor that would prompt the angels to treat him in a special distinguished way.

### The Example of the Prophet of Islam

The history of Islam to-date has been one long jihad (holy war) against non-Muslims. Muslims are exhorted to emulate Muhammad's pattern of behavior (al-Ahzab 33: 21). In the ten years that he lived in Medina (622-632 AD), Muhammad, the prophet of Islam, was the aggressor in seventy-three of seventy-five raids and conflicts he got involved in. He initiated seventy-three raids, military expeditions, full-scale military campaigns, and small assassination hit bands to kill his opponents. This adds up to more than seven slayings, raids or battles for each of the ten years he ruled in Medina in the beginning of the Islamic era. There is a lot of blood on his hands. He did not personally participate in forty-eight of those raids. He personally accompanied his Muslim fighters in twenty-seven raids. In eight of them, he was in the battlefield fighting alongside with them. Muhammad used to order his followers and commanders to kill those who disbelieved in his god, not making any distinction between combatants, and civilians.

The prophet of Islam financed his military expeditions through a variety of avenues. His economic lifeblood was the plunder usurped from defeated enemies, and the jizya tax levied on unbelievers. The majority of the Arabs who adopted Islam and fought in the military battles of jihad did so in order to acquire booty usurped from the conquered tribes and peoples who did not submit to Islam. The Muslim fighters have been motivated mainly by their greed for the booty of wealth and women (al-Fath 48: 19-20). Four-fifths of the booty went to them, and one-fifth to Muhammad, or to the caliph after him (al-Anfal 8: 41). That was how the god of Islam made Muhammad and his followers wealthy (ad-Duha 93: 8; al-Tawbah 9: 74; Bukhari 3.37.495). Muhammad distributed his share of the booty as he wished to close relatives, orphans, the needy, travelers, and new converts to Islam to coax them to stay in Islam (al-Tawbah 9: 60; Bukhari 4.53.373; 4.55.558; Muslim 5.2313).

Sura 8 is titled "al-Anfal," which means "the spoils of war." The entire book no. 53 of Bukhari is called "One-fifth of Booty to the Cause of Allah (Khumus)." The battle plunder included captive women and children who were sold as slaves for profit. Slave trading flourished in Arabia in the early Islamic era. The Qur'an describes the loot as "...lawful and good...," and supports pillaging and plundering infidels, enslaving their children, and placing their women in concubinage (al-Anfal 8: 69; an-Nisa' 4: 24; etc). In fact, the first Islamic raid on the peaceful Meccan merchant caravan at Nakhlah was to loot and rob the caravan. This is what motivates bandits and pirates.

### *The Rules of Jihad*

Based on Islamic jurisprudence derived from the Qur'an, the Hadith, and classical Islamic legal opinions, the principal rules of Jihad are summarized herein. These rules are immoral and exploitative:

1. Muslims may enslave women and children of the conquered non-Muslim populations (Reliance of the Traveler, #o9.13). Islam codifies slavery in its religious law (Sharia). Selling humans into slavery produced a lot of wealth for Muhammad and his followers. Slaying women and children is prohibited, not for mercy, but for profit. However, if a Muslim slays them, he is not censured.
2. The marriages of those women are annulled upon their capture. They may be forced to marry their Muslim masters and added to their harim (an-Nisa' 4: 24).
3. Worse off, Muslim jihadists are allowed to rape the captured female prisoners of war. Ali, Muhammad's cousin and son-in-law, did this abomination, and Muhammad defended him (Bukhari 5.59.637). Islam codifies and legalizes rape for conquering jihadist Muslim men (Muslim 8.3371, 3373-7, 3432). Islam is the only religion in the world that condones and encourages the crime of raping female captives of war as a reward to victorious Muslim soldiers for conquering the infidels.
4. Muslim jihadists are allowed to kill old men and Christian monks (Reliance of the Traveler, #o9.10), and women and children in night raids (Bukhari 4.52.256; Muslim 19.4321-4323).
5. The non-Muslim prisoners of war may be killed, enslaved, ransomed (exchanged for money or a Muslim captive), or released (al-Ahzab 33: 26; Muhammad 47: 4; Reliance of the Traveler, #o9.14).
6. Pagan Arabs were pressured to convert to Islam on pain of death. Enemy men who converted to Islam were allowed to keep their property and children (al-Tawbah 9: 5, 11, 14, 33; Bukhari 4.52.263).
7. The Muslim jihadist invaders may confiscate or destroy non-Muslim civilian property, including homes and groves (al-Ahzab 33: 27; al-Hashr 59: 5, 2; Bukhari 4.52.262, 263; Muslim 19.4324).
8. A Muslim jihadist who kills a non-Muslim in jihad gets his belongings. This is called personal booty. In addition,

he gets his share from the four-fifths of the collective spoils of the battle.

9. The Muslim jihadist invaders give the people of the Book (Jews and Christians) three options (al-Tawbah 9: 29) either to convert to Islam, to keep their faith and pay the submission tax of jizya (poll tax) while living under Islamic rule, or to get killed fighting if they refused the first two options. However, Muslims can mount surprise attacks on the infidels, slay them and usurp their property. This is not censured because the victims are not Muslims, and they are not protected in the Islamic state.

Although Islam permits Jews and Christians to remain in their faiths as dhimmis under Islamic rule (second class citizens in their homelands), from the dawn of Islamic history till the present, forced conversions are widely practiced in the Islamic world. This is because Islamic teachings scorn non-Muslim infidels who are, according to Islamic culture, bound to the Islamic hell. Battle, animosity and hatred directed towards the non-Muslim infidels are part of Islamic mindset.

## The Dhimma

The concept of the dhimma was first introduced by the prophet of Islam. After conquering the Jews of the oasis of Khaybar in 628, he agreed to let them continue to cultivate their oasis only if they gave him half their produce. He reserved the right to cancel out this treaty and expel the Jews whenever he liked (Bukhari 4.53.380). This type of treaty is called a "dhimma."

Peoples that came under Islamic rule and agreed to pay tribute (jizya) in return for Muslim protection are referred to as "dhimmis." They were ultimately reduced to the status of a tiny culturally derivative marginalized minority in their homelands. The only peoples that escaped Islamic dhimmitude were those who were successful in resisting and eventually, after centuries of armed struggle, defeating Islamic imperialistic jihad: the Christians of Europe and the Hindus of India.

The dhimmis (Jews, Christians, etc. under Islamic rule) were not equal to Muslims in dignity and rights. They lived in subjugation to Islamic rule. The terms of the dhimma were first articulated by the second guided caliph, Umar ibn al-Khattab (634-644). The dhimma was an agreement imposed on conquered populations. It required them not to build churches, monasteries, and synagogues, nor restore them. It also required them to wear clothes different from those worn by Muslims, not to acquire weapons, not to ride horses, to refrain from using church bells and from erecting crosses on top of the churches, not to proselytize Muslims, to pay the poll tax (jizya), etc. The jizya indicated the dhimmis submission and inferiority to Islamic rule (at-Tawbah 9: 29). It led to the overall humiliation and abasement of non-Muslims. Payment of the jizya often took place in a demeaning ceremony to ensure the belittlement and humiliation of the dhimmi. The Muslim tax-collector slapped the Christian man on the back of his neck or on his head telling him: 'O unbeliever, pay al-jizya.' This was followed by the Christian man handing him the tax money with his head bowed down and his back bent while the tax-collector held him by the beard. The dhimmi was not allowed to marry a Muslim woman. The penalty for such marriage was death. The dhimmi was barred from public office. The history of Muslim dealings with the dhimmis is one of oppression, random massacres, avaricious greed and plunder, extortion under the threat of persecution, rape, systematic degradation and slavery.

According the Shafi'i school of Islamic Sharia, the dhimma pact is broken if the dhimmi fights the Muslims, refuses to pay the jizya, or disobeys Muslim laws. It is also broken if the dhimmi violates the dhimma's additional stipulations, if any, by having relation with a Muslim woman, leading a Muslim away from Islam, killing a Muslim, or slandering Muhammad and his god. When the dhimma is broken, the rules of the prisoners of war will apply on the dhimmi subjecting him to either death, slavery, ransoming, or release. By denying basic human rights to non-Muslims in Islamic controlled lands, Islam has sanctioned slavery on an unprecedented scale. Jihad slavery in its various forms (slave soldiers, harem slavery, child slavery, etc.) became a powerful tool to both expansive islamization and the support of Muslim society.

The dhimma terms and requirements are codified in Islamic Sharia (Reliance of the Traveler, #o11). Under Western pressure on the weakened Ottoman Empire, the dhimmis were emancipated in the mid-nineteenth century. Although Islamic Sharia is enforced at this time only in a few countries, such as Saudi Arabia, Iran, and the Sudan, many of its elements are practiced in Islamic countries. It is surprising indeed that the dhimmi communities have survived at all despite the Islamic pressures on them throughout centuries of Islamic rule.

## HISTORICAL EXAMPLES OF JIHAD

With the exception of the battle of Uhud in 625 and the battle of the ditch in 627, all the battles of the prophet of Islam were offensive. All jihad wars undertaken after his death were offensive expansive wars. The Persian and Byzantine empires bordering Arabia were not a threat to the Muslim Arabs. In the West, Islamic armies conquered the Levant, North Africa, and finished the conquest of most of Spain by 715. Christians completed the liberation of Spain in 1492. In the East, the Muslim invaders conquered the Persian Empire. By 1206, they had invaded the Punjab, Sindh, Delhi, and beyond. Muslims stopped waging large scale jihad wars after 1683 because the Islamic world had grown too weak. Examples of jihad wars and the atrocities associated with it abound in Islamic history. We cite a few of them herein.

Wherever the Islamic armies invaded, they caused massive destructions, countless systematic massacres of extermination, enslavement and exile of a great portion of the population, and great human suffering. Looting and pillaging the wealth of conquered lands, periodic ransoms, and the jizya tax impoverished and ruined the conquered populations. Economic decline and general impoverishment followed in the conquered territories. More blood has been shed for Islam than for any other cause in history. Some historians estimate that in India alone, more than 80 million people were massacred by the sword of Islam. In addition, 10 million Buddhists, 120 million Christians and African Animists, and many Zoroastrians in Persia were killed by marauding Islamic armies, both during their conquests and in the centuries that followed. The sword of Islam spread death, devastation and dark terror over many lands.

Examples of violent Islamic jihad in modern times are the civil wars in South Sudan, Afghanistan, Lebanon, the Russian war in the Caucasus, and the attacks in the West. To the Muslim fundamentalist, a Muslim terrorist who kills unarmed innocent non-Muslim men, women, and children in the predominantly non-Muslim West is a war hero. What the Islamists could not accomplish by military conquest in the world of today, they are attempting to accomplish peacefully by proclaiming the religion of Islam. The problem is that they do not tell the truth about Islam in their proclamations. Instead, they sugarcoat it in their attempts to sell it dishonestly to unwary Westerners.

### The Early Islamic Era

Banu Qurayza, the last Jewish tribe in Medina, rejected Islam. They remained neutral in the battle of the trench (627). Muhammad, the prophet of Islam, questioned their loyalty, and besieged them. They surrendered. Muhammad appointed Sa'd ibn Muadh, one of his most fanatic followers, to decide their fate. Sa'd was wounded in the battle of the trench and lusted after revenge. He died soon after issuing his verdict. His verdict was that all the men of the tribe were to be killed, and the possessions of the tribe were to be divided among the Muslims. Muhammad ratified this unjust horrific judgment, and in order to justify the bloodbath, he claimed that his god sanctioned it (al-Ahzab 33: 26-27).

Muhammad ordered that a trench be dug in the night across the market place in Medina, and commanded that the male captives be brought forth to the trench in companies of five or six at a time, where they were beheaded and buried in the trench. This continued all day long into the evening till all the men of the tribe, numbering 800-900, were killed. Muhammad observed in person the horrific killings. If is important to stress that these tribesmen were not armed, and were not a threat to Muhammad and his followers. They were murdered in cold blood. Muhammad was responsible for the first Islamic massacre of 627 in the long bloody history of Islam.

The women and children of the tribe were sold into slavery, and its possessions were looted. Muhammad took for himself Rihana whose husband and all her male relatives had just perished in the massacre. Muhammad wanted to remove non-Muslims from Medina and Arabia by the sword, if necessary (Bukhari 4.52.288; 5.59.716; 4.53.392, 380). He started the process, and his followers completed it (Muslim 19.4366). In fact, till this day, it is illegal to build a church in Saudi Arabia. In addition, the religious police will raid a house where Christians are gathered to worship, will arrest the leader of the worship service and torture him in prison.

Muhammad warned the people who harassed him in the market place of Mecca saying that he would come back as slaughterer. The army that Muhammad led in his invasion of Mecca years later had a black flag signifying death with the word "punishment" written on it. Upon conquering Mecca, Muhammad ordered the killing of several persons for making satirical songs against him. In conquering Mecca, Muhammad brought to it death, not salvation. This contrasts with the peaceful triumphant entry of Jesus into Jerusalem riding a donkey, not bearing a sword and without an army.

After the death of Muhammad, the caliph Abu Bakr invaded Syria. During the campaign of 634, the entire region between Gaza and Caesarea was devastated. Four thousand Christian, Jewish and Samaritan peasants were massacred. During the military campaigns of caliph Umar ibn al-Khattab, the second guided caliph, in Mesopotamia between 635 and 642, monasteries were sacked, the monks were killed, and Christian Arabs executed or forced to convert.

In Elam, the population was put to the sword. The Arab invasion of the Middle East was not by any means a joyous liberating experience. It brought a great deal of death and destruction. The inhabitants of towns taken by storm were either killed or led into captivity, and their property was looted. Umar ibn al-Khattab was so brutal and despotic in his retaliation against the Persians for opposing Islam's spread that to this day the Iranians celebrate the anniversary of his assassination with great festivities.

Amr ibn al-As conquered Egypt in 639-642. As he advanced in it, he captured the town of Bahnesa near Fayum and put to the sword its inhabitants, including old men, women and children. He committed the same atrocities in other towns in Egypt. Similar atrocities occurred in North Africa. Tripoli was pillaged in 643. Carthage was razed to the ground and most of its inhabitants killed. The same pattern was followed in Anatolia, Syria, Iraq, and Iran.

Al-Hajjaj, the governor of Iraq (694-714), instructed his commander Muhammad ibn Qasim in 712 to invade India and destroy the unbelievers. After the capture of the port of Debal, the Muslim army took three days to slaughter many of its inhabitants. In the town of Brahminabad, the Muslim army killed more than 6000 men. In subsequent invasions, Islamic armies targeted the Hindu temples and monasteries in an orgy of pillage and arson. Those not killed were captured and sold as slaves. Mahmud of Ghazni (971-1030), the head of a Turco-Afghan dynasty, invaded India destroying, pillaging and massacring. He justified his actions by constantly referring to Qur'anic injunctions to kill the idolaters. At the battle of Somnah, the site of a celebrated Hindu temple, he killed about 50,000 inhabitants.

## The Middle Ages

The Jews of North Africa and Spain suffered several massacres under the Islamic Arab rule, such as the massacre of more than 6000 Jews in the town of Fez (Morocco) in 1033, the massacres of Cordoba and other places in Spain in 1010-1013, the massacre of the entire Jewish community of about 4000 in Granada, Spain in 1066, etc.

The Muslim Berbers Almoravids (1056-1147) arrived in Spain in 1086, followed by the more fanatic and violent Almohad Muslim Berbers who arrived in Spain in 1146-47. Almoravids deported from Spain a large number of Christians to Morocco in 1106, 1126 and 1138. The Almohads (1130-1269) wreaked enormous persecution on both the Jewish and Christian populations in Spain and North Africa, including massacres, slavery and forced conversions.

The Muslim Seljuk Turks invaded Asia Minor over a period of four centuries from the middle of the eleventh century. These invasions were accompanied with extermination of local populations or their precipitate flight. Entire cities, and whole provinces fell into decay. Some fertile districts were laid waste. Impenetrable thickets sprang up in vast areas replacing fertile fields and pasture. This was followed by Ottoman jihad campaigns in the European Balkans. The Turks practiced wide-spread forced conversions which persisted throughout the sixteenth century.

In the fourteenth and early fifteenth centuries, Timur the Lame (known as Tamerlane) launched jihad wars against both non-Muslims and Muslims accusing the latter of lukewarmness towards Islam. He combined Mongol barbarity with Islamic fanaticism. He massacred in the thousands out of Qur'anic piety, as a duty and sacred mission. The following is a sampling of his massacres: his cold-blooded slaughter of 100,000 captive Indians near Delhi in December, 1398, his burying alive of 4000 Armenians in 1400-1, his erecting 20 towers of human skulls at Aleppo and Damascus in the same year, his massacre of 70,000 of the inhabitants of Isfahan in November 1387, etc.

The Wahhabis of Arabia condemned most non-Wahhabi Muslims as infidels, and waged jihad against them. In 1801 and 1802, the Saudi Wahhabis under the leadership of Abdul Aziz ibn Muhammad ibn Saud attacked and captured the holy Shia cities of Karbala and Najaf in Iraq, massacred parts of the Muslim population and destroyed the tombs of Husayn ibn Ali, the grandson of Muhammad, and Ali ibn abi-Talib.

### *The Armenian Genocide*

In the nineteenth century, the Armenians demanded their equal rights and attempted to break out of their Ottoman Islamic dhimmitude peacefully. They sought reforms in the Turkish/Ottoman system of government. As a result, the Armenian genocide began. The Muslim Ottoman Turks massacred more than 200,000 unarmed Armenian civilians in 1894-96 during the reign of sultan Abdul Hamid II (the Sassoun massacre). That was followed, under the young Turks regime, by the Adana massacres of 25,000

Armenians in 1909. This climaxed in the 1915 genocide when additional 600,000-800,000 unarmed Armenian civilians were massacred. The Muslim perpetrators who committed these bloody atrocities were guided by Islamic Sharia prescriptions providing that if the dhimmi requested his equal rights, and freedom from his bondage, he forfeited the protection of the caliph.

The genocide of the Armenian Christians in World War I was an ethnic cleansing of central Turkey by an Islamic jihad wherein Muslim Turks systematically murdered unarmed civilian Christian Armenian males over the age of twelve en masse in 1915. Women and children were deported from their centuries-old Armenian villages. Many of them died or were killed in their arduous journey. Others were given out as slaves, or forced to convert to Islam. The Armenian properties were looted. At the end, about one and a half million Armenian civilians died and were killed in those atrocities. Turkish Armenia ceased to exist. The four elements of the Armenian liquidation in central Turkey—deportation, enslavement, forced conversion, and massacre—reproduced the historic conditions of Islamic jihad carried out from the seventh century on. Successive Turkish governments have consistently refused to acknowledge the historic fact of the Armenian genocide, and to pay compensations to the Armenians.

## *The Sudanese Genocide*

During the brutal civil war between the Muslim Arab North of the Sudan, and the Christian and animist black South (1955-72, 1983-2005), Sudan was the site of the most vicious anti-Christian persecution raging in the world. The Islamist government of the Sudan committed genocide in the South and the Nubba mountains, including massacres, rape, looting, and slavery. Hundreds of Christian villages were razed to the ground. The end result was a devastated economy, a divided country, the death of approximately two million people, and the displacement of over five million people. South Sudan seceded from the Sudan, and became an independent state on July 9, 2011.

Despite the relentless cruel Islamic persecution, the Sudanese Church grew very fast in that period. Many Muslims and animists came to Christ in the Sudan than anywhere else in the world. In twenty years, Christians grew from 5% to over 20% of the Sudanese population (and 80% of South Sudan). South Sudan is the Christian bulwark against the southward advance of radical Islam into central Africa.

In the late nineteenth century, the British General Charles Gordon succeeded in breaking the back of the slave trade in the Sudan. However, the Muslim Sudanese Mahdi, Muhammad ibn Abdullah, that succeeded him in 1885 declared jihad warfare, and restored the slave trade in the Sudan. During the civil war, the soldiers of the Islamic government of the Sudan and the Arab militias armed by the government attacked African villages, kidnapped and sold as slaves tens of thousands of Sudanese Christian and animist men, women and children. There is no doubt that slavery is still widespread in the Sudan, including exporting slaves to Muslim countries in the Persian Gulf.

### *Jihad Atrocity in the U.S.A.*

On Sept. 11, 2001, the Islamist organization of al-Qaeda attacked the U.S.A. this resulted in the death of about 3000 innocent civilians. None of the leading Islamic clerics in the Muslim world condemned the 9/11 atrocities. In fact, some praised it?! Misguided Muslim crowds celebrated it in the streets of the Middle East. Muslim governments, who call for tolerance of Muslims in the West, have never apologized for 9/11 atrocities. The U.S. military was able to locate the leadership of al-Qaeda and destroy it.

## JIHAD AGAINST THE 'ENEMIES OF ISLAM'

The subject of armed jihad runs right through the writings and pronouncements of Markaz spokesmen and is, in fact, the most prominent theme in the Markaz's discourse. Indeed, its understanding of Islam maybe seen as determined almost wholly by this preoccupation, so much so that its reading of Islam seems to be a product of its own political project. The contours of its ideological framework are constructed in such a way that the theme of armed jihad appears as its central, over-riding concern. Not surprisingly, therefore, it constructs a discursive framework that, like Gilani's and the JIJK's, completely denies the legitimacy of the Kashmiri nationalist project, but at the same time goes considerably beyond the limited aims of the JIJK's jihad as Gilani conceives them in his writings.

There has been much discussion on the nature and forms of jihad in writings about Islam. Liberals have tended to explain it in terms of self-defence, while others have taken recourse to certain Sufi positions, where the foremost jihad (jihad-i akbar) is said to the struggle against the nafs or one's 'baser self' or ego. Yet others have suggested that jihad in the path of God (jihad fi sabil illah) can take many forms, and that armed struggle is just one of these. However, in the writings and speeches of Markaz spokesmen jihad appears unabashedly as qital or violent conflict waged against unbelievers. Indeed, it is projected as the one of the most central tenets of Islam, although it has traditionally not been included as one of the 'five pillars' of the faith. Thus, it is claimed that 'There is so much emphasis on this subject that some commentators and scholars of the Qur'an have remarked that the topic of the Qur'an is jihad', and that 'There is consensus of opinion among researchers of the Qur'an that no other action has been explained in such great detail as jihad'.

In order to properly understand the role of jihad for the Markaz's political project, it is necessary to situate it within the broader context of the Markaz's own understanding of Islam. Like other Islamist groups, the Markaz sees Islam as a perfect, all-embracing system and way of life. Islam is said to govern all aspects of personal as well as social life, in the form of the shari'ah. For the establishing of an Islamic system, an Islamic state is necessary, which would impose the shar'iah as the law of the land. This is seen as 'the solution to all our problems'. If such a state were to be set up and all Muslims were to live strictly according to 'the laws that Allah has laid down', then, it is believed, 'they would be able to control the whole world and exercise their supremacy'. Since Islam is seen as the very antithesis of nationalism, it demands the establishment of one universal Islamic state, ruled by a single khalifa. Thus, the present division of the Muslims into many nation-states must be overcome. Since 'the ummah is one', it follows from this that 'the system of khilafah does not recognize the physical borders or the independence of one Muslim country from another'. Hence, 'the state is one, the army is one, the flag is one, the budget is one, etc.'.

Islam is seen as a universal ideology meant for all humankind, and hence its message, and, in other words, the boundaries of the Islamic state, must be extended till the entire world comes under its domination. In order for the Islamic call to reach all peoples, it is the duty of the Islamic state to 'carry it to new lands'. This, it is acknowledged, 'will lead to a conflict with other states and ideologies', which can be resolved either peacefully, through diplomatic means, or by force. The Islamic state must first try the former option, but if that fails it is incumbent on it to take recourse to force and wage a jihad. No one can be forced to accept Islam, however, and jihad is to be waged only to bring 'recalcitrant' states under Islamic control by incorporating them within the ever-expanding boundaries of the Islamic state so that the new territories can be 'provided with the security that comes from the application of Islam', in other words, to be ruled by the shari'ah. The people of the conquered lands, if they choose not to convert to Islam, may continue to practise their own religion. In this way, jihad is seen as 'the method adopted by Islam to protect its lands and save humanity from slavery to man-made regimes'. It is, in short, 'the foreign policy of the Islamic State'.

The global jihadist programme of the Markaz presents itself in a liberationist garb, basing itself on widespread feelings of discontent and suffering of sections of Muslims who see themselves as being persecuted by Western-oriented elites in their own countries, as well as by the West more generally. The greatest problem of the Muslims, says Hafeez Muhammad Sa'eed, head of the Markaz, is their 'subjugation to the West'. Thus, the Markaz is reported to have gone so far as to call for a jihad against the USA. Jihad is contrasted with other forms of war that are pursued for purely worldly concerns, and is described as 'the act of supreme sacrifice to preserve human rights bestowed by Allah'. It is portrayed as a struggle 'to help the oppressed against the atrocities committed by the aggressors', and is compared with 'a surgeon using a blade during an operation'. Jihad is thus a means for challenging oppression and of establishing the rule of Islam.

Eight specific objectives are laid out for this grand jihadist enterprise. These objectives, in the words of an official Markaz statement, are:

- To end persecution and tumult.
- To enforce the Islamic world order.
- To force the disbelievers to pay jizya.
- To protect and shield the weak and the oppressed from oppression.
- To avenge the millions of Muslims who were and are being mercilessly slaughtered in various parts of the world.
- To punish those who have broken covenants made with the Muslims.
- To restore Muslims' possession of territories now occupied by disbelievers, such as Spain, India, Ba'it ul-Muqaddas (Jerusalem), Turkistan (Xinjiang).
- To defend and protect the Muslims continuously facing offensives from the disbelievers all over the world

Jihad is seen as the secret of Muslim power in the past when much of the known world was under Muslim rule, and it is argued that when Muslims 'abandoned jihad and other injunctions they began to degenerate'. In Markaz discourse, jihad is seen as a religious duty binding on all Muslims today. Thus, it is claimed that the prevailing global situation warrants all Muslims to be involved in some way of the other in jihad against non-Muslims. As an official Markaz publication puts its, 'Struggle and fighting against the disbelievers is a comprehensive process, very vast in its nature and scope, and it cannot be carried out successfully and duly unless all the classes of the Muslim community [...] participate in it'. In this grand war there are different roles for different people to play. Those who are ordered by the khalifa to fight must do so, while others may be required to assist the mujahidin by supplying them food, arms and other supplies, providing medical assistance, looking after their families in their absence or even by exhorting others to participate in the war. Thus, every Muslim, man or woman, must be mobilized to assist in the struggle in some form or the other, and if any Muslim has 'never intended to fight against the disbelievers', his or her faith 'is not without traces of hypocrisy'. Those believers who have the capacity to participate or assist in the jihad but do not do so are said to 'be living a sinful life'.

## VARIANT FORMS OF JIHAD

The variant forms of jihad contain two modes of operation: violent and non-violent. The goal of both is identical: to subjugate he non–Muslim population to the Islamic rule of Sharia. The violent mode includes assassinations, devshirme, vigilante justice, torture, etc. Islamists call the non-violent mode "civilization jihad," more appropriately called "stealth jihad." It is a pre-violent jihad. It includes infiltrating the legal system, and the educational, financial, government, intelligence, and military institutions of the West.

### *Assassinations*

Muhammad, the prophet of Islam, was the one who started in the seventh century the trail of blood of Islamic atrocities in Arabia. Muhammad urged his Muslim followers to kill his critics for him in order of silence them, and praised them for doing it afterwards. This led to the assassination of Asma' bint Marawan while she was nursing her baby home (A. Guilaune, The Life of Muhammad, pp. 675-676), 120-year-old Abu Afak (Ibn-Sa'd, Kitab al-Tabaqat al-Kabir, vol. 2, Trans. S. Moinul, p. 31), Kaab ibn al-Ashraf (Buchari 5.59.369; Muslim 19.4436), Abu Rafi Salaam (Bukhari 5.59.371), etc. That practice has been codified in Sharia. Blasphemy, criticizing or defaming Islam, its prophet, the Islamic god, the Qur'an, the Hadith or Sharia are punishable by death in all the schools of Sharia.

In the West, we can critically study Christianity and Judaism. In Islamic countries, Islamist writers attack Christianity. However, Christians are not allowed to criticize and refute Islam objectively. Intimidation and censorship express lack of confidence and weakness in the Islamic religion and its teachings. It cannot defend itself by reason. Therefore, Islamists resort to violence to protect it. Respect should be earned, not forced by intimidation.

Islam forbids anything critical about Muhammad or his god, and condemns anyone that originates the criticism, such as Salman Rushdie—the author of a 1988 book on the Satanic Verses of the Qur'an, the Danish cartoonists depicting Muhammad with a bomb in his bonnet (2005-2006) that precipitated mob violence in Islamic countries resulting in destruction and deaths, Theo Van Gogh who was murdered on Nov. 2, 2004 for producing a short documentary on the oppression of women under Islam, the anti-Islam Dutch politician Geert Wilders who has made a truthful 15-minute documentary on the violence in Islam and the Qur'an, etc. Islamist restraints on criticism of Islam are not directed only to states, but also against individuals.

## Devshirme

Abduction of children in late antiquity was a routine practice of tribes in conflict. These children were released after their relatives paid ransom. Those not ransomed, were sold as slaves.

The abduction of Jewish and Christian Dhimmi children also represented a form of forced conversion. Although illegal, there is substantial evidence that it occurred throughout the course of history, either sporadically — ransoming, supplying harems or as a contribution to the tribute — or in an institutionalized way, as in the devshirme system that functioned over three centuries in the Balkans for Christian children (Bat Ye'or, The Decline of Eastern Christianity under Islam, p. 91).

The Ottoman sultan Orkhan (1326-59) introduced the practice of devshirme in 1330. It was a regular tribute (blood tax) of a fifth of the 7-15 year-old Christian children from conquered Balkan regions exacted every about four years initially. This periodic tribute eventually became an annual tribute. The cruel Muslim Ottoman soldiers literally wrenched the children from their weeping mothers' arms. Those who refused to surrender their sons were put to death on the spot by hanging. Those children were sent in the thousands to remote areas to discourage their escape. They were forcibly converted to Islam and given military training in the janissary corps. The heartless recruiters used to take a surplus of children in the hope of selling them back to their families. If their families were too poor to redeem them, they remained slaves.

The devshirme system enslaved and forcibly converted to Islam an estimated five hundred thousand to one million primarily Balkan Christian adolescent boys. The janissaries became the Muslim power's elite troops, the cruelest soldiers against Christianity and their own people because of the fanaticism taught to them, and the cruelty they lived through.

This regular bloodletting from the conquered peoples increased the Muslim population and correspondingly reduced that of the Christians. The devshirme was theoretically abolished in 1656, but recruitment of ichoghlani continued until the mid-eighteenth century (Bat Ye'or, The Decline of Eastern Christianity under Islam, p. 115).

### *Vigilante Justice*

Islamic Sharia encourages vigilante justice under certain conditions, because a Muslim is not only required to follow the laws of the Islamic god, but is also entrusted to enforce them on earth without needing authorization from the state. Examples on that abound: the 1994 Islamist attempt in Egypt to assassinate Dr. Nagib Mahfouz, a moderate Muslim, who won the 1988 Nobel Laureate in literature for his novel of "Children of Gebelawi" which islamists considered blasphemous; killing Dr. Farag Foda, a liberal Muslim Egyptian professor, in 1992 in Egypt by Islamist fundamentalists; the death fatwa of Ayatollah Khomeini of Iran against the Indian writer Salman Rushdi for his 1988 novel on the Satanic Verses of the Qur'an supported with a million-dollar reward (doubled in 1997) for his death; the killing of the Dutch film maker Theo van Gogh in Amsterdam by an Islamist for producing a twelve-minute film called Submission decrying the mistreatment of Muslim women; etc.

Every Muslim is required to correct the conduct of his fellow Muslims. A killer of an apostate who left Islam, a robber, or an adulterer is forgiven and exempted from punishment for murder under Sharia law. Muslims who commit genocide are spared from punishment if they repent. Individual fatwas issued by Islamic clerics for killing apostates, while not binding on the Islamic state, can be acted upon by any Islamist without getting punished for his crime. Radical Islamists brand all who disagree with them as enemies of Islam and apostates. The violators of Sharia fear vigilante justice by the Islamist public, such as their friends, neighbors, relatives, parents, brothers, or sisters.

Vigilante justice has no restraints and is bound to be abused. It results in relationships between Muslims based on fear and arrogance. It leads to a chaotic society. Death squads or street mobs take justice into their own hands. Mobs stone women accused of adultery. Boys throw acid at girls because they do not like their dress, etc. Muslims are turned against each other. They have to watch their backs. Many of the accusations of apostasy and blasphemy are the result of personal grudges borne by the accusers against the defendants to settle personal scores, or are tools for Islamic governments to silence opposition. Deep-seated distrust plagues Islamic society. Vigilante justice is where Islam gets its power. It is not the power of conviction, but the power of fear.

Many Muslim converts to Christianity in Europe live in hiding fearing for their lives from Islamist violence. However, some European ex-Muslims are summoning the courage to stand up in defense of their rights. They have formed organizations of ex-Muslims in Germany, Britain, Finland, Denmark, Norway, Sweden, and the Netherlands. They no longer tolerate the intolerance of Islam. Mr. Ehsan Jami, the founder of the Netherlands Central Committee for Ex-Muslims (9/11/07) was violently attacked by Muslim fundamentalists on three separate occasions between May 2007 and Aug. 2007. This forced him into hiding.

The Islamists launched a campaign of intimidation including threats of destructive bloody Islamic riots in an attempt to prevent the anti-Islam Dutch politician Geert Wilders from releasing his 15-minute documentary, Fitna, which presented some hate verses of the Qur'an, followed by destructive actions in accord with them carried out by Islamists in the West in recent years. However, Wilders was strong enough not to succumb to pressure, and published his documentary. After 3.6 million visitors had viewed his film on the British website LiveLeak.com, the company announced that "Following threats to our staff of a very serious nature, LiveLeak has been left with no other choice but to remove Fitna from our servers." However, Two days later, LiveLeak posted the film again. Wilders has been living for years under state-provided round-the-clock police protection, because of Islamist threats.

## Legal Jihad

Islamist organizations call for censorship of any criticism of Islam on the grounds of being insulted. This is a common trick of totalitarian movements and governments. They label any objective truthful critique as an insult, and attempt to punish its source. Totalitarian tyrants and movements must not be appeased. Islamic organizations in the West attempt to intimidate people who speak out objectively against Islam by threats of lawsuits in order to silence them. They are well funded by petrodollars. Should the voices of anti-Islamist researchers and activists be silenced, the criticism of radical Islam may end within this generation. This poses a serious threat to the liberty and security of the West. It is becoming rather common in the West that a citizen be dragged to court for his negative views about Islam and Islamists.

## Controlling the Educational System

Before the newly found oil wealth in Arabia, Islam around the globe was in a state of depression. The discovery of oil in Arabia animated the sleeping giant. Using their vast oil wealth, the Arabs of Arabia are funding mosques, Islamic schools, libraries, and academic centers worldwide. They are attempting to make their extreme version of Islam, Wahhabism, the Islamic norm that will eventually dominate the world. Wahhabism calls for enforcing the extreme cruel measures of Islamic Sharia, such as the killing of Islamic heretics and apostates, amputation of limbs, stoning, and decapitation.

An American survey conducted early 2012 by Faith Communities Today (affiliated with the Hartford Seminary) shows that the number of mosques in the United States has grown by 74% in the past eleven years, from 1209 in 2001 to 2106 in 2011. The Greater New City area ranked No. 1 with 192 mosques. According to a Barnabas Fund report, as of 2006, 210 Saudi-funded large mosques and Islamic centers have been built in the key cities of the world, including Washington D.C., New York, Los Angeles, London, Brussels, Geneva, Paris, Bonn, and Rome. It is believed that about half of America's small and large Islamic centers and mosques and six schools of Islamic higher learning have been built, at least in part, with petrodollars. In addition, 1500 small mosques, 202 colleges and about 2000 Islamic schools have been built in the West with petrodollars. In 2007, the university of Michigan installed ritual foot baths to accommodate the Islamic beliefs of the Sharia-adherent Muslims. A publicly-funded charter school in Minnesota was sued by the ACLU on the grounds that it promotes Islam.

The Saudis are buying campus presence by funding programs of Islamic studies and establishing Islamic academic chairs in prestigious academic centers and universities in the West, such as the universities of Georgetown, Harvard, Duke, Berkeley, California, Cambridge, London, Moscow, and Edinburgh. This is creating bastions of non-critical pro-Islamic scholarship within Western academia. In order to retain its Saudi funding, these academic Islamic studies centers are under pressure not to maintain its academic impartiality and integrity of scholarship. That is how the Islamists attempt to control the Western intellect and soul.

Saudi petrodollars provide scholarships for thousands of non-Muslims from the West to study at Islamic universities in Saudi Arabia. The obvious goal is to introduce the Islamic faith to prospective converts.

The American Textbook Council and The Textbook League have reviewed the top-selling textbooks used by thousands of American public schools to teach about Islam.These two highly respected American organizations found those textbooks severely distorted and compromised in their discussion of Islam and Islamic history. They blatantly glorify and promote Islam, while demonize

Christianity. They white-wash the violent bloody history of Islam by omitting the fact that it spread out of Arabia primarily through the military conquests of jihad (holy war). They decouple Islam and Islamist terrorism.

They present Islamic beliefs as facts instead of religious beliefs. And they deny the fact that Islam oppresses and subordinates women. In addition, homework assignments involve exercises that make the students act as if they were already Muslims. This amounts to proselytizing 12-year-old Americans to convert them to Islam stealthily.

Islamic propagandists operating in America influence public school textbooks by threatening charges of racism and xenophobia against textbook publishers. Revising history and leaving out important facts are thought-control brainwashing techniques that were used by the Nazis and the communists in their quest for world dominion. These techniques are used today extensively in the Islamic world.

### *Financial Jihad*

Islamic finance and banking is called financial jihad—jihad with money instead of violence. It is going after the lifeblood of the economy of the West. The oil rich Islamic Arab countries are attempting to take control of the American economy through buying real estate and stocks of American corporations. As of 2008, Sharia finance sector managed assets of more than $800 billion. Standard and Poor estimated that this sector could reach $4 trillion before long. The probable locations for future expansion are Saudi Arabia, United Arab Emirates, Indonesia, Turkey, Singapore, and some Western countries. Britain has a bigger Sharia finance sector than the Islamic countries of Egypt and Pakistan. At least, twenty-two financial institutions offer Sharia-compliant services in Britain, compared with nine in the United States. The British Prime Minister Gordon Brown declared in 2006 that London was going to be the Islamic banking capital of the world.

Some U.S. financial institutions and businesses are engaging in Sharia-compliant financing by accommodating Sharia law (Islamic law) in order to attract Islamic investments and tap into petrodollars. They structure investments and transactions that comply with Sharia requirements that prohibit financial transactions involving interest, excessive risk, or certain assets such as alcohol, tobacco, pork, gambling, or non-Muslim religious entities.

In order to conform to the Sharia (Islamic law) requirements, Western financial companies must submit to "Sharia advisers." Almost all of those advisers are Islamists dedicated to the destruction of the West.

Those advisers certify that the subject financial products have been modified to comply with Sharia requirements. Supporters of Sharia-compliant finance see a golden opportunity for expansion in an economic downturn.

Oil rich Arab Islamists have bought into financially troubled banks, and then demanded that an approved Muslim Imam be installed on their boards of directors to assure that financial products offered to Muslims are "halal"—kosher. Halal finances provide preferential treatment to Muslims, including interest free loans and credit cards.

Sharia finance is an extension of Islamic law. It is a tool of political Islam to control global economies, and to fund violent jihad. Embracing Sharia finance leads to the eventual enforcement of the brutal oppressive Sharia law. Islamic financial institutions are involved in funding Islamist terrorism worldwide. From 1988 to 2001, Bank al-Taqwa (registered in the Bahamas) transferred tens of millions of dollars to the Islamist terrorist organizations of Hamas, al-Qaeda, the Taliban, and others. Bank Meli of Iran is under U.S. and EU sanctions for facilitating Iran's support of Hamas and Hesbollah and funding Iran's Uranium enrichment program. In fact, as of 2010, Iran had six of the ten biggest Sharia-compliant financial institutions.

### *Miscellaneous*

Other forms of jihad include suppression of freedom of religion and speech, the Islamic taqiyya, torture, breaking oaths and treaties, the higher Islamic fertility rates, Islamic immigration into Christian lands, etc.

## ANCIENT BIBLICAL WARS

Religious wars are initiated and carried out within the context of religion. In the ancient world, war was a holy war linked with religion. It was started at the command of the gods, or their approval. It was accompanied by sacrifices, and conducted with the help of the gods who insured victory. Afterward, the gods were thanked by an offering of part of the booty.

The wars of ancient Israel had a definite religious character to them. Before the Hebrew tribes of Israel went to battle, they consulted the Lord God for guidance (Judges 20: 23, 28; 1 Samuel 14: 37; 23: 2, 4; etc.). The warriors who marched into battle had to be consecrated to God, putting aside anything impure. In the battlefield, they brought the Ark of the Covenant that symbolized the presence of God with them. The visible sign of the direct divine intervention in battle was the Ark of the Covenant which the Levites carried. Therefore, the combatants were certain of victory. "The Lord your God, who goes before you, He will fight for you" (Deuteronomy 1:30a). After winning victory, they celebrated the victory by singing songs praising the Lord God. They executed the judgment of God upon the Canaanites for their corruption and decadence. The Canaanites were sinful beyond redemption.

War in ancient Israel was undertaken at the direct command of God. It was not for man's personal advantage or profit. Although ancient Israel was a human state, it was the manifestation of the kingdom of God on earth. God's participation in its historical experience made it his kingdom. Ancient Israel did not fight for its faith, but for its existence.

Following the exodus from the land of Egypt around 1450-1440 B.C., aggressive warfare became virtually a way of life for the Hebrews for several generations. This climaxed under king David (~1010-970 B.C.). The Hebrew nation had reached its zenith. Afterwards, defensive warfare became the norm, as the Hebrew kingdoms sought to protect their boundaries from foreign invaders. The Hebrew kingdoms were required to give their total allegiance to the Lord God. To be a vassal to another state was tantamount to a national breach of the first commandment of the Decalogue. The end of ancient Israel came in war as a result of the sins and apostasies of the Israelites. God judged the evil of his people. The Assyrian army defeated the Northern Kingdom of Israel and captured its capital city, Samaria, in 722/1 B.C. (Hosea 13: 16). In 586 B.C., the Babylonian army defeated the Southern Kingdom of Judah and destroyed its capital city, Jerusalem.

The ancient Hebrew wars of Joshua (~1400 B.C.), Judges (~1380-1050 B.C.) and King David (~1010-970 B.C.) were not undertaken to spread the Jewish religion, or to defend its doctrines and teachings against foreign pagan religions. The God of the Holy Bible never commanded or supported a war to spread faith in Him. The god of Islam is very different in this respect. He instituted the doctrine of the Islamic holy war (jihad), and made it a duty incumbent upon every Muslim to spread his faith by force of arms, and conquer the world for Islam.

About 3000 years have passed since the last battle endorsed by the Biblical God. Those wars have had their day, and have since passed into the dusty pages of the history of antiquity. Those wars took place in the ancient world more than ten centuries before Christ. It was a very different world then in a primitive stage of moral development and evolution. The Christians of the twenty-first-century are not ancient Israel. It is disingenuous to try to use the ancient discontinued practice of Biblical wars to justify the present and continued reality of Islamic jihad. Nevertheless, some Islamists protest that the Old Testament of the Holy Bible allowed religious wars similar to Islamic jihad (al-Baqarah 2: 246-251). They have to contend with a time lag of three millennia. In fact, they choose to ignore the vast differences between the Old Testament ancient wars and Islamic jihad:

1. In the Old Testament of the Holy Bible, God commanded, in divine judgment (Deuteronomy 9: 5), the annihilation of certain tribes, like in the cases of the great flood of Noah, the destruction of the cities of Sodom and Gomorrah (Genesis 6: 1-8: 14; 18: 16-19: 29) and cities in ancient Canaan (1 Sam. 15: 3; Numbers 31: 14-18; Deuteronomy 20: 10-17; Joshua 6: 21; 8: 24, 29; 10: 28, 40; 11: 11). In the

cities of Sodom and Gomorrah, God did not find even ten righteous persons for whose sake He would not have destroyed the cities by fire.The Canaanite societies around 1500 B.C.-1000 B.C. were irreversibly corrupt, degenerate and decadent. They practiced child sacrifice to please their pagan gods, male and female temple prostitution, snake worship and witchcraft in their religious rites and rituals (Deuteronomy 12: 31; 18: 9-12). This was far worse than the moral condition of the surrounding nations in the ancient Middle East. No population that had a hope of repentance, regeneration and righteousness was ever destroyed.

These extreme corrupt pagan practices did not exist in Arabia and the surrounding countries in the seventh century A.D. and subsequent centuries. In addition, Arab polytheists, that Muhammad slaughtered, were not beyond hope of gradual conversion peacefully. In fact, some of them had already believed in Judaism and Christianity. Therefore, the historical milieu, context and culture were very different from those of ancient Canaan. The pagans of Arabia were not so irreversibly degenerate. This is in addition to the fact that Muhammad also attacked Jews and Christians who were ethical monotheists (at-Tawbah 9: 29), and whom the Qur'an had claimed to have worshiped the same God (al-'ankabut 29: 46; al-Baqarah 2: 139).

2. In addition to inflicting His divine judgment on the Canaanites, God wanted to preserve the purity of the Hebrew religion from the corrupt practices of the Canaanites (Deuteronomy 20: 16-18). Sadly, the religious practices of the remaining Canaanite communities that were not destroyed gradually pervaded the Hebrew religion, which brought God's wrath and punishment upon ancient Israel.
3. The twelve tribes of Israel lived in Egypt in bondage and servitude as a nation of refugees for about 400 years (Genesis 15: 13; Acts 7: 6). Their fighting against the Canaanites was to gain sanctuary for the twelve Jewish

tribes—a nation of refugees who had no place to live with dignity. Their settling Canaan fulfilled the divine promise God had made to their forefather Abraham (Genesis 15: 18; Deuteronomy 6: 18-19). As God settled the refugee tribes in the land of Canaan, he commanded them to care for other refugees who came to their land (Leviticus 19: 13).

4. The true living God never commanded the Israelites to spread the religion of the ancient Hebrews by force, or to conquer militarily vast territories far beyond the small territory of Israel/Palestine. The Biblical God gave the Israelites sovereignty only over a specific limited geographical area (Exodus 23: 31; Deuteronomy 11: 22-24). In addition, he commanded the Israelites not to attack certain tribes, such as the tribes of Esau, the Moabites, the Ammonites, etc. (Deuteronomy 2: 5, 9, 19, 37; etc.). In fact, God sent the prophet Jonah, without an army, to preach peacefully in Nineveh, hundreds of miles away. The Hebrew Jewish religion was spread by proclamation, not by the sword. This is very different from what Islam did. It waged wars on nations of distant lands, far beyond Arabia. It sought worldwide military conquest for Islam. This was started by Muhammad and the four guided caliphs after him attacking their neighboring countries which had never threatened them (Bukhari 4.52.267; 4.53.349, 350; etc.).
5. The Qur'anic commands to fight the unbelievers are not restricted to specific time periods in history, locations, or certain populations or tribes. They transcend time and space (Abu Dawud 8.2526). These commands are standardized in Islamic law (Sharia), and are universal and applicable to all times, places and peoples worldwide. This is very different from the divine commands found in the Books of Deuteronomy, Joshua, etc. of the Old Testament of the Holy Bible, which were very specific and restricted to certain times, localities, and tribes within the promised land (Palestine). These commands were intended for the

immediate situation of that period of ancient history only. They were not directed to all future generations to follow. This violence never became standardized and codified in Jewish law. It is a mere history, not theology and doctrine. This violence took place in the ancient world more than ten centuries before Christ. It was a very different world then in a primitive stage of moral development and evolution. The Christians of the twenty-first-century are not ancient Israel. Biblical accounts of violence of ancient Israel are descriptive, not prescriptive.

6. The ancient Hebrews were expressly forbidden from taking booty. When the walls of Jericho fell and they conquered it, its storehouses remained filled. Its children were not sent off into slavery. Its women were not raped as if they were part of the battle's booty. In contrast with that, one of the main motivations of Islamic invasions was taking spoils of war, which included looting, enslaving women and children, raping women, etc.

The true living God of the Bible was clear, precise, and stable in His severe divine judgments of the wicked practices of the Canaanites, and was not dependent on the military strength of the Israelites (Deuteronomy 20: 1). However, the god of Muhammad changed his mind depending on the situation. Muhammad did not fight polytheists sometimes because he was too weak militarily. Therefore, he settled for a treaty. But when he gained military strength, he terminated the treaties unilaterally (at-Tawbah 9: 1-5).

## WARS OF CHRISTENDOM

In contrast with the Islamic doctrine of jihad, the biblical God condemns unjust violence, saying: "When you spread out your hands, I will hide My eyes from you. Even though you make many prayers, I will not hear. Your hands are full of blood" (Isaiah 1: 15; Psalm 5: 6b). Jesus has instructed his disciples to proclaim the Gospel peacefully: "And as you go, preach, saying, 'The kingdom of heaven is at hand.' Heal the sick, cleanse the lepers, raise the dead, cast out demons. Freely you have received, freely give"

(Matthew 10: 7-8; 28: 18-20; Mark 16: 20). As part of their mission to proclaim the Gospel of Christ, Christians are to perform acts of charity and compassion as Jesus had done. Christians are motivated to share the Gospel by their love of God and neighbor.

It is important to emphasize the great difference between the spread of Christianity in the first three centuries of the Christian era, and the process of Islamization under pressure throughout Islamic history. Unlike Islam, early Christianity was not dependent on an earthly state to propagate it by armed expansion. Christ refused to be crowned a king over an earthly kingdom (John 6: 15; 18: 36). He did not incarnate to establish an earthly empire in this dispensation, but to inaugurate the spiritual kingdom of God, the beginning of the new creation. People converted to Christianity out of deep conviction, commitment and love to Christ. He and his apostles after him did not send out invading armies to conquer, rule, and pressure people into Christianity. Instead, he sent unarmed peaceful evangelists to preach his gospel.

In its first three centuries, Christianity spread by preaching the gospel and supportive miracles following the teaching and example of Jesus. The apostles of Christ used words, not swords, in preaching Christianity. Their martyrdom was a living testament of their faith. Some Islamists claim that the verses of Matthew 10: 34-35 and Luke 22: 36, 38 seem to point to holy war. This is the wrong understanding of these verses. Matthew 10: 34-35 speaks allegorically about divisions and disputes arising within the one family from disagreements on Jesus message. These disputes might lead to attacks on those that chose to follow him. Luke 22: 36, 38 refers to a dagger or short sword travelers used for protection against bandits and wild animals. In fact, on the night of his arrest, when Peter struck the servant of the high priest cutting off his ear, Jesus responded by saying: "Put your sword in its place, for all who take the sword will perish by the sword. Or do you think that I cannot now pray to My Father, and He will provide Me with more than twelve legions of angels? How then could the Scriptures be fulfilled, that it must happen thus?" (Matthew 26: 52-54).

When Jesus was threatened, he did not fight back physically. He simply walked away from the threat (John 7: 1; 8: 59; Matthew

12: 14-15; Luke 4: 28-30). He instructed his disciples to do the same when threatened (Matthew 10: 23). They followed his instructions (Acts 8: 1, 4; 9: 28-30; 13: 50-51; 14: 5-7). Jesus refused to punish people for rejecting him (Luke 9: 55-56). He prophesied about the persecution of Christians saying: "They will put you out of the synagogues; yes, the time is coming that whoever kills you will think that he offers God service" (John 16: 2; Revelation 12: 7, 8, 17).

Christianity teaches to live at peace with all (Romans 12: 18; 1 Peter 3: 8-12). It prohibits violence unless it is absolutely necessary for self-defense. In fact, Christ taught that anger is a sin: "You have heard that it was said to those of old, 'You shall not murder and whoever murders will be in danger of the judgment.'

But I say to you that whoever is angry with his brother without a cause shall be in danger of the judgment.

And whoever says to his brother, 'Raca!' shall be in danger of the council. But whoever says, 'You fool!' shall be in danger of hell fire" (Matthew 5: 21-22). Additionally, Christianity prohibits revenge: "Beloved, do not avenge yourselves, but rather give place to wrath; for it is written, "Vengeance is Mine, I will repay," says the Lord. Therefore, if your enemy is hungry, feed him; if he is thirsty, give him a drink. For in so doing you will heap coals of fire on his head. Do not be overcome by evil, but overcome evil with good" (Romans 12: 19-21).

Christ also commanded saying: "You have heard that it was said, 'You shall love your neighbor and hate your enemy.'

But I say to you, love your enemies, bless those who curse you, do good to those who hate you, and pray for those who spitefully use you and persecute you, that you may be sons of your Father in heaven; for He makes His sun rise on the evil and on the good, and sends rain on the just and on the unjust. For if you love those who love you, what reward have you? Do not even the tax collectors do the same? And if you greet your brethren only, what do you do more than others? Do not even the tax collectors do so? Therefore you shall be perfect, just as your Father in heaven is perfect" (Matthew 5: 43-48).

## THE CHRISTAN DOCTRINE ON WAR

Eastern Orthodox Christianity provides two moral options pertaining to war: Justifiable War, and absolute pacifism. Absolute pacifism is the spiritual moral ideal that is fully realized in the age to come. Mercy is its virtue. The mainstream Orthodox justifiable war doctrine is considered a lesser good. Its virtue is justice. Both the absolute pacifism and the justifiable war doctrines insist on the moral principle that we never do evil that good might come. The end does not justify the means.

The doctrine of Absolute Pacifism prohibits violent resistance. It calls for non-violence, non-resistance and universal forgiveness. Pacifists witness to the world around them in the hope of assisting the transformation of its violent sinful kingdoms into the non-violent peaceful eschatological kingdom of God. Absolute pacifists pay more heed to the principle than to consequences. The clergy and monastics are forbidden to participate in any military activity because it is inconsistent with their religious service commitments.

The doctrine of justifiable war provides that a justifiable war may be engaged as a virtuous and righteous act. It is a war undertaken by a legitimate political authority in order to defend the people of God. Its goal is to prevent evil and protect the other. It strives to minimize physical harm to combatants and non-combatants alike, and to achieve its victorious end speedily and efficiently. A justifiable war is based on the proper spiritual intent. It should not be vengeful, self-righteous or bent on conquest. It should have in view the ultimate goals of forgiveness and rehabilitation of the enemy.

Western Christianity (Roman Catholicism and traditional Protestantism) adhere to the Just War tradition. A Just War must comply with six criteria:

1. Competent political authority commanding the war. The political authority should express the will of the people in a just political system (e.g. the sovereign authority of a democratic state, a revolutionary political authority, etc.).
2. Just cause for waging the war. This includes self-defense, defense of the innocent weak neighbor from unjust aggression, preventing massacres, etc.

3. Right intention; such as securing the common good, correcting a suffered wrong, etc.
4. Last resort. War is the only reasonable means to right the wrong. All other peaceful means are impractical or ineffective.
5. Serious prospects of success.
6. A Just war must not produce evils graver than the evil to be eliminated. The anticipated benefits must be proportionate to the expected evils of war.

The doctrine of Just War imposes certain rules of conduct to be observed in war. It prohibits unnecessary violence, needless destruction, looting, raping, large-scale massacres, and acts of vengeance and reprisal. Prisoners of war should not be tortured or otherwise mistreated. A just war is a work motivated by the virtue of the love of God and neighbor. It restrains evil and protects the innocent. The just warrior desires to protect his neighbor from the unjust aggressor because he loves him, and because God hates injustice. "Greater love has no one than this, than to lay down one's life for his friends" (John 15: 13). A just warrior never intends to harm non-combatants. Every effort is made in just wars to minimize civilian casualties, which are unintended if they occur. Just warriors regret that they live in a fallen world where they have to kill the enemy combatants in the battlefield in order to restrain evil. However, it is more upsetting for just warriors to watch others being abused and killed unjustly when they can put an end to that injustice.

## EXAMPLES OF JUST WARS

The sword of Islam was broken in several just wars in history. The following are a few examples:

1. The battle of Tours (southern France). On Oct. 11th, 732, one hundred years after the death of Muhammad, a massive Islamic army led by Abd al-Rahman Al Ghafiqi attacked southern France from Spain. The defending Christian army under the leadership of Charles Martel was outnumbered at least four-to-one. However, Charles Martel defeated the Islamic army in that most decisive battle in history, and

thereby stopped the advance of the Muslim armies in Western Europe. The Muslim army's leader and many of its top commanders were slain in battle.

2. The battle of Kulikovo (Russia). 150,000 Russian troops commanded by Dimitri defeated an invading Muslim Mongol force of 200,000 troops commanded by Mamai on Sept. 8th, 1380 at the Kulikovo field in Russia. The battle had been blessed by St. Sergius of Radonezh, who sent two of his monks, former warriors, to join Dimitri's forces, and prophesied that he would win the battle. The Islamic advance in Eastern Europe was stopped.
3. The battle of Vienna (Austria). It took place in two sieges in 1529 and 1683. In the siege of 1529, a huge army led by Ottoman sultan Suleiman the Magnificent attacked Vienna. The vastly outnumbered Christian forces defeated the attacking Muslim Turkish troops, and broke the siege. In 1683, for the second time, a huge Ottoman army of approximately 150,000 soldiers besieged Vienna for two months. The defending Christian armies were outnumbered about two-to-one. However, they won a decisive victory in the final battle of Vienna on 11 and 12 September, 1683. The battle of Vienna stopped the Islamic advance in central Europe.
4. The battle of Malta. In 1565, the Ottoman Empire attacked the island of Malta in order to gain control over the Mediterranean Sea with a huge fleet of 193 war ships. The Christian defense force was outnumbered more than three-to-one. It withstood a siege that lasted more than four months. At the end, the Christian defense force repelled the massive Turkish attack. The Turkish forces retreated after suffering heavy casualties.

## THE CRUSADES

Some Islamists attempt to draw a parallel between Islamic jihad (Islamic crusades) and the Christian medieval crusades. In fact, the differences between them are vast and extensive:

1. Christ has invited all to follow him willingly, not forcibly. He

never taught his disciples to convert any one to Christianity by force. In fact, he exhorted them to love their enemies (Mt. 5: 44). In the first three centuries of Christianity following his resurrection, his disciples spread Christianity by preaching the Gospel in the face of brutal Roman and pagan persecutions. Jesus and the early Christians did not raise armies to attack non-Christians and force them to convert to Christianity. Christianity spread on the ashes and blood of its peaceful faithful martyrs in its first three centuries. The true almighty God supported his divine Messiah and his message.

The Christian crusades of the Middle Ages were violent and led to atrocities under the banner of the cross and in the name of Christianity. The crusaders did not follow the teachings and example of Christ in conducting their military campaigns. Christ would certainly denounce their atrocities. Instead, they followed the example of the Islamic armies in their conquests. The concept of holy war in Medieval Europe rose as a result of Islamic influence. It is not a Christian doctrine. However, Muslim jihadists, who resort to violence and terror in the name of their Islamic god (Islamic jihad), find a lot of support for their actions in the teaching of the Qur'an and the sayings and example of Muhammad himself, the prophet of Islam. After all, he launched Islamic jihad in the seventh century. Islam spread through violent military conquests since it began in Arabia. In fact, Islamic history is a story of violence and bloodshed from the time of Muhammad to the present day. If the Christian West has anything to apologize for in the crusades, the Islamic world has a lot more for which it should apologize in its jihad wars that had started many centuries before the crusades and still have not ended.

2. The history of the crusades spans about two centuries (1095-1291). We will not get into it here. The initial goal of the crusades was not to force Christianity on any one, and was not to gain booty. Its goal was to protect Christian holy sites in the holy land from Islamic destruction and desecration, and to protect Christian pilgrims from Islamic aggression. Islamic persecution of Christians included plundering monasteries, destroying churches, and killing and extorting Christian pilgrims. The crusades were started for a

just cause. However, they were conducted unjustly. It was a delayed limited response to centuries of Islamic aggression which began more than 450 years before the first crusade was launched, and grew fiercer than ever in the eleventh century. It was a belated unsuccessful effort to liberate Christian lands from Islamic imperialism. The Christians fought to defend and liberate their holy land form Islamic conquest, while the Muslims fought to continue conquering and occupying Christian lands. Muhammad, the prophet of Islam, began the international jihad by his veiled threat in the letter he sent to neighboring non-Muslim leaders telling them to "...embrace Islam and you will be safe..."

The fanatical Islamist Seljuk Turks threatened Constantinople, the capital of Byzantium. Therefore, the Byzantine emperor Alexius I (1081-1118) appealed for military help from the West. That was what set in motion the first crusade.

After a five-week siege, the crusaders entered Jerusalem on July 15, 1099. They killed many of its inhabitants. The crusaders sack of Jerusalem was a heinous act. It was unchristian. They followed the example and the historical record of Muslim armies that had committed similar atrocities when entering a conquered city. This is not to excuse the crusaders conduct, because one atrocity does not justify the other.

Examples of Islamic atrocities of the same historical period abound. In 1077, after conquering Jerusalem, the Muslim Seljuk Turks murdered three thousand Christians and Jews. In 1148, the Muslim commander Nur ed-Din ordered the killing of every Christian in Aleppo. After defeating the crusaders in the battle of Hettin on July 4, 1187, Salah ed-Din ordered the beheading of all the Christian captives. In 1268, after conquering Antioch, the Mamluk sultan Baybars massacred 16,000 Christians, including monks and priests, and sold their women and children into slavery. On May 29, 1453, the Ottoman forces entered Constantinople (Istanbul). The Muslim soldiers slew everyone they met in the streets, men, women and children without discrimination. The blood ran into rivers down the steep streets of the city.

In general, the crusaders let the local Muslims in their territories live in peace and practice their religion freely. In fact, Muslims preferred to live under the rule of the crusaders who treated them justly, than under the Muslim rulers who treated them unjustly. The general level of taxation was lower under the crusaders than under the neighboring Muslim lords. It was not the crusades that put an end to Arab glory; it was the Islamist Turks who turned the Arabs into second-class citizens in the Islamic world. Political and commercial influences on the crusades increased as the years passed by. Christians in both the Middle East and Europe suffered from the latter crusading armies. In fact, the fourth crusade (1202-1204 AD) did not fight Muslims. It fought the Christian Byzantine Empire, and sacked its capital Constantinople (Istanbul now).

## CONCLUSION

The three major branches of traditional Christianity (Eastern Orthodoxy, Roman Catholicism, and Protestantism) are all united on the issue of war.

They all concur that some wars are just, justifiable and virtuous. In addition, Christianity provides the option of absolute pacifism. However, the Islamic doctrine of Holy War (Jihad) to spread religion by force does not exist in Christianity. In fact, this doctrine does not exist in any other major world religion. All major world religions were founded by peaceful men, with the exception of Islam which was founded by Muhammad who was a warrior. The true living Almighty God is not pleased by bloodshed, "When you spread out your hands, I will hide my eyes from you. Even though you make many prayers, I will not hear. Your hands are full of blood" (Isaiah 1: 15). Helping someone to believe in Him is by proclaiming and reasoning without violence, pressure and threats of death.

It is important to make a distinction between the teachings of a religion and the actions of its followers. So, despite the fact that Christ teaches purity of heart, love, mercy and forgiveness, many nominal Christians do not follow his teachings. On the other hand, despite the fact that Muhammad teaches polygamy, jihad, violence, bloodshed and killing, many Muslims do not follow his teachings. Christ's way leads to new life and salvation. Muhammad's way leads to death and destruction.

Christianity is the religion of peace. It has no violent jihadist movement. There is no group anywhere in the world today who is committing violent acts and justifying them by quoting the Holy Bible and Christian teachings. On the other hand, many groups are committing violent acts and justifying them by quoting the Qur'an and Islamic teachings.

Some Islamists argue that Islamic jihad is only for self-defense, and fighting against oppression. The problem with this is that the Islamic definitions for self-defense and oppression are very broad. For instance, rulers that do not acknowledge the rule of Islam are considered oppressors. This is in addition to the fact that all the battles of Muhammad, except for the battles of Uhud (625) and the ditch (627), were offensive. Jihad may be waged defensively to battle tyranny. However, the Islamic definition of tyranny is anything that stands in Islam's way?

The success of building a large Islamic empire in the first century of Islam does not indicate divine support. Great ancient empires, such as the Persian and Roman empires, rivaled it in size, despite the fact that they were pagan who worshipped idols. The Roman Empire was pagan and persecuted Christianity till the edict of Milan in 313 AD. In modern history, within five years, Nazi Germany under the leadership of Hitler built an empire equal to the size of the empire Islam built in one hundred years of bloody conquests. The Nazi were ungodly. They committed many atrocities. In this respect, we need to remember the long decline of the political power of the Islamic nations over the past few centuries with no end in sight, and the repeated military victories of the small nation of Israel over large Islamic armies, which represent a serious challenge to the claims of Islamic supremacy.

The truth is not to be gauged by the number of its followers. Buddhism and Hinduism rival Islam in the number of its followers. But they are pagan religions. Divine success does not necessarily coincide with human expectations and rationality, and is not to be judged by human standards. For instance, king David, the greatest king of ancient Israel, was a successful warrior. He expanded the territory of his kingdom greatly, conquered Jerusalem and made it his capital (2 Samuel 5: 6-10). He wanted to build a temple for the Lord, but God forbade him saying: "You have shed much blood and have made great wars; you shall not build a house for My name, because you have shed much blood on the earth in My sight" (1 Chronicles 22: 8; 28: 3).

The importance of religious war (jihad) against unbelievers is repeatedly affirmed and emphasized in the Qur'an, the Hadith, the example of Muhammad, Islamic history and the ruling of every school of Islamic jurisprudence. The final goal of jihad is that Islamic rule prevails by military force (Bukhari 4.52.65, 196). The purpose of jihad is chiefly political, not religious. It is a historical fact that, with the exception of some Indonesian islands, no nation has ever willingly converted to Islam. Islam was spread with the Qur'an in one hand and the sword in the other. Islam claims superiority over other religions (al-Tawbah 9: 33). It also claims that the Islamic nation is superior over all other nations on the face of the earth (Al-Imran 3: 110). However, the long series of military defeats at the hands of Christians and Jews from Europe and America undermine that claim of superiority. Islam is the religion of the sword.The god of Islam commands jihad warfare to conquer the world for Islam. Therefore, military defeats of Islamic armies in the battlefields, which abound, amount to defeats of the god of Islam? It brings into doubt the truth of the claimed Islamic revelation itself in its entirety?

According to statistics compiled by Bill Warner, the director of the Center for the Study of Political Islam, only a small part of the Islamic foundational texts (the Qur'an, the Hadith, and the Sunnah (life of Muhammad)) is dedicated to religion. The rest of it deals with Political Islam (unbelievers (non-Muslims), politics, and violent jihad). According to Warner, even the Islamic hell is political. There are 146 references to it in the Qur'an. Only 6% of these references are on Muslims in hell for moral failings (murder, theft, etc.). The other 94% of the references to hell are on those in it for disagreeing with Muhammad, which is a political crime. This makes Islamic hell a political prison for those who oppose Islam. The small religious part of Islam serves the function of unifying and mobilizing the Islamic ummah (nation) to launch aggressive warfare against non-Muslims (violent jihad) in order to establish an Islamic Empire that dominates the entire world. This is demonstrated most vividly by the violent Muslim mob demonstrations in Islamic countries, which often follow the Friday mosque prayer. Therefore, Islam could not be classified as a religion. It is a political ideology of predatory imperialism.

Islam is more of a political ideology, than a religion. It is a political ideology hidden under a thin deceptive cover of barren religious rituals, which do not renew the human heart and do not uplift the human spirit. Right after praying the obligatory ritual prayer, a person may do evil because his heart is not touched by the prayer. Islam is a fascist political movement akin to Communism and Nazism invented by the prophet of Islam and his followers. It is a powerful tool of domination and control because, unlike Communism and Nazism, it claims divine authority, which makes it a lot more potent than them. In fact, striking similarities exist between the teachings of Hitler's Mein Kampf (1924) and the teachings of Islam. Tyrants claimed that there can be no true peace without the creation of society that follows their ideologies. For Lenin, everyone had to submit to Communism; for Hitler, to Nazism; for Muhammad, to Islam. They defined peace only in terms of their own ideology. Islam exists not to enhance morality or to improve the life of Muslims. It exists only to perpetuate itself. Islam is not about saving souls. It is about building a world empire.

Stripped of the deceptive veneer of Islam's divine claims, the history of Islam is the history of a warlord (Muhammad) and his followers who conquered and plundered much of the ancient world claiming that their false god wanted them to do so. They devised and used Islam as a tool for conquest and plunder. When Muslims stopped violence against non-Muslims, they turned and started violence against each other. Declaring other Muslims infidels due to insufficient piety is widely practiced by Salafists and Wahhabis to justify the use of violence against them (al-Tawbah 9: 73; etc.).

Islam was born out of violence, propagated by violence, and still practices violence till this day. Although Muslims constitute about a fifth of the world's population, they are responsible for over four-fifths of the world's armed conflicts. More blood has been shed for Islam than for any other cause in history. Some historians (Bill Warner, etc.) estimate that approximately a total of 270 million non-Muslims were massacred by the sword of Islam, both during the conquests of the marauding Islamic armies, and in the centuries that followed. The wounds inflicted by Muhammad and his followers on humanity have been bleeding for about 1400 years.

Muhammad had succeeded in numbing and desensitizing the conscience of his followers by claiming that an imagined divine authority approved, encouraged and commanded the atrocities they committed, and by promising a fictitious fleshly paradise as a reward. The Qur'an has given them a clean conscience for committing the most heinous crimes and cruelties on their helpless innocent victims. As a result, they have killed, maimed, raped, and looted without heeding the cries of their victims, without feeling regret and remorse, and without feeling ashamed and guilty about it. Islam corrupts men so thoroughly that they believe it is good to commit these wicked crimes. Pascal, the French philosopher and mathematician, wrote: "Men never do evil so completely and cheerfully as when they do it from religious conviction" (Sina, Ali, Understanding Muhammad, 2007-2008, p. 208). Lord Acton, a famous nineteenth century historian, said, "Power tends to corrupt, and absolute power corrupts absolutely."

# 3

# Islamic Fundamentalism in Pakistan

Pakistan is situated in a region where fundamentalism has been posed, of late, as one of the most threatening questions. The process initiated by the Islamic revolution in Iran has even been internationalised by the Taliban's victory in Afghanistan. At the same time, the rise of Hindu radicalism in India has further complicated the situation in Pakistan. Recently Islamic fundamentalism has risen as an alternative political phenomenon not only in Pakistan but also in the entire Muslim world. Islamic fundamentalism in Pakistan is partly a link of this international phenomenon and partly caused by specific local reasons. When analysing Islamic fundamentalism, one must understand that the religion of Islam and Islamic fundamentalism are not one and the same thing. Islamic fundamentalism is a reactionary, non-scientific movement aimed at returning society to a centuries-old social set-up, defying all material and historical factors. It is an attempt to roll back the wheel of history.

Fundamentalism finds its roots in the backwardness of society, social deprivation, a low level of consciousness, poverty and ignorance.

Like fascism and national chauvinism, Islamic fundamentalism finds its base in the petty bourgeoisie. But it is not only the petty bourgeoisie that is attracted by fundamentalism; those who have fallen from among the petty bourgeoisie into the ranks of the proletariat and semi-proletariat are also impressed by the movement. Similarly, sections of the proletariat that are newly formed and not yet equipped with class-consciousness and the experience of class struggle are also likely to become supporters of this movement. They correspond to a section of petty bourgeoisie described by the *Communist Manifesto*:

The lower middle class, the manufacturer, the shopkeeper, the artisan, the peasant, all these fight against the bourgeoisie to save from extinction their existence as fractions of the middle class. They are therefore not revolutionary, but conservative. Nay more, they are reactionary, for they try to roll back the wheel of history.

It is possible to distinguish four general causes contributing to the rise of Islamic fundamentalism.

## THE CONTRADICTIONS OF IMPERIALISM

Islam has been a political religion since the beginning. When Arabs invaded other countries, the rationale was jihad (holy war) against infidels, although these wars had economic motives. In the nineteenth and twentieth centuries, when Muslim countries, one after the other, were colonised by the imperialist countries, the resistance movements used religion as well as nationalism as a launching pad for independence struggles. In countries like Indonesia and Malaysia, the national liberation movement was begun in the name of religion.

Of late, as the multinationals have stepped up their super-exploitation of the Muslim world, one of the natural reactions is hatred of the headquarters (i.e. the West) of these multinationals. During the Cold War, imperialism used Islamic fundamentalists against the left. The fundamentalist parties were the closest friends of imperialism in the Muslim world. However, in the post-Cold War era, imperialism does not need them as it did in the past. The CIA has stopped funding Islamic fundamentalists. This changed situation brought Islamic reactionaries into contradiction with imperialism. At the same time, because of the experience of centuries of colonisation and exploitation, a hatred for the West, especially for the USA, is widespread in the Muslim world, as in any Third World country. In the changed situation of the post-Cold War era, fundamentalists turned to anti-imperialist sloganeering and came to the fore as the forces challenging imperialism. Osama bin Laden became a symbol of anti-imperialism no matter what his tactics or the class to which he belongs. The terrorist methods of fundamentalism were seen by the ranks of the fundamentalists as jihad against the USA, while in general the movement was seen as a challenge to the USA.

### The Inability of Capitalism to Solve the Basic Problems

Islamic fundamentalism is spreading especially rapidly in those counties where capitalism has failed to fulfil the tasks of the bourgeois democratic revolution, where it has failed to eliminate poverty and ignorance and where class contradictions are sharpening. Poverty and ignorance are concomitant. A society ridden with ignorance is fertile soil for the growth of fundamentalist ideas.

### The Failure of the Left

It was in Iran that the Islamic fundamentalists had their first major victory. The Tudeh Party (Iranian Communist Party) believed in the bankrupt Stalinist two-stage theory of revolution. Despite having a mass base, the Tudeh Party, in line with its theory, forged an alliance with fundamentalists instead of offering an alternative to the masses. Not only that, but the Iranian left also failed to present itself as an alternative during the democratic movement against the shah and failed or did not attempt to link the democratic movement to the class struggle to overthrow capitalism and replace it with socialism. The alliance with the fundamentalists proved fatal. The fundamentalists on coming to power went on to the physical elimination of the communists, and did it successfully. A golden opportunity for a socialist revolution was lost and the working class had to pay a heavy price, which it is still paying. Afghanistan was the other country where fundamentalists were able to capture power. In Afghanistan, the fundamentalists came to power as a direct sequel to the socialist government. The Afghan revolutionaries who captured power surrendered to the Stalinist instructions and methods taught by Moscow.

Instead of making any genuine effort to consolidate revolution by appealing to internationalism, consolidating workers democracy and laying the material basis to prolong the revolution, they resorted to Stalinist, bureaucratic and class-collaborationist methods of running a transitional state. As a result, they failed, paving the way for the fundamentalists. Similarly in Algeria, where socialists successfully led the national liberation movement against France and remained in power for over two decades, they failed to stop the rise of Islamic fundamentalism. The fundamentalist movement in Algeria is one of the strongest movements in the Muslim world today.

### *Providing an Alternative Society*

The fundamentalists, through their massive network of social services, have built alternative societies in the Muslim countries where they are strong. They provide hospitals, orphanages, schools and many other facilities, which weak capitalist governments have failed to provide to the masses. This adds to their influence as a social force. Their schools are the most influential tool. These seminaries not only provide religious education but also guarantee food and shelter to the children of poor parents who cannot afford education and food.

## THE GROWING RELIGIOUS FUNDAMENTALISM IN PAKISTAN

The religious fundamentalists in Pakistan are once again on the full swing. They are very much encouraged by the outcome of the general elections in Pakistan. In overall, they have got over 16% of the total votes caste in the elections. But in the national assembly, they have emerged the second largest parliamentary group leaving behind Pakistan Peoples Party. Thanks to the support of the conservative Muslim League Nawaz MLN that their nominee for the prime minister Fazal Rehman got 86 votes while PPP trailed behind with 71 votes. The pro military Muslim League Q group was able to fetch the needed 172 votes for the Prime Minister lot.

The upsurge in the fundamentalist support was witnessed on 19th November 2002 when over 70,000 turned up for the funeral of Aimal Kansi in Quetta Baluchistan. This was the largest ever funeral in the whole history of Baluchistan. Aimal, body was brought from US where was awarded the death sentence after found guilty of killing two CIA officers in 1993. Till his last breath, he was very much proud of what he has done to the American imperialism. He has become another hero of the fundamentalists after Assama Bin Laden.

Another sign of the growth in religious fundamentalism was seen on 24th November when activists of Lashkar Tayaba, the banned religious group in Pakistan took over for six hours two temples in Jammu district of Indian held Kashmir. The incident resulted killing of the two and 10 more in the struggle to re-hold the temples by the Indian forces. There have been more incidents like this during the week in Kashmir resulting over 20 deaths mainly of Indian army men. This is no incident. The leader of Lashkar Tayaba Hafiz Saeed was released last week in Pakistan. The Pakistan authorities would not accept at Lahore High Court only a month before that he is held up with them..? Withdraw your writ petition if you want your husband to be released? Was the message of the intelligence agencies to the wife. Later the wife of Hafiz Saeed was forced to withdraw her write petition. Hafiz Saeed as brought to his hometown after being held for over a year and was house arrested. Lahore High Court declared the move as illegal. Since his release on 18th November, he has addressed many thousands in several cities of Punjab. At Faisalabad, the third largest city of Pakistan, he spoke to over 50,000 who came to greet him after his release. Many women threw their children in the air and begged him to take them for Jihad. ? Jihad can not be stopped by any mean,? he declared at the meeting.

Lashkar Tayaba was the main religious group promoted by the military intelligence of Pakistan during the nineties to carry on jihad in the Indian held Kashmir. Many youth were provided the military training at camps set up by the group in different parts of Pakistani held Kashmir. "Suicidal missions are the only way forward to further the message of Jihad" was the main philosophy of the group training. The 11th September 2001 changed the priorities of the military intelligence. The Lashkar Tayaba was asked to wind up the camps. The leader was kidnapped. The military intelligences thought that it would be all over by these actions. That is been proved all wrong. The ghost of religious fundamentalist propped up by the military intelligence is out of control and is in a process of changing its colour. From pro military group, it is fast becoming an anti military group in Pakistan.

In the eighties, the religious fanatics were very closely linked with American imperialism. In the nineties, they left them on their own. From the beginning this century, the fanatics have taken roots among the general consciousness of the masses in Pakistan as an anti imperialist force. ?It is war between Islam and American infidels,? says Samee-ul-Haq, one of the main leaders of MMA, the religious political alliance in Pakistan. He was also the main supporter of the Talban regime.

While in the nineties, the American imperialism has left them on their own but not the major part of the establishment in Pakistan. They wanted to use them against their traditional rival Indians. They had also the illusions that a stable regime in Afghanistan would give them access to the markets of the Central Asia. So the formation and the support for Talban were the main priorities. All that changed with 11th September. The crushing of Talban in Afghanistan by bombing of US imperialism has not curbed the spread of religious fundamentalism. It has spread in a different form in Pakistan at present. Leon Trotsky, the architecture of the Soviet revolution of 1917 in Russia, once quoted ?You can not crush the will of the masses to change the society?. The will of the most of the masses to change the society has not emerged, as was the case in the past, through the left forces in the region. Rather through the religious sentiment. The general elections in Pakistan held on 10th October gives some glimpse how they have emerged as a serious political force in Pakistan. The fundamentalist united in one main group called Mutehida Majlas Ammal MMA (United Action Forum) won the most seats in two provinces. They took considerable votes in all other constituencies. But the most alarming fact was their support in the two major cities, Lahore and Karachi. At Lahore, they won three national assembly seats out of 13 and in Karachi, a neck-to-neck fight against the MQM, the immigrant mass force. MMA got 5 out of 20 seats in Karachi but it was very closely defeated in all the other 15 seats. MQM fetched

12 in the end. The MMA anti US rhetoric, which played a seminal role in wooing voters elsewhere in the country, played important part in their victory. But their campaign in Karachi was also centered on the issues like health and education. Mayer belonging to MMA already rules the local government in Karachi. MMA captured 29 out of 35 National and 52 out of 99 provincial assembly seats in North West Frontier Province (NWFP). In Baluchistan, it got 6 out of 13 National and 14 out of 51 provincial seat. In over all, MMA got nearly 3.2 millions votes. While the main bourgeoisie party MLQ got 7.3 millions. PPP fetched the most votes, nearly over 7.4 million votes. The total vote caste in Pakistan was over 28.9 millions. MMA got over 52 per cent of its seats in the low turnout areas. The fragmentation and disenchantment of the secular vote coupled with increased mobility and motivated election campaign by the MMA are definitely factors that cannot be ignored.

The conservative Muslim League, the main bourgeoisie party in Pakistan was split on the question of the support for military. A large part of it went to support the military rule while the rest under MLN supported the religious fundamentalist on the name of seat adjustment in many parts of Pakistan. MLN was taking revenge from the military as their leader Nawaz Sharif was ousted from power in October 1999. Later he was forced to leave Pakistan and now reside in Saudi Arabia. In the process, the MMA got more votes and seats than the MLN. MLN strategy made the fundamentalist stronger and is now no more close associates of the MLN. In fact MLN is fast becoming a tail end of the fanatics in Pakistan. MMA took more advantage of the lowering of the vote age from 21 to 18 than another political group. The Pakistan Talban from the Madrasas, the religious schools, over 70,000 of them in Pakistan, energetically worked for the successful campaign of the MMA. ? He who has the youth has the future,? Lenin said once. The majority of the youth is fed up with the system. "They are all corrupt", is the argument presented in most of the discussion among youth. ?Only Islamic revolution is the answer? you hear very often.

After the general election, the strategy of MMA was to give an impression to the masses of Pakistan that they are ready to shares the power but it has to be on their principal position. To attract and enlarge their support among the petty bourgeoisie, the MMA in words at least has become champions of the democracy and defendant of the 1973 constitutions.

The constitution, unanimously passed by parliament under Bhutto government, is a combination of capitalist democratic values and religious norms. The MMA also opposed the constitutional amendments by General Pervaiz Musharaf regime to give him more dictatorial powers as president. The Legal Framework Order (LFO) was announced on 21st August 2002, giving powers to president to sack the government anytime he likes and also powers for important postings in the establishment. This strategy has earned MMA some more respect and they are not seen as power hungry as was the impression of them in the past. The religious fanatics have supported most of the military regimes in Pakistan history. Only this time, they opted to remain in opposition in the center. They are more likely to form the provincial government in North West Frontier Province (NWFP) which is next to Afghanistan and could be part of the government in Baluchistan. They have not gone to share the government at the center because of their perspective to become a mass force at national level. ? Had Punjab been awoke like the other province, the Islamic revolution in Pakistan would have been complete in this elections? cried Qazi Hussain Ahmed, the main leader of the most organized Jamaat-i-Islami; JI is a decisive component of MMA. It is JI successful political strategy of forming political alliance of all the religious forces that has won the mass support for the MMA. ?They are never united and can never be united? was the main arguments of the some of the Left intellectuals during the past years. MMA has at least made these intellectuals think twice before they bring this argument against them.

The unity process of the religious forces started long before the 11th September realizing the political vacuum after the failure of the successive civilian regimes to solve any of the basic problems of the masses in Pakistan. The 10 years of successive failed regimes of PPP and MLN after the fall of the last military regime in 1988, has provided the opportunity to the religious forces to exploit the opportunity.

In 1993, the JI formed a Pakistan Islamic Front with some minor Islamic groups to contest the general elections. The PIF failed badly and fetched less than 3 per cent of the total votes. In 1995, Mutehida Jakjehti Council (United Solidarity Council) was formed mainly to address the question of sectarian killings. In 2000, almost 29 religious groups formed the Islamic Mutehida Inqilabi Mehaz IMAM (Islamic United Revolutionary Front. This was mainly to deal with the Western ideas spread by the NGOs in the NWFP and Baluchistan. Jamiat Ulemai Islam under Fazal Rehman played the main role in this group. In June 2001, MMA was founded at the initiative of Jamaat-i-Islami. After 11th September, over 40 different religious groups formed Pak Afghan Defense Counsel. The MMA all eyes are on Punjab, the most populated province with over 64% of the total inhabitants living in this rather prosperous area of Pakistan. Many villages in Punjab particularly in Southern Punjab have young martyrs. Those who have been killed Kashmir or Afghanistan. These ?sacrifices? are laying a strong foundation for the possible growth of the religious political influence on those areas where MMQ is yet to become a majority. MMA activists unlike the main bourgeoisie parties are not driven by careers or greed. They are from the middle and working class background committed for a change. Most of the elected members of MMA from NWFP are from poor background and are seen by many all the time on cycles. This is contrary to elected members of rich parties who are on land cruisers and Mitsubishi Pajeros. The class question is very much in the mind of many who have gone to support the MMA in the recent elections. In the absence of the any significant left force in Pakistan MMA have echoed the class sentiments mixed with religion.

Would the American imperialism tolerate the growing influence of religious fundamentalism in Pakistan? The Americans has so for relied on the military generals to do the dirty job. Musharaf has done it very happily. But the political situations are getting out of control. The formation of the MMA government in NWFP will bring new contradictions between the new government in he center with the provincial government. The under ground Talban will feel easier in surfacing in NWFP under a religious government. Already new social tensions have emerged in the area. Women rights, human rights advocated in the province are under attack. ?NGO, s in these fields must wind up their offices? is the hidden message by the fanatics. The Sunday regular weekly off day will be once again replaced by Friday by the new provincial government. ?Beard is a must,? the new young elected leaders of MMA are advocating for every Muslim. ?Women must obey the Islamic norms and must cover themselves?. It is Talbanisation of Pakistani society in a different form. It is not yet advocating an open Jihad like the Alqaida did. But it is in the oven.

So NWFP and Pakistan could be the next target of all the propaganda of the US imperialism after Iraq. Any attempt by the center to dissolve or suspend the provincial government at NWFP will result in more civil war like situation. In 1974, the united government of the nationalist and religious fundamentalist was dissolved by Bhutto under the pressure of Shah if Iran, a guerilla war started in Baluchistan. Many were killed and many went to Afghanistan in exile. Now nationalist have diminished to large extent for the time being in this election, as they were seen as pro imperialists force. Many of these nationalists supported the American bombing in the false hope that it will crush the religious threat at home as well.

More dark period is heading Pakistan unless new initiatives is been taken by the Left and progressive forces to stop the onslaught of the fanatics.

The handing over the recorded message of Asama Bin Laden in Islamabad to Algezeera tele network shows how things can develop in Pakistan. The possibility of the presence of Asama Bin Laden in Pakistan, the pro Talban provincial government in NWFP, the growing influence of religious fundamentalism in Punjab and Sind can force the newly elected pro Musharaf regime to take drastic actions against them. This in return will make the life of ordinary Pakistani more difficult. And it will make the ideas of religious fundamentalism more popular. Labour Party Pakistan had foreseen the recent growth of religious fundamentalism. It has declined to side with them on any issue. It has opposed the American bombing alongside with the condemnation of religious terrorism. It is adopting the policy to oppose the recently formed new civil pro Musharaf regime. The new civil regime is no change for the masses. It is the continuation of the Musharaf regime in civilian cloths. It will carry the IMF; World Bank dictated policies on the name of reform agenda. The religious fundamentalist will also oppose the reform agenda but only in words. Initially they are showing a very liberal face to the West. They have already said that privatization is a must. But under the pressure of the masses, they can make big noise against the economic exploitation of the people by the Multi nationals alongside with the social and political repressions. The hypocrisy of the fundamentalist can only be exposed with a united action of the trade unions, Left and progressive forces.

## IMPERIALISM AND FUNDAMENTALISM

Islamic fundamentalism provides a glaring example of imperialist hypocrisy. Now the USA and the imperialist West pose as the biggest enemy of Islamic fundamentalism and try to fool the working class in the West by presenting fundamentalism as a big challenge to world peace. But it was the same imperialism that used these fundamentalist forces against the left in various Muslim countries.

In the 1950s and 1960s there was a rise of populist, anti-imperialist and class movements. The USA worked out a plan to patronise the fundamentalists in order to weaken these populist movements, which imperialism feared could end up in socialist revolutions. The CIA, under the guidance of US Secretary of State John Foster Dulles, established a liaison between fundamentalist parties in different countries. According to the plan, a network of Akwanul Muslameen popularly known as Muslim Brotherhood (Egypt), Hamas (Syria), Sarakat ul Islam (Indonesia), Islamic Salvation Front (Algeria) and Jamaat Islami (Pakistan) was established. These parties were given full economic and political support during that period.

This process reached its peak during the 1980s, when thousands of militants or so-called Mujahideen were trained and sent to Afghanistan. The Jamaat Islami of Pakistan provided the main force, but the above-mentioned parties also sent their share.

The shameful alliance of imperialism and fundamentalism was exposed in Pakistan in 1977 during a movement against Prime Minister Zulfiqar Ali Bhutto. The fundamentalists started a movement against Bhutto in 1977 based on his rigging of elections. Some left and bourgeois parties also joined hands with the religious parties. Bhutto was a populist nationalist leader and an irritant for imperialism in the region. During this movement, the dollar was devalued in Pakistan. This was the only such instance in Pakistan, indicating the flood of dollars reaching Pakistan during those days. Similarly, a US official welcomed and waved to a rally of the Jamaat Islami when it passed before the American Center in Lahore while the demonstrators chanted slogans in favour of the USA.

In the Afghan war, thousands of guerrillas fought against the Afghan revolution at the command of the CIA and the Pentagon. Osama bin Laden was a hero then. But the post-Cold War situation, as mentioned, brought them into contradiction for at least three reasons. There was a political vacuum because the collapse of the USSR had hurt the trade union and the left movement in the Muslim world, as it had elsewhere. The imperialist political and economic support for the fundamentalist parties stopped. Imperialism now needed another potential enemy in place of the Communists.

In the new situation, it was in the interest of both fundamentalism and imperialism to become enemies. The fundamentalists started gaining politically by posing as anti-imperialists, while imperialism now had Islamic terrorists to fool its working class and justify big defence budgets. But is this imperialism-fundamentalism enmity real and long-lasting? No. As soon as a working-class movement begins threatening the class structure and imperialism, the old hypocritical alliance of imperialism and fundamentalism will be renewed. However, before that, because of the strong consciousness among the working classes in the West against fundamentalism, imperialism will not openly support any fundamentalist movement. There may be underhanded deals with fundamentalist governments in Afghanistan or Iran, or with Chechen rebels, but not an open alliance. Similarly, after the experience of the Taliban, imperialism would hardly support any fundamentalist movement coming to power. But it cannot be completely ruled out everywhere; because of the internal contradictions of imperialist countries, a section of imperialism may support particular fundamentalist movements while another section of imperialism opposes them. It is most likely that, unless a revolutionary situation arises, the present contradiction between fundamentalism and imperialism will suit both of them, and fundamentalists from time to time may make trouble for imperialism.

## THE WAR AGAINST EVIL EMPIRE AND ISLAMIC FUNDAMENTALISTS

The Soviet military intervention in Afghanistan on 27 December 1979 offered unique opportunity to the United States to weaken its principal adversary, and to General Zia to prolong his obscurantism rule. A resistance movement imbedded with Islamic fervor appeared to be the most effective counter-measure to bleed the Soviets.

The Pakistan ISI and the American CIA masterminded the formation, logistics and action plan of the mujahideen outfits. They secured services of the Jama-at-i-Islami and Jamiat-i-Ulema-i-Islam for inculcating the spirit of jihad and recruiting rank and file to fight what was primarily an American war. Foreign elements, including Egyptians, Palestinians and Saudis, were inducted in the mujahideen groups.

The mujahideen movement thus became a meeting point for Islamic militants of Afghanistan. Pakistan and the Middle East. The United States, without any scruples, promoted and used Islamic militancy to defeat the Evil Empire. Generally the people from Pakistan and abroad professed and practiced the Puritan Schools of Islamic Shariah, where the Jehad is a practiced article of faith.

Unfortunately, after the withdrawal of the Soviet forces from Afghanistan in 1989, the United States consigned that country to oblivion and the Mujahedeen or Islamic Fundamentalist militants became a liability for Pakistan. With its almost entire western borders destabilized as Afghanistan was in turmoil and heavy burden of rogues, Pakistan had no option but to groom the Taliban (students) in its madrasahs to create a force that could restore law and order in Afghanistan.

Islam is a religion of peace but it is being projected as the principal source of international terrorism. The West must distinguish between militancy in the cause of national liberation and the use of force by states to extinguish the spark of freedom. With Muslims being persecuted, maimed and killed from Palestine to Kashmir to Philippines there can be no peace.

### United States War against Terrorism

In the after math of the most inhuman and barbaric acts of terrorism carried out in United States of America by the International Islamic Terrorist out fit, it seems, that country and the civilized world at large, were jolted and came to realize that the menace had grown out of proportion and was bent upon destroying the established order.

The US led coalition, after some preparations and requisite deployments, commenced the War against Terror. Pakistan, as neighbor of Afghanistan and a supporter of the Regime in Afghanistan was in a quandary. It was not left with any options but to support the US led effort against taking out that rogue regime in Afghanistan.

It may not be out of place to mention that, even before the September 11 impasse, the threat perception within the Defense Establishment of Pakistan was going through a rethinking and re-evaluation owing the activities going on inside Afghanistan under the tutelage of Taliban Regime and the Al-Qaeda Movement and its activities inside Pakistan like elsewhere in the world.

The act of the Taliban Regime of destroying the Historic Statues of Lord Buddha, despite best of efforts by Pakistan at persuading them to refrain from such uncivilized act, had not only frustrated Pakistan but also made Pakistan realize that its support for them was in fact emboldening that regime to an extent where the National Interest of Pakistan was being compromised at the altar of their so called Pan Islamic agenda. It was becoming all the more clear that Talebans and Al-Qaeda had expansionist designs and in that regard Pakistan was not an exception. In the after math of the most inhuman and barbaric acts of terrorism carried out in United States of America by the International Islamic Terrorist out fit, it seems, that country and the civilized world at large, were jolted and came to realize that the menace had grown out of proportion and was bent upon destroying the established order.

The US led coalition, after some preparations and requisite deployments, commenced the War against Terror. Pakistan, as neighbor of Afghanistan and a supporter of the Rogue Regime in Afghanistan was in a quandary.

It was not left with any options but to support the US led effort against taking out that rogue regime in Afghanistan, albeit, owing not only being part of the Civilized Society but its own threat perceptions, emanating via the covert and overt activities of Taliban and Al-Qaeda nexus inside Afghanistan, globally and more so within Pakistan.

If anything the event of September 11 only hastened the decision making process in the Pakistani Defense Establishment in as much as the defiant and rigid posture of the Taliban Regime on the issue of handing over UBL and his coterie to the Americans, despite persuasions by Pakistan, acted as a catalyst for Pakistan to arrive at a pragmatic decision. The rigidity, defiance and self-serving stance of the Taliban Regime had placed Pakistan at a crossroad. It had to choose between its own National Interest and its place in the comity of civilized world and Isolation, being branded as a state that was allegedly promoting militancy and terrorism.

The conduct of the Talebans and Al-Qaeda has, if anything caused tremendous damage to the cause of the people of Kashmir. The ground realities dictated that the said elements were, with their expansionist designs, thoroughly indulging in talibanisation of Civil Society in Pakistan. Besides, promoting factionalism and sectarian violence. It was, to say the least, putting the unity of Pakistan at peril.

Having said that, it would be wrong to assume that Pakistan just caved in under the pressure from Washington. The truth would be that the pace of Pakistan distancing itself from what was going on in side Afghanistan was hastened rather accelerated. It could also be said that may be, owing conducive international environment, was fortified in taking that vital decision.

This of necessity should translate into moral and material support for Pakistan to wit stand the fall out of annihilation of that regime from Afghanistan and so also imminent reaction from with in Pakistan from the segment that is sympathetic or allied with the fundamentalist forces.

The short-term objectives set out by the International coalition were attained in matter of months and the Rogue Regime along with its partner Al-Qaeda was dislodged from Afghanistan. An interim set was brought in its place, headed by Karazai.

After being dislodged, the Taliban and Al-Qaeda Forces simply melted away and blended into the local population of Afghanistan and in side Pakistan. The pro-Islamic forces within these two countries, being quite sympathetic appears to have willingly absorbed these forces on the run.

Question is does dislodging the Taliban government from Afghanistan and dismantling the Al-Qaeda network in that country resolves the issue? No.

The ground realities show that the safe sanctuaries for these elements on the run are very much intact, alive and kicking. There is no dearth of sympathetic element within Afghanistan and Pakistan in the so-called respective establishments.

Before 9/11 it was the policy of the Government of Pakistan to support the since deceased Taliban Regime. The Afghan territory was being used as training grounds for members of Al-Qaeda and odd 30 other such out fits from same number of countries to promote militancy in those countries and also to carryout acts of terrorism against the US interests around the world. It is true that those training grounds inside Afghanistan have for now, been uprooted and closed.

It means that immediate and constant threat emanating from Afghanistan may have been addressed. It would be nearer home instead, to say that for now it may be comparably diluted. The capabilities of International Terror may have been in disarray and perceptibly its connectivity may also have been disrupted. It could not be said with any certainty that it has been qualitatively contained to an extent that it has been incapacitated.

The factual position is that there has been significant damage caused to the International Terror Groups. There safe heaven has been neutralized. An environment has been created that has made the lift difficult for the militants and its leadership in side Afghanistan, Pakistan and their respective countries and elsewhere.

However, it is equally true that all these significant achievements could at best be termed as containment. It is equally true that 9/11 has rudely awakened the world to the threat of this millennium. The state of alert is there. The commitment is also there. It is also equally true that militarily the preparation is also there to meet any potential threat.

The respite, if it could be termed as such, ought have been simultaneously put to use to address the causes, which have taken the things to such an impasse that that brand of militancy and terrorism has become the greatest threat to civilized world.

With due deference one dares to say that in the long run the gains so far made would be wasted and the world may wind up with the same problem with more complexities and capabilities.

## LONG TERM REQUIREMENTS

Having said that it would be in the fitness of things to peep in to the History of the Puritan Islamic Movements in the South Asia, Middle East and Far East and so also in the Balkans.

It is also of paramount importance that Islam is viewed as a World Religion side by side with Christianity and Judaism, Revelation being a common source of these religions.

There should be a concerted effort to accept, high light and promote the pacific basis of Islam. The Sufi doctrine of Islam has volumes to offer to Muslims and World at large.

The Islamic Fundamentalist Clergy has to be engaged via the proponents of peaceful, moderate and tolerant Islamic Clergy, which abound through out the world. A meaningful and qualitative dialogue over World Media may be in immediate order. The dialogue being conducted in the Vatican since the early sixties should on the one hand be accelerated and on the other projected globally. Let there be meeting of the minds globally.

Merely by saying that it is not a clash of Civilizations or that it is not a war against Islam would not do. The situation on ground dictates otherwise. The isolating Muslims and relying on the support of the governments in Islamic Countries would not suffice in the long term.

Besides, it also needs to be analysed that time and again the West has tolerated and in some cases abetted or even promoted militancy in the name of Islam. Wisdom of such acts at a given moment in the recent History should be called in question. It should provide a lesson for future course of action. In the case of Pakistan and Afghanistan it is the truth. The menace or monster left by the West in the after math of Soviet defeat has to be annihilated or neutralized. It has to be addressed not only through military means but more so by strengthening the moderate and peace loving citizens of these countries.

Bringing in qualitative and quantitative socio economic in puts in the areas of education, health, economic opportunities and moderate and good governments. It is a daunting task. But there are no short cuts.

## THE RISE OF RELIGIOUS FUNDAMENTALISM IN PAKISTAN

Religious fundamentalism has become a powerful and dangerous force in Pakistan, due mainly to the opportunism of successive political leadership that has pandered to it. Militant sectarian religious groups and parties, led by half-educated and bigoted mullahs, many of them armed to the teeth, are holding our civil society and the state to ransom. They threaten the very fabric of Pakistan society.

Threats of disruption from religious parties have escalated in recent decades. They have steadily grown in strength since the time of General Zia. They now claim that they are the true custodians of Pakistan and that it was they, the mullahs, who had fought successfully for Pakistan, to establish a theocratic state for

Muslims. Facts contradict such claims. With the exception of Ghulam Ahmad Parvez's pro-Pakistan *Tulu-i-Islam,* group, all religious groups and parties, including the *Jamiat-i-Ulama-i-Hind,* the *Majli-i-Ahrar* and the *Jamaat-i-Islami,* had all bitterly opposed the Pakistan Movement and abused its leadership which was secular.

The Muslim League, the Party that led the Pakistan movement, was a party of modern educated Muslim professionals and government job seekers (whom, for the sake of brevity, we may call the 'salariat'). It had little to do with the outlook of bigoted mullahs. It was free of any millenarian ideological pretences about creating an Islamic state. *It was a movement of Muslims rather than a movement of Islam.* Behind it was a new class of English educated Muslim professionals and government job seekers that came into being in the 19 century. It got organised politically by the turn of the century, seeking a better deal for themselves vis-à-vis Hindus who were advancing relatively more rapidly in these fields.

When the Muslim League was founded in 1906 at a meeting convened by Nawab Salimullah at Dhaka, the new party was immediately hi-jacked by the Aligarh group led by Nawab Viqar ul-Mulk. Aligarh was at the vanguard of the new Northern Indian Muslim *salariat* class, the sons of the Muslim *Ashraf,* who were deeply conscious of the loss of their privileges with the advent of British rule and the relatively more rapid rise of Hindu educated classes. The main base of the Muslim salariat was in UP and Bihar for, at that time, its was relatively weaker in the Muslim majority provinces.

The Muslim League was focused entirely on its secular demands of western educated Muslim professionals and the salariat. Attempts to place the issue of Islamic ideology on the agenda of the Muslim League were both rare and invariably unsuccessful. Arguably, the earliest of such attempts was one by Shibli Numani to Islamise the Aligarh syllabus. Shibli was explicitly committed to theocratic values and wanted to shift the emphasis of the Aligarh syllabus away from English and modern sciences, towards Islamic learning and the Arabic language. The response of the Muslim salariat class to that attempt is exemplified by the remarks of Sir Raza Ali, who was a close collaborator of Sir Syed's immediate successors, Muhsin ul-Mulk and Viqar ul-Mulk. With them, Raza Ali was at the centre of the Aligarh establishment. In an article in the daily Statesman opposing Shibli's move, he remarked that the idea of reviving Arabic knowledge was, of course, beguiling for Muslims. But he warned that they should not ignore the demands of our times, for the most urgent need of Indian Muslims was to be offered education that would be beneficial in the affairs of this world; education that would help their coming generations to earn their livelihood. Sir Raza Ali spelt out the principal concern of the educated Muslim middle class at the time. Their concern was not about a hypothetical return to original Islam and the creation of an 'Islamic State', ruled over by mullahs, that Shibli had dreamt about. Shibli had to leave Aligarh, for it was not the place where his theocratic ideas could flourish.

Among the rare attempts to bring the issue of 'Islamic Ideology' on to the agenda of the Muslim League was one that was planned for the Delhi Session of the AIML in April 1943. One Abdul Hameed Kazi (backed by 'Maulana' Abdul Sattar Niazi) canvassed support for a resolution, which he intended to table. That would commit the Muslim League to an Islamic ideology and the creation of an Islamic state. But pressure from everyone around him forced Kazi to abandon the idea. The resolution was not even moved. The Pakistan movement remained firmly committed to its secular concerns. In his keynote speech before the inaugural meeting of Pakistan's new Constituent Assembly, on 11$^{th}$ August 1947, Mr. Jinnah spelt out the *Pakistan Ideology,* namely the secular and tolerant vision of the new state. That speech was not a sudden aberration, as some Islamic ideologists, and General Zia's hacks, were later to allege. It was consistent with what Mr. Jinnah had been saying for decades. The Muslim League had always been committed to a secular society.

Following Mr. Jinnah, his political successor, Liaquat Ali Khan, too reiterated the Muslim League's secular values. When Liaquat moved the Objectives Resolution in the Constituent Assembly in March 1949 he declared that 'As I have just said, the people are the real recipients of power. This naturally eliminates any danger of the establishment of a theocracy.' Despite that clear statement by the mover of the Objectives Resolution, later religious ideologues, notably General Zia and his hacks, have claimed that the Objectives Resolution was a charter for the imposition of the 'Sharia' (as they would interpret it) although the word Sharia does not occur anywhere in that Resolution. Their argument is based on some conventional generalities in the Resolution, which said that 'Muslims shall be enabled to order their lives, in the individual and collective spheres, in accord with the teachings and requirements of Islam as set out in the Holy Quran and the *Sunna*'. That, did not amount to a charter for the creation of a theocratic, 'Islamic' State.

Liaquat's position on the Muslim League's traditional secularism was, however, soon to be reversed. Not so very long after the Objectives Resolution was passed, Liaquat began to change his tune for his political base was threatened by of splits in the Muslim League in the Punjab, which was the power-base of Pakistan's ruling elite. That was due to factional conflict between Daulatana and Mamdot who left the Muslim League to form a rival Party. Liaquat was now in a panic. He decided to exploit Islamic rhetoric, to hold together his crumbling Party. He began to speak of 'Islam in Danger'. He also began to equate loyalty to the Muslim League with loyalty to the state. Those who opposed him or his party were denounced as traitors.

There was, however, a second and a much more important reason why Liaquat decided to abandon his secular stance. Powerful regional movements had arisen in East Bengal, Sindh, Baluchistan and the NWFP, whose people felt that they were not being given their due in a Punjabi dominated Pakistan. They demanded regional autonomy and fairer shares of resources. The Centre, which was seen as 'Punjabi', was in fact dominated by a cohesive bureaucracy, under Chaudhri Muhammad Ali as Secretary General to the Government. It was the centralised bureaucracy that ruled Pakistan whilst politicians, including Liaquat, went through the motions.

Arguably, it was the challenge to the centre from regional movements which was the more important factor in precipitating Liaquat's ideological *volte-face.* Abandoning Mr. Jinnah's (and his own) firm stand against pandering to the mullahs, Liaquat sought to negate regional demands by issuing calls for 'unity' in the name of Pakistan and Islam. We were all Pakistanis and Muslims, it was now argued, and therefore we could not be Bengalis or Sindhis or Baluch.

The bureaucracy, rather than Liaquat, was in effective control, and it was not prepared to make any significant concessions to the mullahs. The mullahs could be given a visible public role, but without any real share in power. For that purpose a *Board of Talimaat-i-Islamia,* was set up. It provided a few jobs for some senior mullahs, the *Ulama.* But the Board was to be no more than a façade for the new found religious rhetoric of politicians. It was not to have any real powers. Its function was purely advisory and that too only on matters that were referred to it. When the Board did make some suggestions they were unceremoniously ignored. Nevertheless, the *Ulama* seemed to be content with the arrangement. They remained quiescent for nearly two decades. Recalcitrant Mullahs, such as Maulana Maududi, found themselves in jail. The mullahs were under control. That basically peaceful scene was disturbed only temporarily in 1953, when Islamic militants launched Anti-Ahmadi riots in the Punjab an d Martial Law was proclaimed. Although religious zealots of the Majlis-i-Ahrar and the Jamaat-i-Islami led the riots, they were in fact being used by cynical political forces, led by Punjab Chief Minister Mumtaz Daulatana. That was done in the context of US attempts to destabilise the Nazimuddin Government at the centre and to counter the Bengal group of MPs in the matter of the proposed Pakistan-US military Alliance which they opposed. That is a long and complicated story.

A decade and a half later, religious rhetoric was indulged in by the illegitimate regime of General Yahya Khan, but without conceding any formal role to the mullahs. General Sher Ali, redefined 'Pakistan Ideology' as 'Islamic Ideology'. The Yahya government's primary concern was to de-legitimise the increasingly powerful Bengali nationalism. Yahya's Bengali adviser, Prof. G. W. Choudhury, had persuaded him and his coterie of Generals, that East Bengali nationalism was limited to only a handful of intellectuals, who were in the pay of the Indians and that the vast majority of Bengalis had no sympathy with them. That tragically false picture could account for the ferocity and reckless manner in which Yahya tried to suppress the Bengali people in 1971. Would they have embarked on that policy if Yahya had even the slightest inkling of the depth of Bengali feelings ?

The mullahs were quiescent, however, until they were stirred into action by the foolish populist rhetoric of Zulfiqar Ali Bhutto who misguidedly decided to exploit religious ideology. Thereby Bhutto sowed the seeds of his own destruction, for the re-activated mullahs became the vanguard of the campaign against him. That set the scene for Gen. Zia's *coup d'etat*.

It was under General Zia that narrow and bigoted religiosity became state policy. The General sought the political support of the mullahs for his illegal regime, for he had no other political base. He also sought financial support from the Reagan regime in the US. Both of these objectives, he thought, could be secured through an Islamic *Jihad* which he proclaimed against the Soviet presence in Afghanistan. The CIA joined took over the task of organising armed religious groups in Afghanistan, in cooperation with Pakistani agencies. When the Russians left Afghanistan, however, the CIA was withdrawn precipitately from the scene, leaving it to Pakistan to deal with the mess that they had created. Foolish Pakistani policies since then, especially under Benazir Bhutto and her successor Nawaz Sharif, got Pakistan even more heavily involved with these once US sponsored 'terrorist groups'.

The present government has done little to turn away from these policies to extricate Pakistan from the mess that was inherited from Zia's Afghan policy. When he seized power illegally, Zia badly needed some source of legitimacy for his regime. Being politically bankrupt, he decided to exploit the credulity of Pakistani Muslims by invoking Allah. He claimed to have experienced *ilham* (a divine revelation) in which, he declared, he was enjoined by the Almighty himself to Islamise Pakistan and to transform it into a fortress of Islam. New 'Islamic Laws' were promulgated that were crude and cruel distortions of Islamic teachings, such as his *Hudud Ordinance* which, for example, had the effect of punishing a rape victim (for fornication) while the perpetrator of the rape went scot-free because of impossible conditions of proof now needed to prove his guilt! Zia also bequeathed to his successors undemocratic Shariat Courts, that are answerable to no one. They issue binding decisions on the state and on the people, in the name of the Sharia. That role, in the name of Islam, is rejected by the philosophy of Sir Syed Ahmad who pointed out that Islam did not decree the office of a Pope with powers to issue binding decrees in the name of the faith. Islam, he said, is a religion of the individual conscience. No person or institution has the right to issue binding *fatawa,* laying down what Islam is and what it is not. Indeed, no other Muslim country has the equivalent of our Shariat Courts. They were set up by Zia's illegitimate regime and should be dissolved.

The *Shariat Courts* are manned by persons who hold rigid religious views. Their most damaging decision so far is an order that requires the abolition of interest, 'in all its forms', by 30th June, 2001. This threatens to bring Pakistan's already very shaky economy to a complete halt. No enemy of Pakistan could have devised a more potent weapon to destroy the country. In arriving at their decision the judges of the Shariat Bench of the Supreme Court set aside the advice of a very large number of scholars who came before it as witnesses, who resisted this interpretation of the *Sharia.* Instead, the Court appears to have been misled by bogus claims of 'Islamic Banking'. They seem to be ignorant of how a modern economy functions and do not seem to have understood at all the obvious implications of their decision in a modern day capitalist economy such as that of Pakistan. They appear to be ignorant of the difference between interest in a modern capitalist economy (*sood)* and usury (riba) in pre-capitalist economies to which Quranic strictures apply. What the Shariat Courts have produced is a time bomb which, if allowed to go off, threatens to blow up Pakistan's economy. The present Government seems to be paralysed in the face of the die hard religious lobby which seems to be triumphant about this. It has poor advisers. As soon as the Shariat Appellate Bench of the Supreme Court announced it decision, the minister of Finance, who is an ex-banker declared, without pausing to think, that the Court's decision would be implemented in full. But, after months of deliberations by several high powered committees, the Government still has no idea whatever of what is to be done. It speaks with two voices. At a recent meeting, the Federal Minister for Religious Affairs declared that the Government has drafted all required laws and regulations, which are ready to be promulgated and that the Government is ready to implement the Shariat Court's decision in full, and without qualifications. But at the same meeting, the Governor of the State Bank of Pakistan (the country's central Bank) declared that they do not as yet know how the Shariat Court decision can be implemented. He said that the Government needs more time to work out viable solutions and that it has asked for an extension of time.

The Government does not seem to understand the gravity of this issue. They should know that they cannot allow the economy to collapse. But they also appear to be too intimidated by religious fundamentalists to overturn the Shariat Court's decree. Meanwhile, the top nine religious parties in the country have declared that they will launch a mass anti-Riba movement, on the lines of the movement that brought down Zulfiqar Ali Bhutto, if the Government fails to abolish interest by the date laid down by the Shariat Bench of the Supreme Court, namely the end of June, 2001. They have declared, ominously, that the time has come for a decisive war between Islamic and secular forces in the country. A major factor in the present situation is a development since the time of Zia. That is the proliferation of *deeni madaris,* religious schools, that have spread throughout Pakistan. They receive generous foreign funding, not least from Middle Eastern states like Saudi Arabia. The *deeni madaris* have little difficulty in recruiting pupils (*taliban*), who are turned into fanatics, ready to die for what they are taught to believe are sacred causes. A factor that has greatly helped their recruitment is the creation of a huge number of unemployed families, people without a livelihood and without hope, as a consequence of farm mechanisation, especially in the Punjab. Every tractor displaces at least a dozen families of sharecroppers. Hundreds of thousands of them are now without a source of livelihood. In that context, the appearance of the well financed *deeni madaris,* who take over their children, give them free 'tuition', accommodation and food, cannot appear to be anything other than a great blessing. The enthusiastic young *taliban,* are taught to recite the Quran. They are also indoctrinated, their minds filled with distorted and intolerant ideas about what Islam is and what it prescribes.

The *taliban* are thus turned into fanatics. Most of the *'deeni' madaris* also give them military training for *jihad* initially ostensibly against the Soviets and now for the liberation of Kashmir. But already Pakistan itself is experiencing the inevitable heavy fall out from this. The armed groups, many of them with battle-hardened *taliban,* are in the vanguard of sectarian killings throughout Pakistan, which are on the increase; killings of members of rival sects, Sunnis against the Shi'a, Deobandi Sunnis against Barelvi Sunnis and so on. They have also begun to issue threats against the state itself and the society in Pakistan. Instead of a viable policy designed to disarm and liquidate such groups, successive regimes in Pakistan have pandered to them. The current military government, unlike the military regime of General Zia, has not indulged much in religious rhetoric, except for the occasional utterances of its Federal Minister for Religious Affairs. Indeed, the Government's liberal interior minister, General Moinuddin Haider, has given calls, from time to time, about doing something to bring the so-called *deeni madaris* under some sort of control, reforming their syllabi to introduce some useful, career related, educational input into their activities. For that he has become the *bête noir* of the religious parties, who have warned the government, firmly, against meddling in their affairs.

The government, for its part, seems to be intimidated by the militant Islamic groups. In December last, for example, one *Maulana* Muhammad Akram, leader of the *Tanzimul Ikhwan,* threatened to march on Islamabad with 'hundreds of thousands' of his followers, to force the Government to promulgate the *Sharia.* The Government's response was to placate him. It despatched the Punjab Home Secretary and the Inspector General of Police to parley with Akram.

That was apparently not enough, for it then sent Dr. Mahmood Ghazi, the Federal Minister for Religious Affairs, as reinforcement. After long drawn out talks, Maulana Akram 'graciously agreed' to defer his plan to storm the capital. It has been suggested by the media that Maulana Akram has 'a lot of influence among middle-ranking officers of the army'. If that is so, that must surely be extremely worrying. Could it be that which explains the Government's apparent paralysis in the face of serious threats from fanatical religious groups? It must know that a do nothing policy will not solve anything. Left to itself, the situation can only get worse.

Theories of the state, democratic or otherwise, are premised on the state's monopoly of legitimate force. But here we have a situation where the state's monopoly of force is undermined by the numerous armed religious groups (who often work in concert) that have agendas of their own. The Government must realise that the more they try to accommodate religious zealots, the stronger and the more intransigent they become. What the situation demands is a firm and well thought out policy to disarm such groups and bring them under control. It is surprising that Pakistan's professional military does not yet seem to have realised the very serious threat that this situation poses to itself as well as to the State and society as a whole. In the meantime, until something is done, Pakistan will continue to stagger towards an uncertain future, with contradictory state policies.

# 4

# Al-Qaida and its Operations

Al Qaida has become the most recognised and evocative symbol of the new terrorist threat. It has provided the fanatical ideology, the operational example and the management model that other groups and individuals have followed. It is the foremost example of the wider phenomenon of transnational extremist-Muslim terrorism. To understand Al Qaida's evolution is to gain an appreciation of this new terrorism. And to understand Al Qaida we need to understand how its philosophy differs from that of mainstream Islam.

## A PLURALIST AND TOLERANT TRADITION

Islam has played a vital role in shaping human civilisation. The classical period of its rich history nurtured and moulded much of our modern scientific knowledge and philosophy. It fostered a tolerant, diverse and pluralist tradition.

Like Judaism and Christianity, Islam traces its faith back to the Prophet Abraham. It accepts all the major Biblical prophets. It accords a special status to Jews and Christians, referring to them in the Quran as 'People of the Book'.

Mainstream Islamic scholars - whose views reflect those of the vast majority of the world's Muslims - have long stressed the Quran's clear endorsement of diversity, its prohibition of coercion, suicide and murder, its instruction to Muslims to act towards others with compassion, forgiveness and restraint. Tolerance of other beliefs has been a key element. Islamic tradition has long encouraged Muslims to respect the sanctity of human life. It encourages them to coexist peacefully with other People of the Book. It advises them to beware of extremism. It has also embraced a wide range of perspectives about ways to approach the faith: Islam is not monolithic. The Quran does contain verses calling on Muslims to defend themselves if attacked, which extremists cite in support of their views. But such verses are usually heavily qualified. It has long been a central tenet of mainstream Islamic scholarship that Quranic verses should not be considered in isolation or divorced from their moral and historical contexts. Mainstream Muslim scholars have argued that, in a time of war, Muslims are obliged to draw a distinction between combatants and non-combatants. Killing innocent civilians is forbidden.

## ISLAM IN AUSTRALIA

Australia is threatened by transnational terrorism, perpetuated in the name of an extremist Muslim ideology. A radical but tiny minority of Muslims have twisted Islamic teachings to further their revolutionary ideals. The overwhelming majority of Muslims are peaceful and law-abiding. The Australian Muslim community continues to make a significant contribution to the struggle against terrorism.

In the early 16th century, Makassan fishermen from the Indonesian archipelago were the first Muslims to visit Australia. They traded with the indigenous Aboriginal community. In the 19th century, Afghan Muslim camel drivers played an important role in exploring and opening up the outback. Today, Islam is one of the fastest-growing faiths in Australia. Muslims are a vital part of the rich mosaic of Australian society.

In the past 25 years, the Australian Muslim community has grown significantly. The 2001 Census counted 281 578 Muslims living in Australia - an increase of 40 per cent since the 1996 Census and an overall rise of 91 per cent in the past decade. These figures may be conservative. Some recent estimates suggest Australian Muslims now number between 350 000 and 450 000. Australian Muslims are ethnically diverse. About 35 per cent of them were born in Australia. The rest immigrated to Australia from over 70 different countries, including Lebanon, Turkey, Indonesia and Bosnia-Herzegovina. There are over 100 mosques and at least 21 Muslim primary and secondary schools in Australia. Islamic community centres, student associations, halal butchers and restaurants are found in every major city in Australia.

Australian Muslims are doctors, lawyers, academics, sportspersons, journalists, diplomats, police officers, members of the Defence Force, entrepreneurs, shopkeepers and labourers.

Muslims have contributed much to our political, economic and social life. They have cemented their place in our religious and cultural landscape. They occupy an increasingly important place in Australian life, and are embracing opportunities to participate in a tolerant, inclusive and culturally diverse Australia.

### *Extremist Ideology*

The ideology and the methods of extremist-Muslim terrorists are far removed from mainstream Muslims' tolerance of other faiths. Only a tiny minority of Muslims support the terrorists' strategy of violence.

Extremists cloak themselves in the language of Islam but, particularly in their advocacy of violence, flout what the overwhelming majority of Muslims accept as fundamental precepts of their religion.

## SOME CONSERVATIVE MUSLIM REFORM MOVEMENTS

### *Salafism*

Salafism is an approach to Islam based on reverence for the example of the 'righteous ancestors' (Al-Salaf Al-Saleh). Some Salafis advocate strict adherence to a literal interpretation of the Quran and the Sunna (the deeds of the Prophet and the Hadith), which they believe contain the source of all necessary guidance. They oppose attempts to interpret Quranic law from an historical, contextual perspective. They reject innovation in faith (bida). 'Wahhabism' is often associated with the Salafi orientation. Its adherents consider the term 'Wahhabism' derogatory; they see themselves as orthodox Muslims and draw heavily on the conservative tribal social customs of the Arabian Peninsula. Salafism is not of itself a doctrine of extremism but groups like Al Qaida draw on strands of an extremist interpretation of Salafism.

### *The Muslim Brotherhood*

Hassan Al-Banna formed the Muslim Brotherhood in Egypt in 1928. It was at first a social and moral reform movement to revive Islam as a way of life and end the separation of religion and state. It complemented government activities by providing valuable community services. Offshoots of the Brotherhood still play an important and legitimate role in some Muslim countries' political processes. Al-Banna combined the Quranic descriptions of qital (fighting) and jihad (struggle) (Jihad does not mean 'holy war'. It means struggle or striving in accordance with the teachings of Islam. There are two forms of jihad: the 'greater' jihad - an inner struggle to better oneself for God - and the 'lesser' jihad - the taking-up of arms in defence of Islam, under strict conditions, when the religion is threatened. The terrorists espouse an aggressively violent or militant interpretation of the lesser jihad) to provide the basis of a call to wage war against non-Muslims who had taken overMuslim lands. Groups like Al Qaida are also influenced by a tradition of religiously based rebellion inspired by the teachings of Ibn Taymiyya and Sayyid Qutb. This contrasts with the more conservative and politically passive tradition of establishment Salafism or 'Wahhabism' found in countries like Saudi Arabia.

## INFLUENCES ON MUSLIM EXTREMIST THINKING

### *Ibn Taymiyya*

Ibn Taymiyya was an important fourteenth century theologian. He cultivated the idea that Muslim rulers who contravened Islam should be labelled kuffar (unbelievers). He developed his ideas at a time when the Muslim world was under attack by the Mongols, and was therefore concerned about defending the Muslim community. He argued that Muslims were obliged to overthrow kuffar rulers like the Mongols. He advocated amending the five pillars of Islam - the obligatory duties of all Muslims - to include militant jihad. His ideas have inspired the worldview of terrorist groups like Al Qaida.

### Sayyid Qutb

In the 1950s, Sayyid Qutb expanded on the thinking of Al-Banna and refined the aims of the Muslim Brotherhood. He argued that artificial nation-states had allowed Muslim countries to lapse into a pre-Islamic state of ignorance and barbarism (Jahiliyya). He advocated the use of militant jihad as a revolutionary instrument to re-establish God's sovereignty on Earth.

### Abdullah Azzam

Abdullah Azzam was a Palestinian activist and mentor to Usama Bin Laden. Drawing on the writings of Ibn Taymiyya, he argued that all Muslims had a compulsory duty to wage uncompromising war to reclaim all lands formerly ruled by the Islamic caliphate. His doctrine was absolute - his motto was 'Jihad and the rifle alone: no negotiations, no conferences, no dialogue'. Azzam helped fund and promote the cause of the mujahideen (fighters engaged in militant jihad) in Afghanistan.

### Ayman Al-Zawahiri

Ayman Al-Zawahiri, an Egyptian radical, is another key ideologist for Al Qaida. Drawing on the works of Qutb, he sees democracy as a form of idol worship. It must be vanquished through warfare. He considers supporters of democracy to be kuffar. He was the driving force behind Al Qaida's 1998 edict instructing Muslims to kill Americans and their allies wherever they found them.

## A Capacity to Harness Opinion and History

Al Qaida and its affiliates employ extremist and selective interpretations of Islam. They use the interpretations that validate their worldview and theologically rationalise their actions, no matter how vicious or out of kilter with mainstream Islam.

The extremists argue that 11 September 2001 victims were not innocent. Because they voted in elections and paid taxes, they were complicit in the acts of an 'evil' US Administration. By extension, any victims in any future attacks are deemed not to be innocent.

Usama Bin Laden, in particular, has been a consummate manipulator of certain frustrations and disillusionment felt throughout the Muslim world. He exploits the depths of resentment that underlie centuries of Muslim history. This resentment is rooted in a sense that the Muslim world has been humiliated by Western colonisation and political, military, economic and cultural dominance.

Other Muslim extremists advocate and take advantage of Bin Laden's assertion that the United States seeks to dominate the Muslim world. They cite the war against the Taliban in Afghanistan and the US-led occupation of Iraq as evidence. The Israeli-Palestinian conflict is perhaps the rawest wound Bin Laden exploits. He demonises the United States by tapping into widespread pro-Palestinian sentiment within the Muslim world and denouncing US support for Israel. Bin Laden also plays on Muslim attitudes towards other theatres of militant jihad, such as Kashmir, Chechnya, Bosnia and the southern Philippines. Many Muslims identify with these causes, and by invoking them Al Qaida swells its pool of potential recruits. But this does not mean they are of themselves root causes of terrorism.

## Al Qaida

### *All roads lead to and from Afghanistan*

The 1979 - 89 war to expel the Soviet Union from Afghanistan was central to the development of Al Qaida. It became a rallying point for militant extremists. The 25 000 or so volunteers from abroad who joined the local Afghan resistance provided Al Qaida with its first recruits. Already susceptible, they were further radicalised in Afghanistan. They adopted the revolutionary visions of Qutb, Azzam and Zawahiri. The majority went home battle-hardened and well trained. Some resolved to spread their new ideas.

The liberation of Afghanistan was supported by a number of countries that opposed the Soviet occupation. The Afghan resistance received financial and logistical support from several countries, including the United States, Pakistan and Saudi Arabia. As well as doing his own share of fundraising, Bin Laden placed much of his own wealth at the mujahideen's disposal.

## A BRIEF BIOGRAPHY OF USAMA BIN LADEN

Usama Bin Laden was born in Saudi Arabia in about 1957. His father, Mohammed, originally from Yemen, was a wealthy businessman with close connections to the ruling Al-Saud.

Usama Bin Laden was one of about 50 children. He had a strict religious upbringing. He attended university in Jeddah and graduated with a degree in administration.

Soon after the Soviet Union invaded Afghanistan in 1979, Bin Laden travelled for the first time to the border areas of Pakistan. It was not until the early 1980s that he entered Afghanistan proper, bringing with him large amounts of cash and construction machinery. In 1984, he built in Peshawar (Pakistan) a guesthouse for militants who were on their way to participate in the resistance to Soviet occupation. Bin Laden and his guesthouse played an important role in the work of Azzam's Maktab Al-Khidamat (services office). They processed and trained large numbers of volunteers on their way to Afghanistan.

When victory over the Soviets looked imminent, Bin Laden created the movement now known as Al Qaida. The aim was to continue the militant jihad globally. Ten years later, with Ayman Al-Zawahiri and others, he formed the International Islamic Front for Jihad Against the Jews and Crusaders.

Bin Laden returned to Saudi Arabia. He used his high public profile there to draw attention to the Afghan victory. He began to criticise the Saudi government for failing to defend Islam.

When Iraq invaded Kuwait, Bin Laden offered to help defend Saudi Arabia using Saudi Afghan veterans. He was rebuffed. The Saudis accepted assistance from US forces.

Bin Laden fled to Sudan, which was governed by the National Islamic Front. He set up Al Qaida's headquarters in Khartoum. Financed by legitimate businesses, including Sudanese government construction contracts, Al Qaida set about establishing its global terrorism credentials. Its primary objective was the removal of US forces from the Arabian Peninsula and the overthrow of the Saudi regime. Eventually, Bin Laden returned to Afghanistan. There, Al Qaida accelerated its operations and intensified its opposition to governments in the West and in the Muslim world that did not meet its standards.

Bin Laden has no formal qualifications as an Islamic scholar. His value to the mujahideen movement - and his impact on it - has been due to his charisma, his leadership, the wealth he inherited through his father's business success, his connections and his administrative skills.

Azzam and others travelled widely, seeking financial support and recruiting volunteers to join the militant jihad in Afghanistan. In effect, they established the global framework for what would become Al Qaida. Recruits came not just from the Middle East, but Central, South and South-East Asia, and parts of Africa; as well as Western countries.

After the Soviet forces were defeated, some mujahideen who had trained in Pakistani camps travelled to other locations, such as Kashmir and Chechnya, rather than returning to their home countries. They had been trained for militant operations beyond the Afghan resistance. Afghanistan was where the careers of Azzam, Bin Laden and Zawahiri intersected. For Bin Laden it was not just an opportunity to experience militant jihad. He also met key figures from other extremist groups and learnt about their causes. In particular, his developing association with Zawahiri gave him an introduction to the wider militant jihad movement. He could now develop his own ideas about the shortcomings of governments in the Muslim world.

### *Learning from Success*

The mujahideen were just one factor in the defeat of the Soviet army in Afghanistan. But they claimed responsibility for it, and for the collapse of the Soviet system soon after.

In the militants' eyes, the Soviet withdrawal proved that a small group of religious extremists with limited resources could defeat a military superpower. For Al Qaida it was a lesson: it could take its fight to other theatres where it faced odds that had seemed impossible. As Zawahiri put it:

The most important thing about the battle in Afghanistan was that it destroyed the illusion of the superpower in the minds of young Muslim mujahideen. The Soviet Union, the power with the largest land forces in the world, was destroyed and scattered, running away from Afghanistan before the eyes of the Muslim youth. This Jihad was a training course for Muslim youth for the future battle anticipated with the superpower which is the sole leader of the world now, America.

Al Qaida drew conclusions, too, about US resolve. They took the US withdrawal from Lebanon in 1983 after about 250 marines died in a truck bombing, and from Somalia in 1993 after a number of its soldiers were killed, as proof that the United States was not prepared to engage in a fight with a determined enemy.

### *Al Qaida's Message*

Al Qaida's fanatical interpretations of Islam place all Muslim societies that do not comply or agree in its sights. Its principal goal - ridding Saudi Arabia of US forces and replacing the Saudi Government - was based on Bin Laden's view that the Saudi Government had forfeited its Islamic legitimacy. That goal has since been extended to the ejection from the entire Muslim world of US and Western influence.

Al Qaida's ultimate message is that all former Muslim lands must be recovered - no matter how long ago they were 'lost' - and their governments replaced by regimes reflecting Al Qaida's interpretation of Islam. All Jews, 'Crusaders' and 'idolaters of democracy' are to be expelled from those lands.

Al Qaida's strategic goals appear to have evolved but are not known to be set out in any consolidated form. Its aims are based on a selective and extremist interpretation of Islamic texts, under which the duty to wage war against the enemies of God is divinely ordained. Bin Laden's 'declaration of war against the Americans' of 1996 declared militant jihad against the United States. It gives a good insight into Al Qaida's worldview and aims. And his so-called fatwa issued in February 1998 at the establishment of an umbrella group called the 'World Islamic Front for Jihad Against Jews and the Crusaders' outlines clearly the true nature of the terrorists' ideology.

Al Qaida's battlefield is global. It will attack its enemies anywhere in the world - its attacks are no longer limited to previous theatres of militant jihad. In their 1998 fatwa, Bin Laden, Zawahiri and their associates tell Muslims that:

> *... to kill Americans and their allies - civilians and military - is an individual duty for every Muslim who can do it in any country in which it is possible to do it, in order to liberate the Al-Aqsa Mosque and the holy mosque [in Mecca] from their grip, and in order for their armies to move out of all the lands of Islam, defeated and unable to threaten any Muslim. This is in accordance with the words of Almighty God.*

This was the first time that Al Qaida identified civilians as legitimate targets. Al Qaida's inclination to take the fight beyond the Muslim world to Western countries has been unambiguously demonstrated in New York, Madrid and elsewhere. And Al Qaida does not consider itself constrained in its methods or choice of targets.

Al Qaida spokesman, Sulaiman Abu Ghaith, said in June 2002:

> *... we have the right to kill four million Americans, including one million children, displace double that figure and injure and cripple hundreds of thousands. We have the right to fight them by chemical and biological weapons ...*

The terrorists oppose secularism and single out democracy for particular criticism. Zawahiri has been notably critical of Muslim groups that have endorsed democracy. He argues that only God can exercise sovereignty over worldly communities. So, in his view, democracy - which renders human beings sovereign - is heresy. It allows mankind to usurp the role of God. Zawahiri characterises democracy as a false religion. For him, people who live in democracies, particularly in Muslim countries, are therefore legitimate targets because, by voting and paying taxes, they participate in the 'idolatrous' democratic process. Similarly, those who seek to promote democracy in Muslim countries are also deemed to be targets. Al Qaida continues to strive for large-scale, coordinated, mass casualty, multiple attacks of the kind seen on September 11 and in the East Africa embassy bombings of 1998.

### *Disseminating the Message*

Al Qaida skilfully conveys its message through the use of modern information and communications technology: pre-recorded video and audio tapes, DVDs, CD-ROMs and the Internet. In 2001, Al Qaida produced a recruitment DVD that was widely copied and made available on the Internet.

The Internet has become an important part of modern terrorism's arsenal. Al Qaida in particular uses it - through websites like the now-defunct www.azzam.com - to spread its ideology and propaganda, and to send messages to sympathisers and operatives. Announcements, edicts and ideological expositions by senior Al Qaida figures are made. Videos depicting terrorist attacks are screened. The Internet is also used for the passage of operational instructions. Certainly, terrorist websites regularly feature calls on Muslims to attack Western targets.

The World Wide Web is also used as a training tool. Various procedural and instruction manuals and general tactical guidance have been posted on extremist websites. Al Qaida also uses the media shrewdly. Bin Laden himself has taken advantage of increasingly globalised communications links to spread his message. His interviews with Time, Newsweek and CNN reached worldwide audiences. They give him opportunities to influence the actions and beliefs of Muslim extremists everywhere.

### *An Evolving, Inspirational Prototype*

Because it is a highly adaptable and complex entity, understanding Al Qaida's structure and behaviour is difficult. During the late 1990s, Al Qaida in Afghanistan took on many characteristics of a hierarchical organisation. It had permanent installations, fixed structures, standardised methods and regular procedures. Since 2001, it has assumed more the character of an ideological movement. Decentralised, semi-autonomous remnants operate independently or follow broad general direction. It remains well funded and ambitious. Apart from the finances of Bin Laden himself, it draws on donors in the Gulf and elsewhere. It developed its own commercial ventures, particularly in Sudan in the early 1990s.

Through Al Qaida's capacity for change and regeneration, some characteristics have emerged over time. Al Qaida is a 'network of networks'. Each of them can operate independently, or with other networks. These networks cover leadership, planning and operations, financial, training and equipment support, as well as propaganda and several other functions. Some networks include a 'hub'. Others are diffuse and decentralised. Since the destruction of Al Qaida's Afghanistan base, many hubs have been shut down, or moved to nearby areas within South Asia. Other networks have evolved to function primarily through electronic media such as the Internet.

### *Just one Part of a Wider Network*

For many Muslim extremists, Al Qaida has become more an idea or ideology than a physical entity. Bin Laden's propaganda skills, and his capacity to exploit Arab and Muslim antagonism towards the West, motivate and direct many militant groups and individuals that may otherwise have few tangible links with Al Qaida.

So, although Al Qaida has been the key influence on the development of transnational extremist-Muslim terrorism, it is not the only element. New adherents to its fanaticism have been attracted by Al Qaida's high-profile successes, its propaganda skills and its capacity to take advantage of deeply felt grievances in the Muslim world.

Some new players have taken up the extremist mantle of their own accord. Others have developed networks independently, and have in turn established links with Al Qaida. And existing, more localised extremist-Muslim terror groups, impressed by Al Qaida's achievements, have absorbed its broader ideological ambitions. They have added their networks to the mix. The shared Afghan experience has accelerated the development of this process. Some such groups share or have adopted aspects of Al Qaida's worldview and developed a similar style. Prominent among them are the Pakistani-Kashmiri terrorist group Lashkar e-Tayyiba, Jemaah Islamiyah and the Al-Zarqawi network.

In this way the Al Qaida experience has been replicated and reinforced. The result is a transnational extremist-Muslim terrorism at once more resilient, more extensive and more difficult to counter. So, as Al Qaida's leaders are eliminated, others will be ready to take their place. Even if Al Qaida itself were wiped out, networks set up in its image are probably capable of continuing its work.

Al Qaida's adaptive networks have helped it survive a sustained US-led military offensive. Since October 2001, a significant proportion of its leadership and rank-and-file has been either captured or killed. Much of the remainder has dispersed and is in hiding. Its communications links and operational capability have been seriously disrupted. But its links with other, similarly flexible networks show how Al Qaida is just one aspect of a larger series of connections, so much so that it retains a potent capacity to strike in diverse locations.

Some Afghanistan veterans have become focal points in their own countries for new and revived groups. They in turn developed their own network structures - echoing the experience of Al Qaida. In other cases, local groups with few or no direct links to Al Qaidahave drawn inspiration, expertise and direction from the movement's public statements.

They act independently in their local areas. Some are attracted to the movement's ideology, some by what they see as its potency against what they resent, some by its propaganda. The aims of groups like Ansar Al-Islam in northern Iraq, Laskar Jundullah in Indonesia and the Abu Sayyaf Group in the southern Philippines have been supported by Al Qaida's global focus.

Irrespective of its own fate, Al Qaida has generated a system of self-sustaining and adaptable networks. It can maintain operational capability because of the autonomous nature of the networks' components. It is likely that some of these networks' functions - training, for instance - have shifted to new geographical and network locations. As Al Qaida's training facilities are damaged, the network is able to adjust. The training function can be continued by other groups. The same thing applies to other network functions, such as finance or operations. It is possible that no overall network for command and control even exists.

The loose links between these networks mean associated groups can operate without central control. Such arrangements are also more resilient to attack. Affiliated groups have adopted in some cases Al Qaida's flexibility and transformative capacities. This extends even more the terrorists' reach and makes their security harder to penetrate.

The networks that originally centred on Al Qaida have become more widespread and less interdependent - with varying degrees of connectedness to each other. They extend throughout the world. There are now active terrorist elements and supporters in the Middle East, parts of Africa, Western countries and in South, Central and South-East Asia.

## THE SOUTH ASIAN CONNECTION

Many individuals and organisations within the complex terrorist 'network of networks' share links with extremist groups in South Asia. These links are mainly historical and ideological, but also include practical and organisational elements.

Historically, many key players within the global militant jihad movement fought the Soviet Union in Afghanistan in the 1980s. They kept in contact after coming home from the war. These links are still strong. For example, the Abu Sayyaf Group in the Philippines is named after a famous mujahideen commander of the Afghan War. Similarly, the Jemaah Islamiyah network draws on strong Afghan alumni links. Many individual terrorists know each other well based on shared Afghan experience.

Ideologically, the diverse transnational terrorist networks share a worldview based on the shared study, indoctrination and experience of the Afghan War. Operating patterns are based upon techniques learned in Afghanistan and then standardised and disseminated through the network. In practical terms, common operational methods have been refined through exchange of information between individuals and groups with shared Afghan experience.

Techniques that appear in one conflict or with one group may later appear in other conflicts. They may be passed via electronic communication or through mobile cadres who train terrorists in specific techniques. Much of this training is centred on Kashmir and the tribal areas of Pakistan. This makes South Asia a key geographical focus for terrorist networks today. The well developed Al Qaida infrastructure inside Afghanistan was destroyed in 2001, but various South Asian groups have copied Al Qaida's organisation and methods. Dispersed groups continue to operate independently, or follow general guidance from key terrorist leaders, with a geographical focus on South Asia.

Of the Pakistani extremist groups, Lashkar e-Tayyiba is the most closely affiliated with Al Qaida. Formed in 1989, Lashkar e-Tayyiba, like Al Qaida, sprang from popular opposition to the Soviet presence in Afghanistan. Through shared experience in Afghanistan, many Lashkar e-Tayyiba leaders had links to Al Qaida. Lashkar e-Tayyiba transferred its efforts to the insurgency in Indian-held Kashmir in the early 1990s. Its activities later escalated from localised actions in Kashmir to international terrorism in India. Lashkar e-Tayyiba performs a critical function in the transnational network as a primary provider of training to the broader transnational terrorist movement, particularly following the destruction of Al Qaida's Afghanistan base in October 2001.

## THE EVOLUTION OF TRANSNATIONAL EXTREMIST-MUSLIM TERRORIST GROUPS IN SOUTH-EAST ASIA

Islam in South-East Asia is predominantly moderate and tolerant. We need to understand the evolution of Muslim extremist terrorist groups in the region in that context. Islam arrived in South-East Asia peaceably, carried to the region in the thirteenth century by Muslim traders from South Asia and the Middle East. Over several centuries, as the religion spread across South-East Asia, it incorporated and adapted elements of pre-existing cultural and spiritual beliefs and traditions.

Reflecting its peaceful evolution, South-East Asian Islam has been traditionally open-minded and accepting of cultural diversity.

Every country in South-East Asia has a Muslim community - from five per cent of the population in the Philippines to around 90 per cent in Indonesia. Within these Muslim communities, Islamic identity or affiliation has grown in recent decades, in line with a global phenomenon. There is a greater observance of Islamic practices and dress codes, particularly among young Muslims. And Islamic organisations have become increasingly prominent and active on university campuses and in politics more generally.

Muslim political and social organisations play a positive role in the countries of the region. Indonesia's two largest Muslim organisations, Muhammadiyah and Nahdlatul Ulama, were central to the successful transition to democracy. They play critical roles in providing welfare and education to their fellow citizens. Both organisations are firmly opposed to terrorism. They expressed support for Indonesia's new anti-terrorism decrees in the wake of the Bali bombings.

The vast majority of South-East Asia's Muslims represent tolerant, mainstream Islam. In parliamentary elections in both Indonesia and Malaysia in 2004, Muslim political parties advocating a moderate and tolerant message outperformed those advocating a narrow conservative interpretation of Islam.

It is important to recognise that support for political Islam or a growth in Muslim piety does not translate into a greater likelihood of Muslim extremism and militancy.

An increase in identification with Islam should not be confused with the emergence of terrorist groups such as Jemaah Islamiyah, which was responsible for the Bali attack. Bali bomber Amrozi no more represents the views of the majority of Muslims in South-East Asia than Usama Bin Laden represents the majority of Muslims in the Arab world. The vast majority of the population of South-East Asia rejects not only the callous violence of terrorist groups but also their goals and ideology.

## Evolution of Militancy-Fusing Local and International Agendas

Terrorist tactics are not new in South-East Asia. Nor are they limited to a particular religious or ethnic group.

Militant separatist movements in South-East Asia since the 1940s have had a range of ethnic, political and religious motivations. And violence against civilians has been perpetrated by followers of a variety of political ideologies and religious faiths. Almost every armed nationalist and communist movement in the region has had such tactics in its repertoire. Across the region, militant sub-national groups have over past decades used terrorist attacks to advance their separatist, ethnic or religious interests.

But the emergence of systematically applied terrorism, associated with a virulent form of extremist Muslim ideology, has transformed terrorist attacks in South-East Asia. A seldom- chosen tactic has become an integral - even primary - choice for interconnected groups. Muslim militancy is not a new phenomenon in South-East Asia. In the post-colonial era, militant Muslim separatist groups formed in countries where Muslims are in the minority - Burma, the Philippines, Thailand- to fight for autonomy from national governments. In Indonesia, where Muslims make up the majority, Muslim militancy has been driven by two goals - to establish an Islamic state, governed by a rigid and doctrinaire interpretation of Islamic law, and to redress economic and political grievances.

A number of South-East Asian Muslim separatist groups have been prepared to use violence or terrorism against their governments. The Moro Islamic Liberation Front (MILF) and the Abu Sayyaf Group continue to operate in the Philippines. The Pattani United Liberation Organisation (PULO) is active in Thailand, and the Rohingya Solidarity Organisation in Burma.

These groups are not primarily anti-Western. Rather, they have had long-standing disputes with national governments based on local socio-political and economic grievances. But Muslim militancy in the region has undergone a dramatic evolution over the past decade. The historical grievances of radical Muslim groups were local in nature. Now, the predominant terrorist threat in South-East Asia is transnational. It draws inspiration and support both from other South-East Asian militant groups and from outside the region.

A volatile fusion of local and international agendas has emerged. Most troubling of all, for some extremist militants, terrorist attacks have become an acceptable part of their strategy. And terrorist attacks have become more lethal, more frequent, more widespread and more focused on targeting Western interests.

Jemaah Islamiyah exemplifies the evolution of Muslim militancy in South-East Asia. It has links to Al Qaida and is strongly influenced by Usama Bin Laden's terrorist ideology and methodology. The threat posed by Jemaah Islamiyah is compounded by its development as a network that ignores national boundaries. It stretches over several regional countries. It has formed links with existing extremist Muslim groups to further its own goals.

In the southern Philippines, elements of local militant Muslim insurgency groups, the MILF and the Abu Sayyaf Group, have established links with Jemaah Islamiyah and to some extent with Al Qaida. Links with elements of the MILF are very important to Jemaah Islamiyah. They give Jemaah Islamiyah access to training camps in Mindanao and a ready- made insurgency to give new recruits combat experience.

Dangerous sub-national groups, who can or want to use terrorism to further their causes, are also present in South-East Asia. Mujahidin KOMPAK, Laskar Jihad (supposedly disbanded) and Laskar Jundullah in Indonesia, and the Malaysian Militant Group (Kumpulan Militan Malaysia - KMM) started out with the ostensible aim of promoting the interests of political Islam. Their transition to more violent methods resulted from their greater identification with, and links to, other radical Muslim movements in the region, in South Asia and in the Middle East.

Driving the increase in terrorist activity in our region has been the exposure of South-East Asian militants to the thinking of Middle Eastern Muslim extremists. That includes the latter's message that terrorism is acceptable. Again, Afghanistan was the crucible. The most significant transmission of extremist ideology and military skills to South-East Asian militants took place in the 1980s, with their participation in the war against the Soviet Union in Afghanistan.

## Origins of the Transnational Agenda: the Afghanistan Connection

South-East Asian extremism took a leap forward when militant Muslim groups - including the leaders of Jemaah Islamiyah - decided to send recruits to training camps in Afghanistan and in Pakistan from the mid-1980s. Their aim was to support their co-religionists in the fight against the Soviet Union.

The Soviet forces left Afghanistan by 1989. But the concept of militant jihad - in this case, a multinational armed struggle by Muslim believers - did not end with their departure. The Soviet - Afghanistan experience was a catalyst for radical activity in South-East Asia. There is an Afghanistan connection to many South-East Asian Muslim militant groups. Up to 1000 South-East Asian Muslims are believed to have received military training with the Afghan mujahideen in the 1980s. In some cases this included battlefield experience. Key leaders of radical Muslim groups in the region are all veterans of the Soviet - Afghan war. They include Jemaah Islamiyah key operative Hambali, Abu Sayyaf Group leaders Khaddafy and Abdurajak Janjalani (now dead), and others.

In the camps in Afghanistan, South-East Asian volunteers were infused with a sense of brotherhood and common cause with those undertaking or supporting militant jihad from other parts of the Muslim world. They were introduced to more advanced terrorist and militant ideology and techniques. They brought them back to South-East Asia and passed them on at training camps in our region.

The returnees formed a natural, transnational network in South-East Asia that is now extensive and well entrenched. This network is at the heart of the terrorist threat in South- East Asia today.

## Education and Advanced Technology

Other external forces are at work to spread extremism in South-East Asia. A significant number of young South-East Asians are studying at religious schools, or madrassas, in Pakistan, Afghanistan and Yemen. They have been influenced by some of the more doctrinaire versions of Islam - particularly the closely-related Salafi and Wahhabi streams. The financial power of Saudi Arabia has also helped promote Wahhabism in South-East Asia through the funding of educational institutions.

Many South Asian and Middle Eastern madrassas teach only a rigid and doctrinaire interpretation of the Quran, with a strong emphasis on militant jihad.

South-East Asia's information technology revolution has hastened the spread of external influences, including extremist ideology. International television and information available on the Internet have led to a greater identification with Muslims in conflict around the world. They have inspired and shaped the behaviour of radicals in South-East Asia. The Internet is not merely a communications mechanism for extremists. It is also an effective vehicle for global publicity and recruitment efforts.

Some madrassas - including those run in Pakistan by the militant group Lashkar e-Tayyiba - emphasise computer literacy, even while teaching few or no other secular subjects. Within South-East Asia itself, large numbers of community-run Islamic boarding schools, or pesantren, operate outside the state control of formal Islamic education systems. Income disparity in many countries of the region has led to poorer youth taking up this option with governments unable to meet the educational needs of growing populations.

A small number of these schools have become a source of concern to regional governments as Jemaah Islamiyah has sought to use networks of pesantren across several South-East Asian countries as a vehicle to propagate extremist ideology and for recruitment purposes. Pesantren vulnerable to these approaches are few in number relative to the majority that emphasise the teaching of moral values. Al Qaida has also recruited and radicalised students with Western secular educational backgrounds. In South-East Asia some of Jemaah Islamiyah's leading operatives have had advanced technical and scientific qualifications from secular universities.

It is important to note that many leading advocates of pluralism and democracy in South-East Asia are graduates of Islamic education institutions. Former Indonesian President, Abdurrahman

Wahid, and prominent Indonesian Muslim intellectuals including the Rector of the State Islamic University in Jakarta, Dr Azyumardi Azra, and the Rector of the Paramadina Mulya University, Nurcholish Madjid, are all graduates of Islamic education institutions.

### *Regional Vulnerabilities*

Transnational terrorist groups, including Al Qaida and Lashkar e-Tayyiba, have demonstrated an interest in South-East Asia. They see it as a base for operations, a safe haven and a source of potential recruits. It is also a source of the kinds of services drawn upon by other transnational criminals. Terrorists look to exploit any vulnerabilities in the region's varied counter-terrorism capabilities. Areas of potential concern in some regional countries include limitations in institutional, governance and legislative frameworks; resource constraints; inadequate coordination arrangements, both internally and between countries in the region; and variable political will. Problem areas also include law enforcement, intelligence, transport security, defence and anti-terrorist financing.

Terrorist groups can also exploit long-standing socio-political and economic grievances that persist in some countries.

The lack of controlled border crossings in some South-East Asian countries is a major impediment to the monitoring and control of terrorist groups. Maritime piracy is a significant problem in the region. Porous borders, combined with massive inbound tourist and business flows, open immigration regimes, limited identity and document fraud detection, inadequately trained or corrupt officials, poor coordination between border control agencies and various security agencies, and limited immigration and customs control capacities all provide an environment in which terrorism can flourish.

All these problems can be compounded by inadequate legislation. Effective laws are important to put governments in the best possible position to investigate, detain and prosecute those involved in terrorism and its financing.

Al Qaida and other terrorist groups are known to have abused charitable organisations. They have used them for fund-raising and have diverted money donated to them towards support for extremist activities. Unregulated and unaudited Islamic charities in South-East Asia are vulnerable to misuse by extremist groups.

## TERRORIST FUNDING IN SOUTH-EAST ASIA

South-East Asian terrorist organisations have received funding through covert means such as couriers, and legitimate and front companies and organisations. It is suspected that Al Qaida provided funding for the Bali bombings and it is known to have provided funding in the past to terrorist groups in the Philippines.

Some Islamic non-government organisations, particularly those based in the Arabian Peninsula are - both knowingly and unknowingly - used as conduits for terrorist financing in South-East Asia. The Australian Government is aware that, while predominantly engaging in legitimate humanitarian and religious activities, some of these organisations have been used by terrorists for the transfer of funds, the purchase of arms and other forms of logistic support. Terrorism has also been supported by other financial activities, including fundraising, extortion, kidnapping and ransom.

## JEMAAH ISLAMIYAH AND THE EVOLUTION OF SOUTH-EAST ASIAN TERRORIST NETWORKS

### *Jemaah Islamiyah - Origins and Development*

Jemaah Islamiyah has its origins in the Darul Islam separatist movement in Indonesia. Darul Islam was involved in regional rebellions in the 1950s and 1960s that sought to impose Islamic law or form Islamic states in parts of Indonesia. The movement was strongest in West and Central Java, South Sumatra and South Sulawesi, areas where Jemaah Islamiyah is most heavily represented today.

After the Darul Islam insurgency was suppressed in the mid-1960s, Darul Islam continued to exist as an underground political movement working for imposition of Islamic iaw in Indonesia. In the 1980s, in the wake of the Islamic Revolution in Iran, the movement became more active and was involved in covert opposition to the Soeharto Government. By the mid-1990s, several armed extremist groups had emerged from the Darul Islam movement, tracing their origins to the insurgencies of the 1950s.

Jemaah Islamiyah evolved as a secretive militant organisation from a faction of the Darul Islam political movement, led by Abdullah Sungkar, who died in 1999. Sungkar and Abu Bakar Ba'asyir, his long-time associate, established the Al Mukmin pesantren at Ngruki, in Central Java, in 1971.

This school became a centre for Muslim radical activity in the area. Many of the Jemaah Islamiyah leaders studied at the Ngruki school, as did Bali bombers Amrozi and Mukhlas. The terrorist who drove the bomb to the JW Marriott Hotel in Jakarta, killing 12 people in August 2003, was also a former Ngruki student.

Both Sungkar and Ba'asyir were jailed several times during this period by Indonesian authorities for seeking to establish an Islamic state. Sungkar and Ba'asyir fled to Malaysia to escape a crackdown by Indonesian authorities on Muslim militancy in the mid-1980s. Malaysia then became the centre of the group's activities. Jemaah Islamiyah - in the form in which it is known today - was established around this time, in the mid- to late-1980s. Sungkar led Jemaah Islamiyah from Malaysia, preaching a doctrine of attaining an Islamic state in Indonesia through militant struggle on the three-fold basis of strengthening faith, Islamic brotherhood and military capability. The Luqmanul Hakim madrassa in the Malaysian state of Johor, since closed down by Malaysian authorities, was a base for Ba'asyir and Sungkar while in Malaysia. Bali bomber Mukhlas taught at the Luqmanul Hakim school during this period.

These Indonesian exiles developed a radical religious following in Malaysia. At the same time, they were developing links with the Muslim separatists in the southern Philippines. They adapted their preaching to their new circumstances. They began to promote a pan-Malay Muslim ideology calling for a unified South-East Asian Islamic state.

Probably the most important factor in the development of South-East Asian extremism was Sungkar's decision to send recruits to militant training camps in Afghanistan and Pakistan from the mid-1980s.

Both Sungkar and Ba'asyir returned to Indonesia in 1998 following the fall of President Soeharto. After the death of Sungkar, Ba'asyir took over leadership of the major Darul Islam faction in Central Java. Ba'asyir used it as a platform to launch the Indonesian Mujahideen Council (Majlis Mujahidin Indonesia - MMI) - a political organisation campaigning openly for the implementation of an Islamic state in Indonesia.

While the MMI has a broad membership, including many members who seek to bring about an Islamic state through peaceful, democratic means, its leadership core is closely linked with Jemaah Islamiyah and seeks to use the MMI as a political front.

### *Abu Bakar Ba'asyir*

Abu Bakar Ba'asyir is the spiritual leader of Jemaah Islamiyah. Indonesian police arrested Ba'asyir on 30 April 2004 under Indonesia's counter-terrorism law, and declared him a suspect in the Bali and JW Marriott Hotel bombings.

Ba'asyir incites and supports terrorism. He has repeatedly stated his support for Usama Bin Laden.

In an interview on the SBS Insight program on 9 March 2004, Ba'asyir gave unflinching support to the Bali bombers, describing them as defenders of Islam and Indonesia. In an interview broadcast on Channel 7 on 17 March 2004, Ba'asyir claimed that 'sooner or later, America and the countries that assisted will be destroyed in the name of Allah'.

### *Jemaah Islamiyah - Operations and Training*

Using the skills gained in the crucible of the war in Afghanistan, Jemaah Islamiyah has developed a formalised structure to provide systematic training for its new recruits from across the region.

Jemaah Islamiyah established Camp Hudaibiyyah within the MILF's Camp Abu Bakar in Mindanao, in the southern Philippines, from about 1998, using some of the original graduates from training in Afghanistan and Pakistan. Camp Hudaibiyyah was closed down by the Philippine military in 2000, but there is evidence that

Jemaah Islamiyah training has continued in alternative locations in the southern Philippines.

While many of the more senior Jemaah Islamiyah operatives gained their terrorist training and expertise in Afghanistan and Pakistan, others have developed the bulk of their skills in South-East Asia.

Training camps are not required at all for competent individuals to pass on the bomb-making skills and techniques needed for terrorism. Graduates of Jemaah Islamiyah's militant training may well have the operational, logistic and administrative skills required to plan and stage another terrorist attack like Bali or the JW Marriott Hotel bombing.

## ABU BAKAR BA'ASYIR

Abu Bakar Ba'asyir is an Indonesian cleric of Yemeni descent who was born in Jombang, East Java, in 1938. Ba'asyir was active in advocating an Islamic state in Indonesia from his student days, and he joined radical Islamic youth movements. He started, but did not complete, an Islamic legal studies course at a university in Solo. He appears to have gradually become attracted to more extreme ideas during his university days.

Ba'asyir met Jemaah Islamiyah founder Abdullah Sungkar - also an Indonesian of Yemeni descent - in Solo. Here the two established an Islamic radio station that, by 1971, had evolved into an Islamic boarding school, Al Mukmin, located at Ngruki, outside Solo. Ba'asyir and Sungkar both spent four years in jail (1978 - 82) on charges related to their ongoing covert agitation for the establishment of an Islamic state in Indonesia. Ba'asyir's original nine-year sentence was reinstated in 1985 and he fled to Malaysia with Sungkar. From exile, they directed their followers to the anti-Soviet militant jihad in Afghanistan. Jemaah Islamiyah - in the form in which it is known today - was officially formed during this period.

Ba'asyir took over the spiritual leadership of Jemaah Islamiyah after the death of Sungkar in 1999. In 1999 he helped found the Rabitatul Mujahidin (Mujahideen Association) in Malaysia. In 2000 he founded and was elected head of the Indonesian Mujahideen Council (MMI).

In April 2003 Abu Bakar Ba'asyir went on trial charged with attempting to cause the collapse of the Indonesian Government, forgery, perjury and immigration offences. He was not charged in relation to the Bali bombings. The first charge included allegations Ba'asyir had led a plot to assassinate Indonesian President, Megawati Soekarnoputri, and that he had authorised the Christmas 2000 church bombings in Indonesia.

In September 2003, Ba'asyir was convicted of treason and immigration offences and sentenced to four years in prison. This sentence was reduced on appeal and the treason conviction overturned. Ba'asyir was rearrested under Indonesia's counter-terrorism laws on the same day he was released from jail: 30 April 2004. He faces questioning and possible new charges as a suspect in terrorist activities, including the Bali and JW Marriott Hotel bombings.

Jemaah Islamiyah's emphasis on training has several benefits for the organisation. It provides a flow of extremists, bolstering Jemaah Islamiyah's ranks or replacing its losses. And coordinated training helps to cement transnational organisational bonds within Jemaah Islamiyah by throwing together recruits drawn from different geographic regions.

### *Jemaah Islamiyah - Links to Global Terrorism*

In looking for global partners to advance its terrorist campaign, Al Qaida has found a willing ally in South-East Asia in Jemaah Islamiyah. And now that Jemaah Islamiyah has global recognition as an actor in transnational extremist-Muslim terrorism, support from Al Qaida and other sponsors of terrorism in the Middle East is likely to continue to flow to South-East Asia.

Financial and operational links to Middle Eastern extremist groups, especially Al Qaida in the early 1990s, were important in the development of South-East Asian radical Muslim groups, including Jemaah Islamiyah.

While Jemaah Islamiyah and Al Qaida operate largely independently of each other, there are close and direct links.

Jemaah Islamiyah leader, Hambali, who was captured in Thailand in August 2003, is widely understood to have been Al Qaida's South-East Asian operations chief, and certainly provided ongoing contact between Jemaah Islamiyah and Al Qaida. The relationship between Jemaah Islamiyah and Al Qaida is more a loose alliance forged through a shared ideology, rather than a hierarchical structure of command and control. But Al Qaida is a potent inspiration and example to South-East Asian Muslim militants, and has provided resources for their terrorist operations.

Jemaah Islamiyah's transformation from a radical Muslim organisation focused on local grievances and with local ambitions to a transnational terrorist network is of key concern to Australia and other governments in the region.

## *Jemaah Islamiyah - A Distorted Vision*

Jemaah Islamiyah promotes its vision of a unified South-East Asian Islamic state encompassing Indonesia, Malaysia, Singapore, the southern Philippines and southern Thailand. Jemaah Islamiyah has also identified Australia as a region in which to expand its network.

But Jemaah Islamiyah's concept of a South-East Asian super-state, forming part of a global Islamic caliphate, governed by Taliban-style religious extremism, is flawed. The overwhelming majority of the population of Indonesia - and indeed of South-East Asia more broadly - appears to reject Jemaah Islamiyah's vision and its use of terrorist attacks to further its aims. There are other large obstacles to Jemaah Islamiyah achieving its goal, not least the fact that all governments in the region reject the idea. Nation-states and nationalism are obvious major hurdles. And Jemaah Islamiyah's attempt to provide a transnational framework for radicalism in the region is not always at one with the deep historical roots and distinct agendas of its potential allies in South-East Asia. Local agendas and the jealously guarded independence of partner groups get in the way.

Jemaah Islamiyah relies on operational cooperation with other extremist organisations in the region, based on shared values, family links and ties forged overseas or while waging militant jihad in inter-communal conflicts in Maluku and Sulawesi. But Jemaah Islamiyah does not command the obedience of these other organisations. The various extremist groups are beset by personal rivalries, differences over the appropriateness of targeting civilians, and the acceptability of traditional Indonesian Islamic practices.

Even within Jemaah Islamiyah there is division. Some elements focus almost exclusively on bringing about an Islamic state in Indonesia. Others work to an anti-Western or anti-US agenda.

The region has seen how Jemaah Islamiyah is prepared to damage regional economies in pursuit of its own ideological goals, regardless of the impact felt more broadly across society. The Bali bombings are estimated to have taken 1.5 per cent off Indonesia's gross domestic product.

The fall-out from terrorist attacks in Bali, Jakarta and the southern Philippines shows how Muslim-inspired terror strikes also at mainstream Islam and mainstream Muslim countries. The ultimate manifestation of the contempt that South-East Asian Muslim extremists have for the people of the region is their repeated, indiscriminate killing of citizens of South-East Asian countries. Westerners, Christians and Jews are priority targets, in line with Usama Bin Laden's so-called fatwa. But 34 Indonesians were killed in the Bali bombings and 11 in the JW Marriott Hotel bombing, among them both Hindus and Muslims.

Extremist-Muslim terrorism is likely to remain a feature of the security environment in South-East Asia for the foreseeable future. The major factors underlying the severity of the terrorist threat - the strong intention and capability of terrorist organisations to strike, and the varying counter-terrorism capabilities of regional governments, which in turn enhance the attractiveness of the region to terrorist groups such as Al Qaida - will not soon, or easily, change.

## JEMAAH ISLAMIYAH STRUCTURE

Jemaah Islamiyah established a geographically based hierarchy with defined responsibilities and decision making procedures.

The leader (Amir), a leadership council (Markaz) and consultative councils (Shura) oversaw four geographic divisions

(Mantiqi). Each Mantiqi divided into smaller sub-groups which administered Jemaah Islamiyah activity appropriate to their area.

- Mantiqi I and IV were focused primarily on fundraising.
- Mantiqi II was focused primarily on leadership and recruitment.
- Mantiqi III was focused primarily on training.

While parts of this structure have been disrupted since late 2001, including through the arrests of key leaders, Jemaah Islamiyah retains a flexible hierarchical administration. Amir Markaz Shura Mantiqi III Sabah, Sulawesi and South Philippines Mantiqi IV Australia and Papua New Guinea Mantiqi I Singapore and Malaysia Mantiqi II Indonesia Wakalah Wakalah Wakalah Kirdas Kirdas Kirdas Fiah Fiah Fiah

## THE THREAT TO AUSTRALIA AND AUSTRALIA'S INTERESTS

### *Australia - A Terrorist Target*

Australia is a terrorist target, both as a Western nation and in its own right. Intelligence confirms we were a target before the 11 September 2001 attacks, and we are still a target. Our interests both at home and abroad are in the terrorists' sights. Al Qaida leaders threaten publicly and frequently. Their declared rationale is often misleading, but their intentions are clear.

Before 11 September 2001, Usama Bin Laden referred to the United States and its allies, mentioning Israel and the United Kingdom by name. Since then, he has more clearly identified those countries he considers to be 'allies'. Australia has been referred to in six separate statements issued by Bin Laden himself or his deputy, Ayman al-Zawahiri:

- On 3 November 2001, Bin Laden said: The Crusader Australian forces were on the Indonesia shores ... they landed to separate East Timor, which is part of the Islamic world.
- In an interview released in mid-November 2001 concerning the war in Afghanistan, Bin Laden said: In this fighting between Islam and the Crusaders, we will continue our

jihad. We will incite the nation for jihad until we meet God and get his blessing. Any country that supports the Jews can only blame itself ... what do Japan or Australia or Germany have to do with this war? They just support the infidels and the Crusaders.

- Bin Laden made further reference to Australia in a videotape released in the United Kingdom in May 2002 in which he said: What has Australia in the extreme south got to do with the oppression of our brothers in Afghanistan and Palestine?
- On 12 November 2002, Bin Laden made a statement that gave more prominence to Australia than any other non-US Western country and reaffirmed Australia as a terrorist target: We warned Australia before not to join in [the war] in Afghanistan, and [against] its despicable effort to separate East Timor. It ignored the warning until it woke up to the sounds of explosions in Bali. Its government falsely claimed that they were not targeted.
- On 21 May 2003, in an audiotape, Ayman al-Zawahiri said: O Muslims, take matters firmly against the embassies of America, England, Australia, Norway and their interests, companies and employees.
- On 18 October 2003, in an audio message addressed to the American people concerning the war in Iraq, Bin Laden stated that: We maintain our right to reply, at the appropriate time and place, to all the states that are taking part in this unjust war, particularly Britain, Spain, Australia, Poland, Japan and Italy.

Another statement attributed to Al Qaida was issued through Al Jazeera television in December 2002. This statement reinforced the threat. It stated that Al Qaida would attack vital economic centres and strategic enterprises of the 'Jewish - Christian Alliance', including operations on land, at sea and in the air. Australia has also been mentioned in statements attributed to Al Qaida on the Internet.

Jemaah Islamiyah also has Australia in its sights. It perpetrated the October 2002 Bali bombings - a stark testament to the threat it poses to Australian people and interests. The bombings were a deliberate attempt to inflict mass casualties on Western civilians. Australians were clearly likely to suffer the heaviest impact. We do not know whether direct targeting of Australia was part of the original intent but this has been subsequently claimed by some of those convicted.

The Bali bombers - including Mukhlas and Amrozi - have spoken to the media about their actions. Mukhlas stated in an interview with Australian television in May 2004:

> *... In Australia ... this [is] a curse from God that they be afraid of their own shadow ...It's the victory for the terrorists.*

There are almost certainly other groups seeking to harm us, both in Australia and overseas. Most are likely to draw influence or inspiration from the likes of Al Qaida and Jemaah Islamiyah, but their secretive methods mean that we may not be aware of their existence until they attack.

### Why are we a Target?

Australia is a target for complex reasons. But we can distil all the invective and rhetoric to a basic premise. These terrorists feel threatened by us, and by our example as a conspicuously successful modern society. We are in their way.

Transnational extremist-Muslim terrorists imagine us as part of a Zionist - Christian conspiracy aimed at bringing impiety, injustice, repression and humiliation to the Muslim world. Weakening the influence of the West would advance their political goals by helping undermine those Muslims they view as corrupt and open to Western influence. We are seen as standing in the way of their goal to transform the Muslim world into a Taliban-style society. According to their simplistic worldview, we are part of the Christian West which, to them, is un-Islamic and therefore illegitimate.

The core values we hold and which are intrinsic to our success as a liberal democratic culture are anathema to these extremists. For them, our beliefs in democratic process, racial and gender equality, religious tolerance and equality of opportunity are mere human inventions at odds with God's law. These values impede their political goals. They are confronted by the reality that it is not only people of the West who value such freedoms.

And we advance our values through an active foreign policy. We energetically support democracy, human rights and religious freedoms in our international contribution and through our participation in international forums like the United Nations. Our close alliance with the United States, our role in East Timor, our early and active engagement in the war in Afghanistan, and our involvement in the Coalition in Iraq are often cited by transnational terrorists as reasons for targeting us.

## THE BALI BOMBINGS

On 12 October 2002, two bombs exploded at Kuta in Bali. The first, inside Paddy's Bar, was detonated by a suicide bomber. It was apparently intended to move people onto the street towards a second, larger device in a van outside the Sari Club. This device, also triggered by a suicide bomber, was detonated within a minute of the first explosion. Less than a minute later another device exploded, without causing casualties, near the US Consulate in nearby Denpasar.

The official death toll for the Bali attacks was 202, including 88 Australian citizens. The Bali attack was a sophisticated operation. The team that conducted it was coordinated by Jemaah Islamiyah member, Imam Samudra. It brought together logistics specialists, bomb makers, a support team, and the actual attackers - including two suicide bombers.

The attack was a Jemaah Islamiyah operation, but it is thought that Al Qaida helped with advice and training. Al Qaida and senior Jemaah Islamiyah member Hambali (arrested in Thailand in August 2003) provided funds. Jemaah Islamiyah leaders, including Hambali and Samudra, received training in Afghanistan - probably from Al Qaida.

The Australian Federal Police and the Indonesian National Police conducted a joint criminal investigation into the bombings. This led to the identification and arrest of most of those who took part in planning or executing the attack. By April 2004, 33 people had been convicted by the Indonesian courts for involvement in the attack. Three have been sentenced to death and four were given life sentences. Indonesian authorities have arrested several others who provided assistance to the Bali bombers.

Our actions are cited as evidence of the imagined conspiracy against Muslims as the terrorists attempt to draw support for their extremist views. They do this cleverly, invoking causes which resonate strongly and authentically in the broader Muslim community. But the essence of their objections is not our actions. Rather, it is our example as a people and as a society, and the values we stand for.

## Australia's Global Interests

Australia's interests are global. As a fully integrated member of the international community, we have a major stake in the global campaign against terrorism. To protect our interests we need the support of other countries that share our values, just as they need ours. The terrorist threat to our global interests can only be defeated through a comprehensive and effective international response. There is no room for complacency.

Australians have a significant presence abroad. Over 3.5 million of us travel overseas each year - around one million at any one time. Some 720 000 Australians or almost 4 per cent of the population live overseas. About 120 000 of us move overseas on a long-term or permanent basis each year.

Australia has an extensive diplomatic network of 86 overseas posts as well as other official representations. About 2000 Australian Defence Force personnel are deployed on more than ten operations and training activities around the globe, including in the Middle East, Europe, Africa, South-East Asia and the Pacific. The Australian Federal Police maintains a significant overseas presence, through its International Network and with personnel currently deployed in Cyprus, East Timor and Solomon Islands. Australian non-government organisations also maintain significant overseas representation. A total of 2289 Australians worked overseas through a non-government organisation in 2003.

We have extensive global economic and business interests. Australia's trade and foreign investment is a key to our economic prosperity. Exports account for around 20 per cent of annual gross domestic product. The jobs of one in five Australians now depend directly or indirectly on the export of Australian goods and services. In 2003, Australia's two-way trade in goods and services was valued at $304 billion, including $140 billion of Australian exports. In the same year, Australia invested $152 billion abroad while international investment in Australia totalled over $233 billion. The Australian dollar is the world's seventh most traded currency.

These figures show that terrorism threatens not only the physical security of Australians travelling and living abroad. It also threatens our international economic and commercial interests. The threat of terrorism raises the cost of trade and travel and undermines investor and consumer confidence. Lower rates of economic growth are the result, particularly in an economy like Australia's, with our heavy reliance on trade and foreign investment. And the interdependence of national economies means economic disturbance is felt throughout the global marketplace.

## ECONOMIC COSTS OF TERRORISM

Terrorism impacts on world economic activity in several ways. The immediate impact includes loss of life, damage to property and infrastructure and disruption to financial markets. Other short-term costs include rescue efforts and post-attack consequence management as well as the costs of remedial measures.

In the medium to long term, terrorism creates uncertainty, reduces confidence and increases risk perceptions and insurance premiums. Investors seek lower risk and shorter-term investments. These typically have weak rates of return. The cumulative effect is to reduce overall investment and slow rates of economic growth. The IMF estimates that the loss of US output resulting from terrorism-related costs could be as high as 0.75 per cent of Gross Domestic Product, or US$75 billion per year. Any decline in US real GDP compounds and prolongs the adverse impact of economic uncertainty on Asian countries and Australia.

Increased spending on counter-terrorism may provide a boost to some businesses. But there is an overall decline in economic productivity as resources are diverted to security from more productive activities. Pressure is also exerted on state budgets. Productivity losses from the threat of terrorism can be offset by improving risk perceptions. If properly managed, security measures can facilitate and secure trade and investment. New technologies introduced to strengthen trade security can increase efficiencies in trade and decrease trade costs through reduced theft, shorter delays and lower insurance costs.

Economies which fail to adopt new trade security measures or fail to cooperate in multilateral counter-terrorist measures run the risk of marginalising themselves from many international transactions.

Terrorism also places Australia's international relations under stress. Well established international practices, relationships and conventions are challenged by the threat of terrorism. The need for a robust response to terrorism challenges long-standing international patterns of behaviour. Australia's relationships with other countries can come under pressure because of the need to respond to situations which, while internal to a particular country, can affect our security. Overall, the international system becomes less predictable and less easy to manage.

## THE NATURE OF THE TERRORIST THREAT TO AUSTRALIAN INTERESTS

### *Overseas*

The threat to Australian interests is higher overseas than at home. Australian interests overseas are often less well protected and within easier reach, making them an easier target. Our interests are at particular threat in South-East Asia, South Asia and the Middle East. The extent and complexity of the overseas threat is recognised in the travel advisory system developed by the Department of Foreign Affairs and Trade. The volatile international security environment has resulted in raised threat levels for Australia's interests overseas in recent times. Australian interests are at threat from terrorists wherever Western interests are targeted. A more dangerous international environment also means Australians may accidentally get caught up in attacks directed primarily at others. Terrorist attacks against Western interests in

Europe or the United States could involve Australian casualties - as in the 2001 World Trade Center attack.

Australian interests can be targeted directly. This was the case in December 2001 when a Jemaah Islamiyah plot to bomb the Australian, British and United States diplomatic missions in Singapore was foiled by the Singapore authorities. Similarly, in June 2003 the Thai police uncovered a plan by Jemaah Islamiyah to bomb the Australian Embassy in Bangkok together with the embassies of the United States and United Kingdom. Australia has also been named as the primary target for terrorists in Indonesia by an Al Qaida manual titled Targeting the cities.

Australian counter-terrorism activities abroad may also be targeted. Also, peace-keeping, military, law enforcement and development cooperation projects, and the people who carry them out, can challenge the capacity of terrorists to operate freely. Threatened by this, terrorists may target these activities in an attempt to break Australian resolve. Australian interests can also be attacked if they present a 'soft' target. Should a non- Australian higher-profile target be too difficult to attack, Australian interests could be targeted instead. In these circumstances, our interests may be seen as an easier option for the terrorists.

### *South-East Asia*

Australia has significant engagement with the countries of South-East Asia and we have a major stake in the region's security.

Despite the Bali tragedy and ongoing terrorism concerns, the region remains a popular destination for Australians. Four of the top ten destinations for Australian travellers are in South-East Asia. Around 45 000 Australians live in the region and many Australians have family there.

Australia has substantial commercial and diplomatic interests in South-East Asia as well as an overall interest in the region's security. Trade between South-East Asia and Australia now exceeds $40 billion a year - Singapore, Indonesia, Thailand and Malaysia feature in the top 15 destinations for Australian exports. The region encompasses important communication links, air routes and sea lanes vital for our trade.

Terrorists in South-East Asia have demonstrated an interest in targeting Australia and our overseas interests. As well as the threat from Jemaah Islamiyah and other known groups, there is a more diffuse threat from tomorrow's terrorists - militant groups that may commit terrorist acts in the future.

Since September 11, information indicating terrorist plans to attack Australian embassies in South-East Asia has come to light. The symbolic value of bombing diplomatic missions will ensure that they remain a likely terrorist target.

Key economic and commercial interests, including airports, airlines, shipping and transport infrastructure, have also been identified as targets. In April 2002, regional authorities disrupted a Jemaah Islamiyah plot to hijack a plane and crash it into Singapore airport. The magnitude of the terrorist threat to Australia's interests in South-East Asia depends on the effectiveness of action by countries in the region to counter that threat. Jemaah Islamiyah and other terrorist groups in the region will look for and exploit any weaknesses in the region's counter-terrorism response. The precise nature and location of the threat to our interests is likely to vary.

### *Pacific Islands*

There is no current evidence of terrorist activity in the Pacific island countries but they remain vulnerable to exploitation by terrorist networks and even terrorist attacks. Apart from its direct consequences, a terrorist attack in the Pacific would also have a major impact on the region's important tourism sector, along with possible longer-term economic and social damage. Pacific island countries recognise their vulnerability and are working with Australia and other countries to rectify them.

### *At Home*

The terrorist threat extends to Australia's shores and a terrorist attack on our soil is possible. This reality underpins Australia's National Counter-Terrorism Plan - to prepare for, prevent and respond to acts of terrorism and their consequences within Australia.

In the past, Australia was geographically insulated from areas that were a focus of terrorism, including the Middle East, North Africa and parts of Europe. This helped protect it from the terrorist threat. But globalisation means we are within easier reach. Today geography is no defence. The protection once afforded by the so-called 'Sea-Air Gap' no longer exists.

Terrorists do not necessarily need to enter Australia in order to launch an attack against our territory or our interests. This means that Australia's security environment has become less predictable since September 11 and the Bali bombings.

Extremists with links to transnational extremist-Muslim terrorist groups have shown interest in undertaking terrorist attacks in Australia. Al Qaida explored possible targets in Australia in 2000 and an associated group has recently been active. This suggests a serious intent to undertake terrorist attacks here.

In May 2004, Australian citizen Jack Roche pleaded guilty to charges of conspiracy to commit offences against the Crimes (Internationally Protected Persons) Act 1976. Roche was sentenced to nine years' imprisonment. Roche associated with Jemaah Islamiyah in Australia, trained in Afghanistan, and met with and took direction from Hambali and other extremist identities, including Khalid Sheikh Mohammed. Roche videotaped the Israeli embassy in Canberra and the Israeli consulate in Sydney in June 2000 as a preliminary measure to support a possible future terrorist attack in Australia.

Following the listing of Jemaah Islamiyah as a terrorist organisation by the government, the residences of individuals with suspected links to Jemaah Islamiyah were searched in October 2002.

Although no evidence of operational planning in Australia was found, these searches confirmed links between Jemaah Islamiyah members in Australia and senior Jemaah Islamiyah figures in South-East Asia.

References made by Al Qaida and affiliated groups, targeting Western countries in general and Australia in particular, highlight the enduring terrorist threat to Australian domestic interests.

Some transnational terrorist groups have small numbers of supporters in Australia. A small number of Australians have trained in terrorist camps in Afghanistan and Pakistan. The prospect of Australia being a source of funds for overseas terrorist activities is also of concern.

Strong border control measures are essential in securing Australia against external terror threats. But the terrorist threat to Australia does not only come from external sources. It can also come from people living and working in Australia.

Although we have much greater control of our security at home than abroad, the threat of the unknown remains. We have identified and successfully disrupted the activities of some groups but we must remain alert and adaptable to deal with new threats should they emerge.

### The Threat from Chemical, Biological, Radiological or Nuclear Terrorism

The acquisition of chemical, biological, radiological or nuclear weapons by transnational terrorist groups would add a new dimension to the terrorist threat to Australia. It would seriously compromise the physical security of the Australian community. Although the range of damage that can be inflicted by this form of terrorism varies enormously, even a small incident would cause significant alarm.

We know Al Qaida has shown interest in both acquiring and developing expertise in chemical, biological, radiological and nuclear terrorism. The growing black market in the technology to support these weapons underscores the need for quick international action against proliferation threats.

### The Threat to Australian Values

Muslim extremist terrorists threaten Australia's core values as much as our security. The views they espouse challenge our way of life as a tolerant, open and diverse society. Terrorists attack democratic societies by using their very openness as a weapon against them. They prey on both fear and ignorance. In threatening us, they challenge us to abandon our fundamental freedoms, community tolerance and the open nature of our civil society. They present us with the risk that, in framing a counter-terrorist response, we may sacrifice, prejudice or compromise our basic values.

## *The Long-term Threat*

The ambiguities of the longer term present us with the most difficult challenge. The transnational terrorist threat is evolving rapidly. The structure and capacity of groups such as Al Qaida is changing and new terrorist groups are emerging. Some of these new groups are acting autonomously and adopting new tactics.

The existence of highly capable transnational terrorist groups means Australian interests will continue to be at heightened threat from terrorist attack. Together with our global partners, we have had significant successes in disrupting the operations of transnational terrorist groups. But Al Qaida and terrorist groups associated with it retain the intent and capacity to carry out sophisticated attacks. Both their rhetoric and their behaviour signal that they are in for the long haul.

Intelligence is one of our best defences. It provides us with an understanding of our security environment, allowing us to work effectively with like-minded countries to disrupt and defeat terrorist attacks before they occur. It gives us early warning of threats as they develop but it will never be able to provide the complete picture. The further we look into the future, the more difficult this becomes. No defences are foolproof.

And as we become more accustomed to living under the shadow of transnational terror, we also face the threat of our own complacency. We cannot allow further tragedy to be our wake-up call.

# 5

# Nuclear Jihad

However, in sharp contrast with the optimism and confidence of the "Indian-and-Pakistani-states-as-rational-actors" proponents, the anti-state actors could care less if nuclear prevention breaks down and results in large-scale and unprecedented death and destruction. To understand their perspective in its proper context, a brief historical overview is in order before we examine the views and impact of anti-state actors on nuclear prevention in South Asia.

Much like other worldwide ideologies, Islam and its followers also divide the world into two regions: the world of believers, *Dar-ul-Islam*, or the House of Islam, and *Dar-ul-Harb*, or the House of Infidels and non-believers containing all territories ruled by non-Muslims, against whom no-holds-barred jihad is to be waged by the believers (true followers of Islam) who are destined to dominate and rule over the non-believers. Such concepts promote ideas of "us versus them" and generate hatred, hostility, enmity and a permanent state of war. Interestingly, this concept of continuous struggle (holy war against non-believers) bears remarkable resemblance to Mao's concept of permanent revolution against his perceived enemies—rightists and capitalists—during the Great Proletarian Cultural Revolution (1967–76) in China. The division of the world into two blocs is also similar to the one made by the followers of other totalitarian ideologies—Fascism and Communism—which ruled out peaceful coexistence with other belief systems. As Cathy Young observes: "Perhaps every belief system that lays claim to the ultimate truth carries the seeds of violent fanaticism and intolerance. This is true not only of religions but of secular ideologies such as Communism." The Islamists see the growing economic interdependence, globalization, Western cultural penetration, and the notions of liberty (freedom of speech, expression, and movement) and equality (especially equality of religions and sexes) as posing a serious threat to the basic tenets of Islam.

Historically, jihad in the Indian subcontinent was primarily waged against Hindus, Sikhs and Buddhists and later against the Christians during and after the British rule. In the nineteenth century, Sayyid Ahmad Barelvi took the struggle one step further and launched an "eternal jihad" against *kafirs* (infidels) with his call to Muslims: "Fill the uttermost ends of India with Islam, so that no sounds may be heard but Allah Allah Allah!" The long-term objective of Islamists is to spread the frontiers of Islam eastward to the whole continent of Asia and beyond. During the 1980s and 1990s, Afghanistan and Pakistan became the jihadis' destination of choice, as Islamist warriors coalesced in the two countries to battle the enemies of the faith (first the Soviet Union, then the United States, Israel, and India). As noted earlier, Saudi Arabia, in its self-appointed mission to protect and promote Islam, especially the puritanical Wahabi version, has been providing much of the financial and ideological support to religious schools, charities and organizations around the world at which students are taught to develop their hatred for non-believers such as Christians, Jews and Hindus. They are taught that Islam cannot coexist with other religions and that to kill in the interests of Islam and the Shariat is a religious obligation and not a sin, even if the killing involves the use of WMD. Verse 191, Sura 2, of the Holy Quran explicitly enjoins upon the Ummah to punish enemies of the faith in this fashion: "And slay them wherever ye catch them, and turn them out from where they have turned you out." Coupled with "the Medina Syndrome" (the perception that Islam is perennially in danger from powerful enemies), the only answer for pious Muslims in despair is "unity, faith and war." To put it simply, solidarity for jihad and jihad for solidarity. As Therese Delpech observes:

Their declared ambition is to annihilate not just religions other than Islam (the destruction of the ancient Bamiyan's Buddhist statutes in February 2001 is an eloquent testimony), but also anyone who does not accept its perverse version of Islam (bin Laden's people have burnt Shi'ites alive in Afghanistan)...No concession, however great, would be enough to end [their] "mission" because, unlike many previous terrorist organizations, *it does not intend to create a state nor does it wish to introduce political reforms. Its objective is metaphysical: a titanic struggle between "good" and "evil" forces, in which any means can be used to achieve the end.*

In the India-Pakistan context, the Islamists argue that Kashmir is a symbol, not the root cause of the India-Pakistan conflict. They point to General Parvez Musharraf 's statement made as the Chief of Army Staff in April 1999: "Even a settlement of the Kashmir issue will not usher in peace in the region. Low intensity conflict against India will continue because India is a large hegemonic power." This reinforces the view that the India-Pakistan conflict is rooted in history, religion, culture, and the politics of revenge, epitomizing clashing worldviews and a divide along religious, civilizational fault lines. Many Islamists are convinced that India, like its erstwhile friends, the Soviet Union and Yugoslavia, is doomed to further partition and Balkanization. In the aftermath of the Soviet collapse in the early 1990s, there was great optimism in Pakistan about "the coming collapse of India," which would enable the creation of a large Islamic state in Central and South Asia with Pakistan as its core. The leader of *Jamaat-i-Islami* Pakistan, Qazi Hussain Ahmad, speaking in Rawalpindi in February 1992, declared, "a great Islamic State spreading from Kashmir to Central Asia would emerge after the independence of Kashmir." Islamists contend that Prophet Muhammed is said to have singled out India as a special target for jihad—the land of idol worshippers: "Slay the idolaters wheresoever you find them" (Sura 9:5). "Whosoever will take part in jihad against India," *Markaz* leader Muhammad Ibrahim Salafi claims that the Prophet had declared, "Allah will set him free from the pyre of hell." Interestingly, notwithstanding their conflicting perspectives and interests, both Hindu and Islamist fundamentalists seem to have an identical interpretation of Indian history: that the ultimate game plan is not limited to "liberating

Kashmir" but to subsume "Hindu India" into Islamic civilization. In this context, they point out that Zulfiqar Ali Bhutto's threat in 1971 of a thousand-year war with Hindustan (repeated by his daughter at the height of the 1990 crisis) was not hyperbole. Since the beginning of the second millennium, Hindu India has been subjected to repeated invasions by the armies of Islamic faith. As a result of Islam's eastward march over the last one thousand years, ancient India has already been successfully broken up into four states—Afghanistan, Pakistan, Bangladesh and India. Hopefully in another one thousand years, so the argument goes, the objective of either an Islamic India or the creation of more Islamic states will be achieved by the end of the third millennium.

Indians oppose this by saying that their country, one of the oldest civilizations in the world, has not only survived but thrived during millennia of invasions, whereas Pakistan could not survive the first twenty-five years of its existence and is unlikely to survive over the next twenty-five years if it continues with its self-destructive policies. The Islamists respond by saying that Ghauri and Ghaznavi may have lost war several times but they won eventually to subjugate Hindu India. Likewise, Pakistan may have lost to India in 1971 and 1999 but that does not mean the end of their attempts to expand Islam's frontiers eastwards. Islam, *if not Pakistan,* will eventually prevail. To this end, "pro-*jihadi* cells" armed with weapons are being established throughout India's minority regions ready to unleash terror and communal bloodbath at an appropriate time in the future when India is faced with a series of domestic crises and/or external aggression and is headed by a weak leader (in the mold of Indonesia's B. J. Habibie) unable to resist international pressure. Islamists also note that Pakistan still draws inspiration from the medieval period when Muslim warriors from Afghanistan used to invade ancient India, evident by the fact that all of its nuclear-capable ballistic missiles— Ghauri, Ghaznavi and Abdali—are named after the three prominent Afghan warlords who attacked India frequently between the eleventh and eighteenth centuries in an attempt to expand their empires. As Zaffar Abbas notes: "he symbolism highlights the official mindset in the country. For Islamabad, the present conflict with India is a continuation of the battles of the past, wars that are described in Pakistani history books as the just causes of Muslim invaders against infidels."

From the perspective of Hindu nationalists, nothing could be more provocative than Pakistanis (including Bhattys, Chaudharys, Dhillons, Khokars, Naiks, Ranas, Shahs, Sethis, among others) seeing themselves as "direct descendants" of Muslim invaders and plunderers (such as Ghauris, Ghaznavis, Abdalis and Babbars who looted Lahore, Multan, and laid waste to the cities in Sindh—all now in Pakistan) and wanting to wage a no-holds-barred holy war. In Hindutva's discourse, Islamic religion and people are portrayed as intolerant, hostile to Hindu values, proselytizing, expansionist, repressive, and violent. The Indian response is articulated by a former chief of the Indian Army: "If a nuclear war can bring an end to the thousand years of invasions of India by the armies of Islamic faith, so be it. Let's fight a nuclear war and destroy Pakistan once and for all." Apparently, both countries have become infected with the virus of religious-based nationalism, increasing the "death or glory" spirit within their armed forces. For their part, right-wing Hindu nationalists have also not given up their dream of regaining the "lost territories" ("the sacred lands of Hinduism and Buddhism lost to Islam during the second millennium," as the *Vishwa Hindu Parishad* or World Hindu Council puts it) and restoring the Hindu supremacy over the entire *Akhand Bharat* (Undivided India). The growing ascendancy of Hindutva forces in Indian politics is an indication of the radicalization of Indian society as a result of a two-decade long, Pakistan-backed proxy war. Meanwhile, Islamist extremism continues to haunt Pakistani state and society. Pakistan is, in the words of former Italian foreign minister Gianni De Michelis, "the fuse of the world." The provinces close to the Afghan border and home to the U.S. armed bases are now controlled by Islamist parties that created the Taliban and are openly sympathetic to the aims and ideals of al-Qaeda. The concern is that the radical Islamist worldview of groups like the *Jamiat Ulema Islam*, which is supportive of both the Taliban and al-Qaeda, could become the country's leitmotif. Violence levels in Indian Kashmir also continue to rise. Many observers believe that Washington may have to rethink its strategy vis-à-vis Islamabad if the war on terrorism is to be won decisively.

The complete dismantling of the al-Qaeda terrorist infrastructure in Pakistan seems unlikely because of the apprehension within Pakistani armed that doing so would devalue Pakistan's importance in the U.S. security strategy and once again make the United States turn its back on the country and make the country vulnerable to Western pressure and sanctions over Islamabad's WMD proliferation activities. It would also deprive Pakistan of invaluable Western aid and leverage vis-à-vis Washington and New Delhi.

As long as anti-state actors donate to to the "Islamic Caliphate" and Pakistan to the two-nation theory, and as long as political power in Pakistan is exercised by the army, the mullahs, and the feudal lords in the name of jihad, Islam, and Kashmir, there cannot be peace in the region. A noted author and commentator, M.J. Akbar, in his book, *The Shade of Swords*, concedes that Pakistan's anger against India is larger than the problem over Kashmir, but contends that the anger of the "Muslim Street" is not merely socio-economic, as some are positing. Muslim anguish is essentially about departed glory, contrasted to Hindu resurgence after one thousand years and Jewish revival after two thousand years backed by the secular, but Christian, West. As has often happened in the past, Muslim radicals have latched on to certain enemies to explain the current decay because they need someone to blame, apart from themselves. This partly explains why and how Pakistan, a homeland for Muslims, "turned jihad into an instrument of state policy from its inception and became the breeding ground for the first international Islamic brigade in the modern era." The fall of the Taliban has transformed the frontline state of Pakistan in the war on terrorism into its next battlefield, as fleeing al-Qaeda/Taliban jihadis and their supporters take refuge in Pakistan's Wild West with many slipping down into the cities, using networks of associated groups and sympathizers to reorganize to fight another battle another day. The Islamist fundamentalist groups have repeatedly demonstrated their power with a series of terrorist attacks in

India and Pakistan seen as warnings to Musharraf that abandoning militants in Kashmir and siding with the infidel West would have disastrous consequences. In the worst-case scenario, radical Islamic extremists, especially those who sympathize with al-Qaeda in the armed establishment, could gain control of the nuclear weapons and delivery systems and launch nuclear strikes. The threatened use of nuclear weapons by irrational anti-state actors will carry greater credibility than the threatened use of nuclear weapons by nation-states. India's nuclear deterrent can deter neither nuclear attacks nor cross-border terrorism conducted by anti-state actors. Interestingly, one perceptive commentator has argued that in Pakistan's destruction lies al-Qaeda's salvation because anti-state actors can survive and thrive only in failed, collapsed and war-torn states:

[Since] al-Qaeda has long used Pakistan as an ongoing base for its command and control and training functions, it has a deep interest in Pakistan's future. Paradoxically, al-Qaeda's and Pakistan's national security interests are not at all the same. From al-Qaeda's point of view, a war with India—even one that led to the destruction of an independent Pakistan— would be highly desirable for three reasons:

1. As al-Qaeda sees it, the government of President Pervez Musharraf has become a tool of the United States, supporting U.S. efforts to destroy al-Qaeda in Pakistan. While Musharraf's support has been far from wholehearted, al-Qaeda is aware that Musharraf cannot be relied upon to protect the network, particularly while under heavy pressure from the United States and India.
2. A stable Pakistan with a strong central government poses a threat to al-Qaeda's security [because] a strong government is less manipulable ...[and] less predictable. It can turn its power against al-Qaeda quite easily. *A Pakistan whose armed has been smashed and whose government ceases to function creates a situation in which al-Qaeda can stake out* and defend remote areas of the country from encroachment. From a geographic point of view, India has the ability to smash Pakistan. Occupying and pacifying the country, particularly the regions that al-Qaeda uses for its bases, is far more difficult...With an Indian army stretched to the limit and no meaningful Pakistani force to face, al-Qaeda

becomes more secure. Even U.S. operations against al-Qaeda in remote areas without Pakistani collaboration would become extremely difficult.

3. Al-Qaeda has, as its core argument, the idea that Islam is under attack from other religions. *If India were to attack Pakistan, al-Qaeda would be able to make the argument—convincingly in the Islamic world—that the Jews, the Christian West and the Hindus have allied to strangle Islam.* The plausibility of this argument would, al-Qaeda hopes, galvanize the Islamic world into united resistance. That unification is al-Qaeda's goal.

From al-Qaeda's viewpoint, an Indian attack on Pakistan would be highly desirable. *Even an attack involving nuclear weapons would be acceptable... That is why Pakistani-based Islamic militants aligned with al-Qaeda have persistently exacerbated the crisis between the two countries. In the long run, they see a war, even one that is ruinous to Pakistan, as an acceptable price to pay for their ultimate goals.* What is unacceptable is a settlement between India and Pakistan that would leave the United States in a dominant position in both countries as broker and arbiter. Islamic militants have done everything possible to foment a conflict.

The perspectives and interests of state and anti-state actors and this, in turn, makes India-Pakistan nuclear prevention highly unstable. In fact, the two frameworks are so markedly different that mere institution of confidence-building measures alone will not address the problem. None of the political, technical or situational conditions identified by Lewis Dunn apply to anti-state actors. Thus, the entry of anti-state actors makes the situational context vastly different from that of the Cold War era. Undoubtedly, the greatest disruption to the equilibrium of the nuclear balance of terror emanates from anti-state actors that may come to acquire "a level of power and technological sophistication once associated only with nation-states." The multinational mercenary terror network that al-Qaeda and others have assembled could be regarded as a malignant and mutated form of the "virtual state" that requires a reconsideration of conventional strategies of prevention based on retaliation. The traditional theories of prevention may apply to other states but certainly do not apply to anti-state actors and rogue regimes. Nuclear weapons were never meant to deter transnational terrorists. Religious zealots bent on martyrdom have turned on its head a nuclear doctrine that was based on the deterrent value of mutually assured destruction.

## NUCLEAR PREVENTION IN SOUTH ASIA

THE PRECEDING ANALYSIS of the perspectives of anti-state actors shows that prevention in South Asia may not work in the context of asymmetric and unrestricted warfare based as it is on surprise, shock and deception and waged by those who have little or nothing to lose, particularly when suicide is used as a weapon. The instability argument points to the following reasons:

1. The history of four wars, and the intensity, duration and complexity of the animosity, coupled with growing domestic pressures in each country for action against the other, make nuclear prevention unstable. The war on terrorism has encouraged brinkmanship on both sides with both seeing the U.S. presence in the region as a safety net. The next nuclear confrontation could be even more dangerous if the two sides follow the Cold War-era U.S.-Soviet standoff model—with nuclear missiles on alert, aimed at each other and ready to launch on warning. As Lee Butler, former head of the U.S. Strategic Command, has said, it was "no thanks to prevention, but only by the grace of God" that the United States and the Soviet Union survived their crises. India and Pakistan may not be lucky next time.
2. Whereas the Cold War was ideological, the India-Pakistan conflict is historical and religious. More than disputed borders, India and Pakistan share disputed histories. The United States and the Soviet Union never engaged in direct armed conflict with each other. Nor did they have a history of armed conflict or animosity prior to the 1940s. Nonetheless, they still came close to war more than once.
3. Territorial disputes and the sharing of a border are rooted in the deep religious divide going back one thousand

years, for example, to the desire to re-establish Islamic or Hindu supremacy over the entire subcontinent. Indians and Pakistanis have bitter memories and highly emotional issues too long to list: invasions, partition, three wars, religious and border disputes, volatile political cultures, inflammatory media, and two decades of low-intensity conflict. In contrast, none of these factors existed as potential fuses to light the nuclear powder keg during the U.S.-Soviet nuclear standoff. The United States and Soviet Union never shared common or disputed borders. The geographical proximity also means lack of adequate time to rectify a mistake or for early warning of an accidental missile launch.

4. Neither India nor Pakistan possesses accurate intelligence or warning systems, nor do they have the ability to assure a second strike. The fear of a decisive first strike "use it or lose it" option, with short distances, poor warning systems, and small stockpiles amidst the talk of "nuclear jihad," makes prevention very unstable. As a result, the possibility of a nuclear conflict in South Asia—by design or accident—cannot be entirely ruled out. Their weak, untested command and control systems and relative inexperience in managing nuclear weapons, plus a lack of knowledge about each other's armed processes, means the "line in the sand" could be crossed unintentionally. For example, Islamabad has made it clear that it will use nukes first and in the early stages of conflict, hoping this threat will prevent an Indian attack across the Kashmiri. Line of Control. While India follows a no-first-use policy, a number of strategic analysts during the recent armed standoff called for a reconsideration of the NFU policy in the context of Pakistan. Others claim that India's armed forces are "prepared to try to destroy Pakistan's nuclear capability before it is used, and seek their own capability to launch a nuclear attack if they believe that enemy nuclear missiles are armed and ready for launch or already on the launch pads or are in booster phase. Pakistan, in turn, may seek

to preempt such a situation by using its nukes even earlier in a conflict rather than losing them." There are also serious concerns over lax security controls in that part of the world.

5. Crisis stability based on prevention does not apply to South Asia, where brinkmanship and one-upmanship is part of political life. The United States and the Soviet Union painstakingly avoided issuing either open or veiled threats over nuclear weapons—even though the U.S. nuclear doctrine implied a willingness to do so. (The Cuban missile crisis of 1962 was the sole exception.) In contrast, Pakistan has publicly flexed its nuclear muscles on four occasions in recent history—in 1987, 1990, 1999, and again in 2002. Likewise, India has repeatedly warned that it would survive a nuclear war but Pakistani would surely disappear from the world map. (The world has not heard such a threat since the 1950s when Mao Zedong argued that enough Chinese would survive a nuclear confrontation with the United States to usher in a communist revolution.) In short, neither periodic threats of nuclear annihilation nor nuclear blackmail bode well for stable nuclear prevention.
6. The conventional armed imbalance, or the lack of prospects for victory, did not seem to deter Pakistan from initiating three wars, all of which resulted in clear and quick Indian victories. While India is a *status quoist* power, Pakistan is the revisionist power, extremely dissatisfied with the territorial status quo and frustrated and resentful for lacking the means to overturn it. Emboldened by its nuclear deterrent since the late 1980s, Pakistan believes it can undertake such confrontations without risking severe Indian punishment. Besides, there is a view in armed circles that India no longer enjoys a decisive armed edge that it did a decade or two ago. The idea of a limited nuclear war may be embedded in Pakistani nuclear thinking but not in Indian strategic planning. If Pakistan's armed keeps multiplying provocations as in the past, a weak and unpopular regime may well stumble into a war that neither wants.

7. There is no greater fallacy than the hope that Pakistan can continue to engage in low-intensity conflict while relying on its nuclear capabilities to deter the Indian retaliation. Post-September 11, India believes that it has every right to launch pre-emptive strikes—much like the United States—against the terrorist bases and jihadi infrastructure. But many in the Pakistani armed are convinced that "Hindu India" would continue to bark but never bite. This could lead to miscalculation and misperception resulting in a catastrophe. A "failing state" or a collapsing regime may not behave like a responsible, rational nuclear weapon state—an essential prerequisite for successful nuclear prevention. One can imagine a scenario in which the so-called "Kashmiri freedom fighters," armed with a couple of nuclear weapons provided by disgruntled Pakistani army officers, threaten to nuke New Delhi if Indian security forces are not withdrawn within forty-eight hours, and set off a nuclear device in the Himalayas for demonstration effect. The nightmare scenario that we must consider is a collapsing Pakistani state that might have someone with a finger on the nuclear trigger and a fanatical desire to destroy its enemies. A loss of control of either Pakistani or Indian nuclear weapons could be a potential trigger of a wider nuclear confrontation between India and Pakistan. Alternatively, "clashes between security forces and hostile groups at nuclear installations might even result in release of nuclear material or even conceivably a partial nuclear detonation."
8. At the "anti-state actor" level, individuals or groups may violate security rules for reasons of profit, settling a grudge or religious and ideological motives. They may try to transfer sensitive items to some anti-state actors. Two retired Pakistani nuclear scientists with alleged al-Qaeda connections are currently under custody. The possibility of a civil war fought with nuclear weapons in the Indian subcontinent cannot be completely ruled out. Another concern is the possibility of yet another coup in Pakistan.

In conditions of civil war and internal chaos in a nuclear weapon state, nuclear materials could conceivably be used as bargaining chips in a struggle for internal power, or as negotiating leverage with external powers. If there were two rival claimants to the government in Islamabad, for example, we would be inclined to support the side that claims to control that country's nuclear forces. The scenario of Pakistan in splinters, with one piece becoming a radical Muslim state in possession of a nuclear weapon, is a concern, should al-Qaeda/Taliban declare jihad against Pakistan—the weakest ally in the U.S.-led anti-terrorism coalition. Furthermore, the breakup of states creates the danger of WMD falling into the hands of separatists and religious fanatics. In short, power struggle and instability in Pakistan also could lead to attacks on the Pakistani armed's nuclear arsenal by anti-state actors and the theft of nuclear weapons.

9. The freelance factor of terrorism changes the situational context completely in the sense that anti-state actors may have vested interest in provoking a war between India and Pakistan. With relatively little radioactive material, obtained from low-level waste from a power plant or medical facility, terrorists could easily construct a "dirty bomb" using simple explosives. Such devices, hidden in a truck or ship-borne cargo container headed for Karachi or Bombay, could inflict considerable casualties followed by widespread radiation poisoning.
10. Finally, the China factor further adds to unpredictability, complexity, and instability in the subcontinental nuclear power balance. China has long been the most significant player in the India-Pakistan-China triangular relationship. The Sino-Pakistan armed alliance (in particular, the nuclear and missile nexus) is aimed at ensuring that the South Asian armed balance of power is neither pro-India nor pro-Pakistan but pro-China. Most war-gaming exercises on the next India-Pakistan nuclear war end in a Chinese armed intervention to prevent the collapse of Beijing's most allied ally in Asia. For Beijing, the most worrisome

scenario would be one which brings the United States and Pakistan on a collision course, with or without India acting as a U.S. partner.

## RELIGION, TERROR AND SACRIFICE

To disenchant terrorist discourse also means, in a multi-religious and multicultural society, the necessity of disenchanting the state and public rhetoric. The turn to talk of religion and spirituality, that talk of re-enchantment and desecularization, not only serves to act as public space for religious diversity to state their claims of communal legitimacy, it also provides a public space for the religion of terror and terror discourse. To disenchant is not to dismiss the various religious claims or affiliations, but to effectively seek to secularize them into the realm of privatism. Yet in order to do this we need to be also aware of the claims of the sacred, especially in claims of sacrifice and transgression that *exist still* within our society – and which are repositioned into the public sphere by acts of terror.

Georges Bataille offers a provocative take on the challenges of sacrifice and transgression, in which the sacred unleashes itself in acts of passion which are contrary to reason. He notes the links of horror, terror and the sacred and how, in the contemporary world, with the reduction to symbolic passion in our religion we have attempted to domesticate our fascination with death and destruction that sits at the heart of religion. This is the basis of the *religare* of terror – our fascination with death as *sign and symbol* of the sacred. Therefore the challenge of terror is the return of the sacred as transgressive in a world seeking to limit and contain it, to reduce it. The problem is that we fail to see acts of terror as acts of exaltation and intoxication in the sacred, failing to acknowledge Bataille's claim for the transgressive eroticism of terror:

> The inner experience of eroticism demands from the subject a sensitiveness to the anguish at the heart of the taboos no less great than the desire which leads him to infringe it. This is religious sensibility, and it always links desire closely with terror, intense pleasure and anguish.

This is why terror has become the new global religion. It reflects and provides the religious sensibility in the contemporary world – it transgresses the space given to religion in the postmodern turn and rejects both the restraints of controlled plurality and the turn away from plurality in the turn back to a new modernity. Today, terror is a religion that acts as transgression and taboo to *both* modernity and postmodernity. In a sense, following the Nietzschean nihilism of *Beyond Good and Evil* we now exist in a world of taboo and transgression, a world of sacred violence. As Bataille notes: "the transgression does not deny the taboo but transcends and completes it". In this we need to now view the transgression of terror as that *which transcends and completes* both taboos – those of death and of religion/sacred in public space – in the modern world. As "the taboo is there to be violated" and is "at the very least...the threshold beyond which murder is possible", our taboos on public death and public religion are in fact those which paradoxically issue a form of demand *for* the transgression of terror – and the terror of transgression. In effect, notes Bataille, for our profane world to exist we require the complementary acts of transgression that exceed its limits but do not destroy it: "the profane world is the world of taboos. The sacred world depends on limited acts of transgression".

This means that acts of terror are acts of transgression for the expression of the reality of the sacred world. In other worlds, acts of terror are a form of sacrifice. What the act of sacrifice does is not a killing but rather a relinquishing and a giving. What is sacrificed is what is useful – it "restores a lost value by relinquishment of that value". As bin Laden would have it:

When you talk about the invasion of New York and Washington, you talk about the men who changed the face of history and went against the traitors....These great men have consolidated faith in the hearts of believers and undermined the plans of the crusaders and their agents in the region. Terrorism against America deserves to be praised because it was a response to injustice, aimed at forcing America to stop its support for Israel, which kills our people. The acts of terror are, from a religious viewpoint, acts of sacrifice: they give up what is useful – the life of the terrorist, the life of the believer, the sacrifice of people in the profane world – in a manner of transgressive action that seeks to transcend the taboo on violence, death and the sacred. As Bataille notes: "The sacrificer declares ...I call you back to the *intimacy* of the divine world, of the profound immanence of all that is...".

The spectacle of terror is therefore on one level the intimacy of sacrifice in the intimacy of our daily lives, in the intimacy of our living rooms, in the intimacy of our public and private spaces. It is on one level, as Bataille states of sacrifice, "the communication of anguish". So what is this anguish? Perhaps it is as Slavoj Zizek notes, the cry of anguish of sacrifice, of terror, of violence. Furthermore, that our transgressive avidity for these is our passion for the "Real" – that which he notes Alain Badiou as claiming is "the key feature of the twentieth century".

This passion for the Real is what sits at the heart of Loos' call for the overthrow of unnecessary ornamentation; this passion for the Real sits at the heart of the Futurist worship of the cleansing effect of technology, war and death; this passion for the Real is what lies in modernity's rejection of transcendence – and in Postmodernity's rejection of modernity's secularity. In effect, the dualistic battle in modernity between what is seen as order and what is seen as chaotic *is* this battle over what is Real and where the Real is located. Violence, taboo, transgression and sacrifice are those acts that serve as both statements of the Real – and the rejection of what is perceived to be non-Real. Acts of terror, made possible by the space given in postmodernity for the articulation of varieties of transcendent "Real", are an act of the rejection of these possibilities in a challenge of what is seen as the Real. Yet in their symbolic intention, they participate in the postmodern spectacle as an attempt to evangelize by effect. The passion for the Real and the attempt to represent it are actually transgressive to modern world where we attempt to keep the Real controllable by not confronting it. The response to the rise of transcendence as the location of the Real was not to confront it but rather to seek to splinter it by postmodern tolerance. Yet all this did was to give consent to those who sought to destroy even the possibilities of competing Reals.

In effect, contemporary terrorism is the Real of modernity (a battle beyond good and evil, of order and chaos) confronting itself with the non-reality of terror and spectacle that act as transgressive to that which we seek to hold as Real. The effect is not concerned with the reality of the chaotic act, but rather with the chaos that is the response to the reality of the act. In effect we say "we cannot believe this act has occurred" and this stating of our inability to believe in the Real is the chaos that the act of terror seeks. We then search to ascribe a meaning to the event that may mean *we claim to see the reason behind the act*, the "cry of anguish" that caused this act. To ascribe meaning to the act is to order it, in effect to attempt to "make it real" – and in making it Real paradoxically giving a form of inverted value and meaning to the actions and beliefs of those who undertook it.

Yet often what happens in response is the turn away from the liberal tolerance of dissenting beliefs that (perhaps) marks off a Western sense of the Real: a form of order that exists by ordering chaotic elements within pluralism. Yet the act of terror is a rejection of Western liberal pluralism, a rejection of the type of Western order that secularizes its taboos and transgressions.

## THE RESPONSE TO TERROR

The type of modernity in which we currently find ourselves is, in a Zizekian sense, one where we have a series of competing claims as to both the validity and location of the Real – and a series of competing claims as to what are acceptable actions to institute its recognition by the wider population. Fundamentalist terror sees what it seeks to destroy as chaotic, as unnecessary, as an affront to what is Real, what is ordered, what is necessary. Fundamentalist terror is the violence of the Real in the service of what is seen as the *necessary alternative*. The type of symbolic violence undertaken is a reflection of the type of claims of reality being made. Symbolic action as has been undertaken so far in New Zealand reflects a society that is secular by inclination. The Real is contained in symbolic action that can be reported and represented as secular in effect and motivation. Other acts of symbolic action in New Zealand such as desecration of Jewish graves, and graffiti attacks and vandalism of mosques and synagogues can, in a secular society, be contained as criminal acts of a non-legitimate extreme minority. The challenge presented by Destiny Church is not its symbolic nature, but rather the media response that gives credibility to religiously motivated symbolic events as being effective – and as being a means of effecting a form of legitimacy. Yet paradoxically, what will keep Destiny under control is its obsession with a gospel of prosperity – they will not seek to destroy the type of society that they believe will reward them. The danger to a country like New Zealand is the recourse to symbolic violence by those marginalized by both belief and culture – and yet given postmodern tolerance for their intolerant beliefs. The Real of the modern secular pluralist state is ever open to the challenge of the competing modernity of the religious Real that understands the nature and efficacy of symbolic violence. As Paul Piccone and Gary Ulmen noted in response to September 11: The first thing that will have to go is the criticism of the concept of tolerance for the intolerant – and therefore of its pseudo-universalism. Tolerance is a particular western value, which applies only to those who practice it. It excludes not only those who reject it, but also those who tolerate its rejection.

The religion of terror is linked to the religion of modernity, the belief in the pluralist secular nation state, the belief in a future that unfolds through rationality and progress – and in particular to a distinct form of western modernity. The failure of the postmodern can now be seen as the failure of the extension of tolerance to the intolerant, to those who seek to reject that which enables them to dissent. The recourse to symbolic violence is the challenge of the transgression of the taboo of intolerance; that which seeks a response that will assert the validity of the claims of the Real being made by the terrorist. As Baudrillard notes: "The tactic of the terrorist model is to provoke a surplus of reality and to make the whole system collapse under it".

To oppose the surplus of the reality of taboo and transgression that is to be found in the act of terror, the system under attack needs an alternative Real that can neutralise any attempts to impose any religious Real upon the general public and the nation. This occurs either by the symbolic actions that terrorise the liberal State's fear of being viewed as intolerant, or in specific actions that by act of violence seek to spread the terror of the Real through the *religare* of the mass media and so constitute the grounds for a new *religare* of terror. The challenge is that it is the freedom of the mass media that allows the circulation of the spectacle of terror – yet to limit the spectacle is to enforce the control of image and truth of the kind sought by the fundamentalist terrorist.

Contemporary terrorism is not a challenge against modernity, but rather a challenge that rejects the offer of postmodernity, an offer made by the post-Christian West and yet rejected by those who that West sought to include. What is offered in the act of fundamentalist terror is the challenge of an alternative modernity, an alternative way of ordering the chaos of life, an alternative belief system that uses the synthesis of mass media and terror to provide a new *religare* of terror that, in our response, serves to validate, from the point of view of the terrorist, the sacred necessity and justification for the act of terror: "We realized from our defence and fighting against the American enemy that, in combat, they mainly depend on psychological warfare. This is in light of the huge media machine they have".

To oppose the *religare* of terror the state may opt to secularize symbolic recourse as criminal behaviour, as has been the case in New Zealand, in effect trying to neutralize terrorism claims to efficacy as religious act and as *religare,* through a response of indifference. Secondly, it may be recognized that the privatization of belief and culture that occurs in modernity can also serve to allow the legitimization of intolerance within those groups. A cosmopolitan society is therefore confronted with the reality that calls for religious and cultural difference which can locate and express themselves in statements and actions of intolerance. Thirdly, this means that the secular *religare* of a cosmopolitan society *will* result in symbolic acts by those who seek to reject it. With the increasing recourse to religion as a form of identity politics (beliefs and communities as tangible *religare*), the state's dismissal of these to the privatist sphere may force the recourse to further symbolic action and this will be seen by some as a necessary risk. The alternative will be understood as responding *as if* the global *religare* of terror paradoxically legitimizes the unnecessary ornamentation of communal religious expression *within* the public sphere.

As Baudrillard notes, already the West is responding to "the spectre of terrorism" by terrorizing itself. In effect we are unsure how to respond to what he notes is the inversion of the master and slave relationship because the non-terrorist is "deprived of death and destiny" while the terrorists, the ones who control death, are the symbolic master. The western terrorising of "itself" occurs when, seeking to remain "tolerant" it provides the symbolic space for the terrorist "master" impose a hyper-real condition of REAL EVENT-DEATH as a permanent condition of the *religare* of fear and "*eschaton* expectation" – the "crystallization" of "all the ingredients in suspension".

The dilemma for the secular, cosmopolitan society is therefore when the private belief attempts to act within the public domain in a manner that seeks to impose its particular values and identity *upon all* within the society, this is particularly true of any recourse to religious fundamentalism. To avoid the self-terrorism that is the common response, perhaps in the end all private beliefs are to be equally unequal – and so exist in a form of oppositional equality. This is because in a Loosian-derived modernity, unnecessary ornamentation is itself the location of definition in a pluralist society. To proceed from locating *all* religious identity as unnecessary ornamentation is perhaps the only way to achieve equality, but also the groundwork toward the articulation of a pragmatic common narrative of modern identity. To privatize religion may protect an individual's identity, but it may also impede it. So, on the one hand the state may attempt to reply to fundamentalist terrorism with indifference. But what about the terrorism of the state and the uncertainty that the state – terror relationship bring to any discussion of either?

Jean-Luc Nancy, who raises the question of "what is to be done?" also offers a possibility which in its articulation of the necessity of the provisional possibility is a possible (non)solution:

Perhaps though, we know one thing at least: 'What is to be done?' means for us, how to make a world for which all is not already done (played out, finished, enshrined in a destiny), nor still entirely to do (in the future for always future tomorrows).

This challenge sits against the claims of necessity and certainty, the dualist battle that "terror" and "the war on terror" encompass. That this is a war of rhetoric – a rhetorical war – is also beyond a doubt. This is a point acknowledged by Kevin Roberts, CEO Worldwide of SAATCHI & SAATCHI Ideas Company in his recent "presentation to various U.S. Defense Intelligence Agencies". Robert's claim was the need for the rebranding of the rhetoric of "the War on terror", with the aim to create a new "loyalty beyond Reason", what Roberts calls a Lovemark: "these are brands that make deep emotional connections with consumers. Passionate connections that go inside people's lives and make a difference". These are brands that have "High Love, High Respect" such as Harley Davidson, Apple and JFK. For Roberts "brand America" currently has "High Respect, Low Love". His rebranding of "brand America" and of the "War on terror" is based on his "Lovemark" credo: "Mystery, Sensuality and Intimacy". This could be termed the seduction, the eroticism of the brand, the pornography of global capital.

Roberts' rebranding is to what he terms the "fight for a better world", a fight launched alongside the war on terror that seeks to tackle geopolitical issues such as "global AIDS, malnutrition and malaria". But Roberts' call "to create America as a lovemark" is a response that needs to be added to the already empty rhetoric that "terror" inspires. This is capitalism as hyper-real benevolence, a simulacrum of compassion that is pushing a global product. It merely swerves to emphasise Zillah Eisenstein's critique that: "Anti-terrorism rhetoric fits well with global capitalism ...there is no single country that houses terrorism...or capitalism. Both are networked transnationally.

What this demonstrates is that the *religare*, the religion of terror has already become just another product, something to be consumed in a form of globalization. Baudrillard encourages us to think about the problem of fundamentalist terrorism by reversing several of our standard assumptions. What if it were Islam, he asks, that were spreading through the West and rising to dominate the globe? Baudrillard tells us that if this were the case then "...terrorism would rise against Islam, for it is the world, the globe itself, which resists globalization".

What we need to consider, perhaps even confront, is the challenge that the *religare* of globalization is the *religare* of terror which is both product and consumption of capitalism and its other – terror. For terror is the inside of capitalism; that which acts as perhaps the "lovemark" of the inverted fight against the global. This link of religion, modernity and capitalism was noted by Marx in his call that "the criticism of religion is the prerequisite of all criticism". One could perhaps invert and expand it and say also that "the religion of criticism is the prerequisite of all terror". This dualism is what perhaps sits under all questions involving the modern, capitalist state and terrorism. Both the state and terror are built on certainties – yet both are certainties under attack from their other within the *religare* of the global. As Nancy has also noted: "Where certainties come apart, there too gathers the strength that no certainty can match.

The collapse of certainty is perhaps the collapse of the real, or rather the collapse of the belief in the real, a collapse that forces a struggle to assert the claim of the real (terror/war on terror) over and against the uncertainty and the indifference that the collapse of the real engenders. As Baudrillard notes: "There is no corpse of the real, and with good reason: the real is not dead, it has disappeared.

The unacceptability of terror is only as unacceptable as the *religare* of modernity, of the global, of global capital, as the drive to non-ornamentation. All are drives for the real arising out of claims of certainty as to the location and representation of the real. The *religare* of the real is the religion of terror – and of the war waged against it – a war of mutual rhetoric that by transgressive public religion/*religare* and public death affirm the Manichean centrality of modernity itself. Baudrillard's aphorism that "He does not have room for both the world and for its double – but no one knows which will have the last word" sits under any consideration of a response. Perhaps the only response is not to fall into the impatience of desiring a response, for out of impatience could possibility eventuate that which we do – but deny – desire:

Impatience is a millenarian passion which desires the immediacy of the end. Now today, wherever time has been abolished by the operation of 'real time', events no longer come to maturity, either immediately or with a delay. But impatience is not consoled by that: having nothing left to devour, it devours the remains of the real.

The immediacy of the end, the desire to immediately end "terror/the war on terror" or that which terror strikes at, are reminiscent of the drive to hygiene of futurism, the banishing of ornament, the self-implosion of Modernity at Pruitt-Igoe. The state that desires the immediate end to terror by self-terrorising itself is itself devouring what it believes is the remains of the real (itself as bureaucratic state) out of a millennial passion for the end. This self-terror of the self-devouring response has, as Baudrillard notes, its immediate prior expression in the West's hyper-real Iranian *Fatwa* it carried out for the Iranian state on Salman Rushdie: "The Iranian strategy consists in inflecting Western culture with fear, duplicity and self-pity".

Perhaps the issue is the centrality of the Loosian modernist rejection of disorder – a pursuit of order as *religare* that terror seeks to deny and discredit. Writing of the 1988 Libyan terror bombing of the plane over Lockerbie, Baudrillard notes: "What fascinates thought is this terrorist enchanting of things, the symbolic disorder of which terrorism is merely the visible epicentre".

The choice is therefore a degree of no-choice, the enchanting of terror by the state, the enchantment of terror by the terrorist, both symbolize a disorder against the Loosian claims of the realised real in ordered modernity, in the systems of order that the bureaucratic state now activates to self-terrorise itself, in effect to institute its internal *Fatwas* on its own citizens in the recognition that: "Every society must choose itself an enemy, but it must not try to exterminate it".

The state and the self-instituting terrorist act both have each other as enemy, but cannot act for a final extermination, a fulfilled millennial, apocalyptic passion for then their claims of and for the real are finished. The act of extermination is the internal destructive act of Pruitt-Igoe, the real terror is that turned by the state upon itself, to clear the space for the self-transcendence of its prior claim for the real.

As the French novelist Frederic Beigbeder notes in his mediation on the final hours of the twin towers: "Since September 11, 2001, reality has not only outstripped fiction, it's destroying it. It's impossible to write about this subject, and yet impossible to write about anything else. Nothing else touches us". The Western *Fatwa* has been extended – we all now live as Rushdie: self-imprisoned not by the original action but by our (Western) reaction to the original event-death. The Irony is that the modern Western dismissal of the ornamentation of religion has been supplanted by a *religare* of terror that ornaments us continually in the hyper-real self-*Fatwa*. Maybe our best case scenario is to hope that Baudrillard is right when he says: "terror is dissipated by irony" Neither are in short supply today.

## TERRORISM AND NUCLEAR WEAPONS

Former Director of Central Intelligence George Tenet reports in his memoirs that A.Q. Khan rebuffed several approaches by Osama bin Laden for access to nuclear know-how, although it was not clear why. Perhaps Khan understood that cooperating with the renowned terrorist leader was a bridge too far as it risked contributing to a scenario of nuclear Armageddon that could cause mass destruction and loss of life in his own country.

Although A.Q. Khan avoided engaging al-Qaeda on nuclear issues, earlier revelations about a group of former Pakistani military officials and nuclear scientists who met with Osama bin Laden around the time of 9/11 remind us of the continuing threat of the intersection of terrorism and nuclear weapons in Pakistan. On October 23, 2001, acting on an American request, Pakistani authorities detained Bashiruddin Mahmood and Abdul Majeed, two retired Pakistan Atomic Energy Commission (PAEC) officials. They had been involved in relief work in Afghanistan since their retirement from the PAEC in 1999 through a non-governmental organization (NGO) they established called Ummah Tameer-e-Nau (UTN). In November 2001, the coalition forces found documents in Afghanistan relating to the UTN's interest in biological weapons. This prompted Pakistani security forces to arrest seven members of the UTN's board, most of whom were retired Pakistani Army officials and nuclear scientists.

George Tenet speculates in his memoirs that UTN's contacts with the Taliban and al-Qaeda may have been supported by some elements within the Pakistani military and intelligence establishment.

Tenet says Pakistani interrogations of the seven board members were initially insufficient. He further notes that despite CIA warnings to Pakistani officials about UTN's activities before 9/11, it was only when President Bush dispatched him to Pakistan in November 2001 following revelations of a meeting between Bin laden, al-Zawahiri, and UTN leaders that Musharraf took serious action.

### Outcome of Khan Investigations

Similar foot-dragging by the Pakistani authorities was evident in the case of the A.Q. Khan proliferation network. U.S. officials had repeatedly raised their concern about A.Q. Khan's activities with President Musharraf, but it was not until Washington provided indisputable proof of its knowledge of Khan's activities and threatened to go public with the information in late 2003 that Musharraf took direct action to halt Khan's activities.

Even after details emerged on the tremendous damage done by the A.Q. Khan proliferation network, there was no formal prosecution of the Pakistani associates of Khan, and Khan himself is merely under house arrest. President Musharraf claims he cannot formally prosecute Khan or allow him to be questioned by U.S. or international authorities because of the hero status Khan enjoys for contributing to the development of Pakistan's nuclear weapons program.

### U.S. Policy Recommendations

There are steps the U.S. can pursue to help ensure nuclear weapons do not fall into the wrong hands in Pakistan and to prevent a dangerous nuclear arms race between Pakistan and

India. Washington has already begun to pursue such initiatives but will need to increase its attention and resources on expanding and strengthening such measures.

## *Leveraging, not Conditioning, U.S. Assistance*

Based on the negative consequences brought by the U.S. cut-off of assistance to Pakistan in 1990, it is unlikely that a narrow policy of cutting or even conditioning assistance to Pakistan through U.S. legislation now would help meet the above goals. The 1990 aid suspension cost the U.S. valuable leverage with Islamabad, damaged military-to-military relationships, and stoked strong anti-U.S. sentiment that still exists in the country. Efforts to publicly condition assistance to Pakistan could actually weaken Musharraf's hand in convincing his military commanders that the U.S. is a reliable partner. President Musharraf already contends with public opposition to his support for U.S. counterterrorism goals in the region, and conditioning aid through legislation would awaken memories of 1990 and weaken Pakistani public support for pursuing relations with the U.S.

Instead of conditioning aid on specific actions by Islamabad, Washington should target its assistance programs more effectively to accomplish specific goals. On the nuclear issue, the U.S. should seek to implement programs that help improve safety and security at nuclear facilities. Press reports indicate that the U.S. may already be cooperating with the Pakistanis on this front, but given Pakistani sensitivities on the issue of maintaining sovereign control of its nuclear assets, such cooperation will remain largely out of the public eye.

Perhaps over time, as the U.S-Pakistan partnership solidifies, it will be possible to develop a Nunn-Lugar Cooperative Threat Reduction (CTR) program with Pakistan similar to what the U.S. has established with Russia. Potential areas for cooperation with Pakistan include nuclear reactor safety, safeguarding nuclear material, rapid response to nuclear-related emergencies, and expanded export control cooperation. The Pakistan parliament adopted export control legislation in September 2004 for nuclear and biological weapons and their delivery systems.

Tailoring a CTR program of assistance for Pakistan would be challenging since Pakistan is not a signatory to the Nonproliferation Treaty. The U.S. is prohibited both by legal and treaty obligations from assisting the nuclear programs of states outside the nonproliferation regime. Another obstacle is the basic premise of the Nunn-Lugar legislation that requires recipients of CTR assistance to make "substantial investment of its resources for dismantling or destroying such weapons." It would be impossible to develop a CTR program with Pakistan along these lines without addressing the fact that Indo-Pakistani rivalry is what drives Pakistan's nuclear program.

### Encourage India-Pakistan Nuclear Confidence Building

India and Pakistanhave made significant strides in their dialogue over the last three years, including the maintenance of a ceasefire along the Line of Control that divides Kashmir since November 2003; the opening of rail and bus links across their borders; and increased people-to-people exchanges. Efforts to build confidence on nuclear-related issues have been slow, however. Addressing the Indo-Pakistani nuclear issue also relies, to some extent, on perceived progress in resolving the Kashmir dispute as well as the status of China's nuclear programs.

Talks over the vexed Kashmir issue were expected to make progress this year, following President Musharraf's announcement of forward-leaning proposals to resolve the dispute last December. However, the judicial crisis in Pakistan sparked by the Government's March 9 dismissal of the country's chief justice and ensuing street demonstrations have sidetracked the Musharraf government and raised concern in New Delhi about negotiating with Islamabad during the political uncertainty.

Preventing Pakistan's nuclear weapons and technology from falling into the hands of terrorists should be a top priority for the U.S. Revelations about the devastating impact of the A.Q. Khan proliferation network and nuclear black market will prevent Washington from considering a civil nuclear cooperation agreement with Pakistan similar to that being pursued with India. U.S. policy toward Pakistan's nuclear program should instead focus specifically on nuclear safety and security cooperation and encouraging India-Pakistan dialogue that will improve Pakistan's regional security perceptions.

Washington needs to maintain a robust partnership with Islamabad based on mutual trust and understanding. U.S. policymakers should refrain from compartmentalizing our myriad interests in Pakistan but instead integrate the various components of U.S. policy toward Pakistan. In other words, pursuing nuclear safety and security and nonproliferation in Pakistan should not be viewed as "competing" with other U.S. goals such as denying Taliban and al-Qaeda safe haven on Pakistani territory; shutting down madrassahs that feed terrorist groups; encouraging peace talks with India; as well as pressing for steps toward democracy. These goals are interrelated and mutually reinforcing and will eventually encourage the country toward a stable and moderate path.

## "NUCLEAR SECURITY IN PAKISTAN: REDUCING THE RISKS OF NUCLEAR TERRORISM"

Today's frightening instability in Pakistan comes in a world in which global terrorists are actively seeking nuclear weapons and the materials and expertise needed to make them, a quest that has been underway for more than a decade. Rapid action is needed to keep the Taliban's advances in Pakistan from creating new opportunities for these deadly adversaries.

Yet, assessing nuclear security in Pakistan should not be viewed in isolation. The challenges faced by Pakistani authorities must be seen in their broader context to be properly understood and effectively countered. All countries in possession of nuclear weapons are concerned about the possibility of losing control over a bomb or weapons-related material. Consequently, states must pay utmost attention to securing these means of mass destruction. Recent years have seen increased international cooperation on nuclear security, improvements in international material protection control and accounting procedures, and increased funding for nuclear security-related initiatives. Despite increases in the scope and sophistication of security measures, much work remains to be done in order to lock down all nuclear materials to a Fort Knox standard. The fact remains that missing weapons-usable material turns up regularly on the nuclear black market. The most worrisome aspect of these recurring incidents is that facilities from which the materials originated did not report them missing. In addition, there have been some notable lapses in warhead security, even in the United States.

Despite such troubling developments, global security efforts until now have been good enough to avert a nuclear catastrophe. The bad news is that nuclear threats are growing.

According to former CIA analyst Bruce Riedel, "Pakistan is the most dangerous country in today's world."

### *Daunting Security Task*

Ensuring complete control over nuclear equipment, material, and technology is more difficult now than at any time in the past. There is a burgeoning global interest in all things nuclear. More states are seeking nuclear technologies, power, and weapons. Production, transportation, and storage of nuclear materials will expand throughout the 21st century. The presence of more material in more places increases the odds of a security breach leading to the loss of a bomb or the theft of materials to make a bomb. The anticipated global renaissance in nuclear energy will pose new challenges in this regard unless the associated proliferation risks are fully taken into account in decisions on materials processing, transportation, and storage. In this light, it is essential to secure not only weapons-grade plutonium and uranium from military programs, but also plutonium, highly enriched uranium, and other materials from civilian programs. Materials that would not meet the standards required for a nuclear weapon developed by a state might be usable in a terrorist's yield-producing bomb.

Thus, a zero tolerance standard must be adopted for the loss of any nuclear weapon or of materials that may be fashioned into a bomb. Terrorists know that they can exploit any vulnerability to their advantage. In December 1998, Osama bin Laden expressed al Qaeda's intent when he stated in an interview, "Acquiring weapons [of mass destruction] for the defence of Muslims is a religious duty." In November 2001, he added, "I wish to declare that if America used chemical or nuclear weapons against us, then we may retort with chemical or nuclear weapons. We have the weapons as deterrent."

In its efforts to achieve the stature of a state, a terrorist group is most interested in producing a nuclear yield-a mushroom cloud. Consequently, a terrorist group would improvise a nuclear device or essentially build a crude nuclear bomb, one that has a low yield and may be unpredictable, inefficient, and unsafe in comparison with the complicated weapons systems in a national nuclear arsenal. To counter this qualitatively new threshold of nuclear-related threats, states must ensure that terrorists do not acquire any nuclear materials. This risk increases the demands that must be placed on security measures for materials at all stages of their use, i.e., production, processing, transportation, and storage, in research reactors as well as weapons facilities. The bottom line is that it is not enough to preclude terrorists from getting their hands on a bomb. States must eliminate any possibility that terrorists will acquire sufficient materials to build a bomb or successfully attack or take over a facility containing weapons or materials.

After the September 11 attacks, for example, the United States raised the level of the security for nuclear weapons and nuclear materials. As a centerpiece of this effort, President George W. Bush signed a National Security Directive in August 2006 establishing the U.S. government's Nuclear Materials Information Program. This program directed the consolidation of all U.S. information pertaining to all nuclear materials worldwide, in all forms and at all levels of enrichment. It included radioactive sources that could be fashioned into a dirty bomb. Every country was considered as a potential source of a crude terrorist weapon, including the United States. The directive prescribed a systematic approach to assessing the security status of all nuclear materials in facilities and in transit. It required the construction of a forensics database containing all U.S. holdings.

In addition, substantial new investments were made in upgrading security throughout the U.S. nuclear establishment. To that end, security planners in the Department of Energy and the

Nuclear Regulatory Commission made assumptions about the likelihood that malicious insiders at nuclear sites would work with outsiders to allow access to facilities and materials. The Energy Department and the FBI dramatically increased intelligence and counterintelligence efforts to mitigate threats posed by malicious insiders. Defence in depth-multiple, reinforcing layers of security-was strengthened to catch any leakage of materials or information that could enable an outside group in its pursuit of a bomb. In spite of such upgrades, serious security lapses have occurred in the U.S. nuclear establishment over the past several years. Others will surely happen in the future because no security is perfect. Thus, constant vigilance is required; it is important to strive continuously toward the elimination of nuclear threats, knowing that it may never be possible to achieve this ideal standard. The surest way to fail is to become complacent, to believe it cannot happen here.

That is certainly true in Pakistan. Nevertheless, all signs indicate that the professional and disciplined Pakistani military establishment that maintains control over the nuclear arsenal understands the dangers of a breakdown in nuclear security. Senior Pakistani military officers have consistently expressed a high degree of confidence that they are prepared to counter a range of plausible threats in this regard.

These officers have a lot to worry about, notwithstanding high-level reassurances from Pakistani authorities that everything is under control. Three worrisome trends are exerting mounting pressure on the Pakistani military's ability to secure its nuclear assets and prevent a nuclear catastrophe. First, growing extremism in Pakistan increases the odds of insiders in the nuclear establishment collaborating with outsiders to access weapons, materials, or facilities. Second, the rapid expansion of Pakistan's nuclear weapons program will introduce new vulnerabilities into the security system. Finally, growing instability within the country could lead to unanticipated challenges to nuclear command and control procedures, resulting in a "loose nuke" scenario, a takeover of a facility by outsiders, or, in the worst case, a coup leading to Taliban control over the nuclear arsenal.

## Collaboration Scenarios

The greatest threat of a loose nuke scenario stems from insiders in the nuclear establishment working with outsiders, people seeking a bomb or material to make a bomb. Nowhere in the world is this threat greater than in Pakistan. Pakistani authorities have a dismal track record in thwarting insider threats. For example, the network run by the father of the Pakistani bomb, Abdul Qadeer Khan, channeled sensitive nuclear technologies to Iran, Libya, and North Korea for years under the noses of the establishment before it was taken down in 2003, to the best of our knowledge. The Umma-Tameer-e-Nau (UTN), founded by Pakistani nuclear scientists with close ties to al Qaeda and the Taliban, was headed by Sultan Bashiruddin Mahmood, who had been in charge of Pakistan's Khushab reactor. He discussed al Qaeda's nuclear aspirations with bin Laden. According to Mahmood, bin Laden asked him how he could construct a bomb if the group already had the material. It is stunning to consider that two of the founding fathers of Pakistan's weapons program embarked independently on clandestine efforts to organize networks to sell their country's most precious secrets for profit.

Although the UTN network apparently was neutralized before it had a chance to fulfill al Qaeda's long-held aspirations to obtain what bin Laden has called a "Hiroshima bomb," this was the first known case in which a "WMD for hire" network had been created specifically to provide weapons of mass destruction to terrorist and extremist groups. In this context, members of the UTN group represented the broad set of scientific-and engineering-related capabilities necessary to construct an improvised nuclear device. They had an international reach. Most importantly, some prominent members of the group had once held positions in the Pakistani establishment and had connections to people on the inside with access to nuclear materials. It is not certain that this group had the wherewithal to have succeeded in its desire to enable al Qaeda's quest for a bomb, but it is encouraging that resolute Pakistani and U.S. follow-up action apparently nipped in the bud a potentially serious threat. There are troubling indications that these insider threats are not anomalies. In the Khan and UTN cases, the rogue senior officers and their cohorts in the nuclear establishment were not caught by Pakistan's security establishment. It would be foolhardy to assume that such lapses could not happen again. The Pakistani military, intelligence, and nuclear establishments are not immune to rising levels of extremism in the country. There is a lethal proximity between terrorists, extremists, and nuclear weapons insiders. Insiders have facilitated terrorist attacks. Suicide bombings have occurred at air force bases that reportedly serve as nuclear weapons storage sites. It is difficult to ignore such trends. Purely in actuarial terms, there is a strong possibility that bad apples in the nuclear establishment are willing to cooperate with outsiders for personal gain or out of sympathy for their cause.

### *Relying on Secrecy*

Pakistani authorities certainly recognize the gravity of this problem. One of the ways they are coping is to emphasize secrecy and clandestinity over the more visible manifestations of nuclear security. The U.S. and Russian model of nuclear security relies on redundant layers of high walls, gates, and guards at sites in order to produce a highly visible image of impenetrability that will deter those seeking to gain access to them. Essentially, Pakistan has sacrificed some of the advantages of the traditional approach to security in favour of reducing unique vulnerabilities and threats arising from the circumstances in which it finds itself.

The thrust of the Pakistani military's strategy is to reduce its vulnerability to a nuclear security incident by systematically denying outsiders opportunities to gain illicit access to nuclear weapons. Consequently, the nuclear establishment is distributed geographically: Materials processing and weapons production facilities are consolidated in sites near Islamabad in areas under tight government control. Special nuclear material is reportedly stored apart from the weapons themselves. Warheads are reportedly stored separately from delivery systems.

Another precaution taken by the Pakistani military is to maintain strict secrecy over the location of storage sites and to transport and deploy weapons clandestinely rather than in convoys that have a stronger, highly visible security profile. These security precautions produce fewer visible signs of movements, thereby lowering the risks associated with possible theft of or attack on weapons at their most vulnerable point, in transit.

Paradoxically, this dependence on secrecy over physical security could backfire in the event a malicious insider gained access to locations of weapons storage sites, transportation routes, and similar insider information, especially because more moving parts are involved in assembling weapons when they are being deployed. In such a case, there would be fewer barriers between an outside group and the bomb.

The emphasis on maintaining clandestinity and secrecy in nuclear activity may hold other unintended consequences. For instance, Pakistan's development of indigenous weapons-use controls-permissive action links (PALs)-for partially disassembled weapons systems is more challenging than for PALs built into a fully integrated weapons system. Moreover, although unpredictability in nuclear-related movements and activity is good from the standpoint of frustrating would-be attackers, it could conceivably increase the chances of a dangerous miscalculation of Pakistan's actions by India, especially in a crisis in which Pakistan's archrival interpreted a nuclear terrorist incident as a threat against its security.

Another trend that militates against achieving perfect nuclear security is the rapid expansion of the Pakistani nuclear program. Pakistan's nuclear arsenal roughly doubled from 1998 to today's total of a hundred weapons, in round numbers. In the coming years, as new plutonium-production capacity at the Khushab site comes online, the total number of nuclear weapons could increase dramatically. Using plutonium as the nuclear-explosive material also would allow Pakistan to build smaller nuclear weapons.

The expansion of the nuclear weapons program will mean more material, more construction of facilities for processing material and manufacturing weapons and delivery systems, and more demands for waste storage and transportation. More of everything means more vulnerabilities, more places for something to go wrong.

Finally, Pakistan's expanding nuclear program and the insider threat that accompanies it is taking place in the context of the broader trend of increasing instability in the country. In terms of assigning probabilities to a potential nuclear meltdown, the most likely scenario that Pakistan may confront is not a loss of control over one of its nuclear weapons, although that risk certainly must be addressed. Rather, threats are more likely to emerge from the increasing number of potential pathways to a bomb, specifically, the increasing threats posed by a slow hemorrhaging over time of technology, design, and construction knowledge and materials that might ultimately cross the threshold and produce a terrorist bomb. This phenomenon is more complicated and subtle and more difficult to counter than the scary, well-hyped scenarios involving loose nukes stolen by terrorists from a storage site or in transit.

## Rising Risks

Unfortunately, there is growing rationale and shared motivation for insiders and outsiders to cooperate out of shared hatred toward the United States.

This kind of externally directed hostility may not be readily recognized in its formative stages by those guarding the nuclear weapons arsenal, because these threats are not being directed against the Pakistani government. Countering such insidious trends will require not only a strengthening of defences, but also a weakening of the threats, the sources of anti-U.S. antipathy that contributes to the possibility that al Qaeda will be able to convince an insider to help its cause. In terms of assessing any spike in these risks, the overall direction of pro-Taliban and anti-Taliban sentiment in the country should be closely watched.

The National Command Authority (NCA) that controls the use of nuclear weapons remains under the tight reins of the Pakistani military, not the civilian leadership. It is not obvious how effectively the military might respond to unprecedented challenges to its nuclear command and control procedures. The bifurcation of civilian and military roles seems to have been left deliberately ambiguous under the NCA; certain responsibilities that nominally have been given to the civilian leadership may be carried out by the military. The potential discrepancy between constitutional authorities and actual execution of those authorities raises the risks of uncertainty and confusion in a crisis. For example, the Pakistan civilian leadership, especially if a more extreme government assumed power, might issue orders or make statements concerning the status and control of nuclear forces contradicting those made by the Pakistani military commander-in-chief.

Confusing and chaotic conditions would likely accompany a deterioration of the general security situation in Pakistan.

One can only imagine how difficult it might be for the military to respond effectively to an unanticipated challenge to command and control communications that results from a surging Taliban offensive. Worse yet would be the potential uncertainties caused by an extremist bid to seize power. In such cases, some elements of the military's loyalties might be divided, even in the event that overall control over nuclear forces continues to be assured. By way of example, if a colonel in charge of hundreds of troops decided to take over a nuclear weapons site, would the military be able to resolve such a situation in a way that did not lead to catastrophe?

It is not likely that the Pakistani military and nuclear security establishment can fully consider all such challenges to its authority in advance or, even if it can, that such scenarios would unfold precisely as anticipated. For example, how would the military be able to respond to a breakdown of security involving a loose nuke, an ambushed convoy, or a takeover of a nuclear facility? Even if the military managed to resolve any threats on the ground immediately, there are questions concerning the military and civilian roles in the NCA that are not well understood outside Pakistan or perhaps even within the country. It is possible that, in extreme circumstances, the Pakistani government would be hard-pressed to reassure the outside world, especially India, that all its nuclear assets are under the full and authoritative control of the military.

Fortunately, it appears that the odds of such a security breakdown are very low, at least from an assessment based on the current realities of the security situation in Pakistan. The authorities appear to be serious about countering Taliban advances in the country.

That is vital because ensuring continued stability and law and order is the most important factor in averting the possibility of a nuclear catastrophe. As Pakistan moves forward to face an uncertain future, the government faces an ongoing challenge to its authority and myriad threats against which it must defend. With the passage of time, the odds steadily increase that Pakistan will face a serious test of its nuclear security.

For its part, the United States must be fully prepared to respond to this eventuality. The United States should continue to do all it can to assist Pakistan in upgrading its nuclear security. U.S. government assistance to Pakistan has been a wise investment, even without full transparency into the expenditure of funds. The United States should be satisfied that anything that helps upgrade Pakistan's nuclear security is an investment in its own security. No country, including Pakistan, can be expected to risk exposing the details of its nuclear security posture and readiness to another country. Most importantly, U.S. assistance has improved bilateral nuclear ties between Washington and Islamabad, engendered trust, established more reliable lines of communication, and enhanced the possibility of more effective consultation and coordination in a crisis.

Pakistan and the United States should be prepared to take cooperation one level higher. Both countries should consider unprecedented ways to address the more extreme contingencies on a cooperative basis to the extent that such action is feasible and realistic. In the interest of bridging gaps in nuclear security planning, senior-level officials should use existing channels of communication to discuss, behind closed doors, their specific concerns, including various security vulnerabilities that may emerge. Having such a dialogue early on, before an incident occurs, might help lower the risks of either side making a serious misstep based on miscalculations arising from inadequate information, misplaced assumptions, or the sensitivities that inevitably accompany nuclear-related decision-making. In addition, Pakistan should receive high-level reassurances concerning U.S. nonintervention in a crisis, possible means of assistance, and so on. Moreover, senior officials in both countries should agree to pursue specific joint actions and special communications mechanisms to be activated during a crisis, such as responses to a stolen or missing nuclear weapon or takeover of a nuclear facility.

Finally, increasing the level of transparency and predictability between India and Pakistan is absolutely vital. Neither party can afford to make a miscalculation in the heat of the moment that might escalate into a nuclear confrontation.

# 6

# Terrorism in Pakistan

## INTRODUCTION

Terrorism has emerged as the most ominous threat to the global peace and security. Transcending of the geographical boundaries, this growing menace has directly or in-directly affected most of the countries with having varying degrees of terror, havoc, destabilization and devastation. Pakistan is the major victim and worst hit owing to its contiguity with the epicenter of terrorism i.e. Afghanistan. It has posed an extremely serious threat to the integrity, stability, progress and internal security of the country. Besides our internal vulnerability, competing interest, intrigues and nefarious designs of external players in the region have profoundly compounded the milieu. We have, therefore, no option but to thwart the heinous design of the internal and external enemies by facing this challenge squarely.

The phenomenon of extremism and terrorism is extremely complex, fraught with awesome socio – economic, politico-religious and military implications. It is politically destabilizing, economically crippling and militarily devastating. Having fathomed the perils of this menace for the integrity of Pakistan, our government has taken a bold and principled stand to root out terrorism from our soil.

In pursuance of our national policy and resolve to combat terrorism with all our might, a large number of army formations and troops are engaged in war against particularly in FATA, Swat, Baluchistan and some other areas neighboring of Afghanistan.

Pakistan is front line state in war against global terrorism. Pakistan Army has played a key role in breaking the back of Al-Qaeda and foreign Taliban by killing and apprehending most of the militant leaders, busting their bases and destroying their sanctuaries. In the accomplishment of this noble and sacred task, army has made unprecedented sacrifices.

While our operational preparedness and battle worthiness attained through sustained training our the year for conventional operations have stood us in good stead in undertaking myriad operations successfully in the war against terror, we have also suffered heavy causalities in some of the operation due to the inadequate training in LIC. In order to minimize our losses in life, weapons/ equipment, to rejuvenate our traditional fighting spirit and successfully combat terrorism. Our grey areas on LIC training and conduct of counter terrorism operations need to be addressed at priority.

## HISTORICAL PERSPECTIVE OF TERRORISM

Terrorism is often understood as new form of warfare and relatively a modern technique to operational engagement. In fact it was documented 2000 years ago by a Jewish sect known as Zealots:-

a. Terrorism appears in the Bible's Old Testament, and there were frequent incident of political murder, even systematic assassination, e.g. the murder of 'Julius Caeser'

b. During 8 century, the group of assassins called Fida'I led by Hassan Bin Sabbah, a pronounced pioneer of suicide terrorism, perpetrated the killing of governors, prefects, caliphs and crusader king of Jerusalem.

c. Terrorism continued to be active right from the Middle Ages up to the Modern Times wars of Thirty years (1618-1648) including the Napoleonic Wars (1799-1815)

d. Between 14 and 17 centuries, the Peasant Revolution spread throughout Europe particularly in Britain and Germany. In early 19 century (1808-1813), the first major guerrilla band appeared in Spain against the

French rulers. This movement introduced the term 'guerilla'.

e. The high tide of terrorism rose toward the end of the 19 century. Among the main active groups were the Irish Rebels, the Russian Socialist Revolutionaries and assorted anarchists all over Europe and North America. But secret societies were also actively spreading terrorism in Egypt as well as in India and China, aiming at national liberation.

f. The violence of 19 century terrorist's was noteworthy; they killed a Russian Tzar (Alexander II), American president (William McKinley in 1901 and before him in 1881, James Garfield) and King Umberto of Italy.

g. One particular terrorist act, the assassination of Austrian Archduke and heir to the throne, Francis Ferdinand and his wife Sophia on 28 June 1914 perhaps altered the course of world history, resulting in death of millions of people, leading to the fall of four imperial dynasties (German, Russian, Austro-Hungarian and Ottomans).

h. Post World War II historical perspective reveals a world with high potentials for violent conflicts. Since then there have been 160 or more armed conflicts around the world, of those, perhaps three quarters have been of so-called "low Intensity nature".

## TERRORISM ACTS IN PAKISTAN

Numerous terrorist acts also took place in Pakistan some of them are as under:-

a. In Pakistan, sporadic acts of terrorism can be traced back from the assassination of Mr. Liaqat Ali Khan.

b. Indian sponsored "Mukhti Bahni" in East Pakistan can also be termed one of the organized terrorist movements resulting in creation of Bangladesh. Insurgency in Baluchistan was yet another event involving Pakistan Army to such an environment

c. Pakistan was subjected to foreign sponsored terrorism for its moral support to afghan Mujahedeen against Russian Intervention.

d. The activities of RAW in collaboration with other anti Pakistan elements/ agencies worked on Afghan refugees in particular to create harassment and lawlessness in various parts of the country.

e. Recently the assassination of the Benzair Bhutto is one of the brutal act of terrorism in Pakistan

### *Post 9/11 Environment*

After 9/11 the direction of terrorism in the world changed its face some salient aspects are:-

a. The environment of 9/11 was a direct confrontation between America and the Forces against America/ America interests. Non state actors mainly Al Qaeda worked as a magnet for all those who were In search of an allying point/ base. This was future compound by direct onslaught of Americans forces in Afghanistan. Iraq and Afghanistan played major role in dragging Pakistan onto this quagmire. Interests of extra regional forces compounded the situation further. Subsequent event drew Pakistan into international lime light due to its geographical location bordering Afghanistan and Iran.

b. Since Taliban who were Pashto speaking residing mostly in southern part of Afghanistan adjacent to FATA, were the target of American forces, hence on Pakistan side of Pak Afghan border, Sympathies with them rose to the highest point among the locals. Afghan militants were welcomed and assisted by locals. However, international environment were against this nexus. American President remarked on the rubbles of World Trade Center "America today is on the bended knee in prayers for people whose lives were lost here.... The rest of the world hears you. And the people, who knocked these buildings down, will hear all of us soon". They declared Taliban responsible for the tragedy because Al Qaeda's main leadership in Afghanistan, which according to USA was organizing, planning and initiating anti American activities from the soil state ruled by Taliban.

c. Pakistan, due to its own compulsions, having recognized Taliban regime was justifying its stance at various international forums. However 9/11 surprised the whole world including Pakistan and this blatant act of terrorism could not be justified. Pakistan principally condemns terrorism in all its forum and manifestations. It was the need of the hour to work with international community to rid the world of this peril.

d. The government of Pakistan took a considered decision to support Global War against Terrorism, safeguarding own national interests. Revenging attack on World Trade Center, USA retaliated and because of its operation in Afghanistan (Tora Bora), Pakistan Army was deployed on the western border to seal it and prevent influx of militants into Pakistan. It was a golden opportunity to open "No Go areas" in FATA and bring it par with the rest of the country.

## UNDERSTANDING PAKISTAN'S APPROACH TO THE WAR ON TERROR

Although Pakistan has been a frontline state in the war on terror since the tragic events of September 11, 2001, there is no doubt that General Musharraf initially cast his lot with the United States mainly as a result of deep fears about what U.S. enmity might imply for Pakistan's long-standing rivalry with India, its efforts at economic revival, its nuclear weapons program, and its equities in the conflict over Kashmir. Desirous of protecting Islamabad's interests in these areas and to avoid Pakistan becoming a target in the campaign against terrorism, Musharraf reluctantly cut loose Islamabad's ties with the Taliban— a force it had nurtured, trained, and equipped for almost a decade in its effort to secure control over Afghanistan— and stood aside as the U.S.-led coalition assisted its detested antagonist, the Northern Alliance, to rout its own clients and their al- Qaeda accomplices and seize power in Kabul. Because the al- Qaeda elements in Afghanistan during the 1990s were never directly dependent on the Pakistani Inter-Services Intelligence Directorate (ISID) for their success (despite maintaining a significant liaison relationship), the ejection of their Arab, African, and Central Asian mercenaries was viewed with fewer misgivings than the flight of the Pashtun- dominated Taliban, who were tied to Pakistan directly in terms of both patronage and ethnicity.

Islamabad's ties to the Taliban were so strong and so important that throughout the initial phase of Operation Enduring Freedom, General Musharraf and his cohort implored the United States to desist from decisively destroying Mullah Muhammad Omar's regime in Afghanistan. When this objective could not be secured, Pakistani leaders argued against all coalition military operations that would result in ejecting the Taliban's foot soldiers from their traditional bases in the southeastern provinces of the country. When these entreaties were also disregarded by the United States and the comprehensive defeat of the Taliban appeared inevitable as a result of joint U.S. and Northern Alliance military operations, Islamabad responded by covertly exfiltrating its army and intelligence personnel seconded to the movement— along with some key Taliban operatives, if Indian intelligence sources are accurate— while permitting the defeated stragglers to cross over to safety across the frontier and into Pakistani territory. Taliban forces and their al- Qaeda guests thus found their way across the highly porous Afghanistan- Pakistan border into the FATA. While Pakistani border patrols concentrated their efforts against the latter group, resulting in the seizure of numerous low- level al- Qaeda elements, these operations nonetheless were never rigorous or watertight enough and were, in any event, frustrated by other factors: the old tribal tradition of extending succor to strangers who ask for protection; the region's history of providing foot soldiers, first, for the anti- Soviet jihad and, later, for the war against the Northern Alliance in Afghanistan; the absence of a strong Pakistani state presence in this area; and the utterly hostile topography consisting of remote and difficult mountain terrain with poor lines of communication, all of which combined to bestow on the defeated remnants a substantial measure of sanctuary and assistance.

The U.S. inauguration of the "global war on terror" soon compelled General Musharraf to make good on his "principled" decision to join the U.S.-led coalition. This inevitably required Musharraf to confront the sources of terrorism that had developed internally in Pakistan, most of which ironically resulted from his own army's previous decisions to nurture radical Islamist organizations because of their utility to Islamabad's military campaigns in Kashmir and Afghanistan.

Four different terrorist groupings were implicated in this regard. The first were the domestic sectarian groups like the Sunni Sipah- e- Sahaba and its offshoot the Lashkar- e- Jhangvi and the Shia Tehrik- e- Jafria Pakistan and its offshoot the Sipah- e- Muhammad, which were engaged in violent bouts of bloodletting within the country. Although many of these groups had enjoyed the support of the Pakistani government, the military, and the intelligence services previously, their unexpected growth in power over time had become not only an embarrassment to their sponsors but also a serious challenge to domestic order. As Christine Fair has summarized it, "The scale of sectarian violence in Pakistan is staggering, with hundreds of people killed or injured in such attacks each year." The New Delhi–based Institute for Conflict Management has documented sectarian violence alone as claiming close to 5,000 lives in Pakistan since 1989, with incidents involving everything from targeted killings of high-profile civilians, to bombings of mosques and drive- by shootings of innocents, to pitched gun battles in major population centers. In one incident, for example, sectarian hostility in the town of Parachinar in the Kurram Agency involved a five- day war, where small arms, mortars, rocket launchers, and antiaircraft missiles were all used in a convulsive spasm that claimed hundreds of lives and injured many more.

Confronted by such challenges to the writ of his state, Musharraf was only too happy to exploit the opportunities offered by the war on terror to crack down on these groups and suppress them once and for all. He did so, however, only selectively. Focusing the government's energies primarily on those Deobandi and Shia groups whose objectives were out of sync with the military's perception of the national interest, he targeted Sunni groups such as the Lashkar- e- Jhangvi, the Sipah- e- Sahaba Pakistan, the Harkat- ul- Mujahideen al- Alami, the Jundullah, and to a much lesser degree the Harkat- ul- Jihad- e- Islami, as well as Shia threats such as the Sipah- e- Muhammad, primarily because they were engaged in "anti- national" jihadi violence within Pakistan rather than in support of Islamabad's external ambitions vis-à- vis India and Afghanistan. Using the entire panoply of coercive state capabilities, these entities were therefore put down with a heavy hand through arrests, targeted assassinations, and aggravated intergroup massacres. Although many of the tools used to defeat these perpetrators of sectarian violence were often unconstitutional, Musharraf shrewdly judged that the aggressive dismemberment of these groups would not evoke either domestic or international condemnation. He was right.

Using the opportunities therefore afforded by the global war on terror, the Pakistani security services systematically eliminated many sources of sectarian violence within two years of the campaign's initiation, even though they have been unable to conclusively eradicate the cancer of sectarian bloodshed within Pakistan itself. In part, this is due to the selectivity of Musharraf's antisectarian campaign. But the continuing fragmentation of these violent groups; their links to the wider networks of international terrorism now resident in Pakistan, various foreign sponsors abroad, and the flourishing madaris within the country; and the continuing utility of their gun- toting membership to different political parties and occasionally to governmental organs themselves imply that sectarian threats will be impossible to extinguish so long as "state policies of Islamisation and [the] marginalization of secular democratic forces" continue to persist in Pakistan.

The second set of groups, the terrorist outfits operating with Pakistan Army and ISID support against India in Kashmir, was treated in a remarkably different way compared with the anti-national sectarian militants inside Pakistan. These groups, such as the Lashkar- e- Toiba, the Jaish- e- Muhammad, and the Harkat-ul- Mujahideen, for example, were the long lances in the Pakistani campaign to wrest the disputed state of Jammu and Kashmir from India. Since the late 1980s, the Pakistani military has financed, trained, armed, and launched these cadres on their murderous missions into Kashmir and elsewhere inside the Indian union. Because the struggle for control over the disputed Himalayan state was fully under way by the time the global war on terror was inaugurated, these terrorist groups were more or less exempted from Musharraf's domestic campaign against violence and extremism.

This exclusion was justified both on the strategic rationale that Pakistan's participation in the war on terror was intended, among other things, to protect its freedom of action in Kashmir and on the repeated, though fraudulent, assertion that these groups, far from being terrorists, only personified the legitimate Kashmiri struggle for self- determination against India. In fact, of all the Pakistani- sponsored Deobandi terrorist groups operating against India in Kashmir and elsewhere, only one entity— the Hizbul Mujahideen— began life as an indigenous Kashmiri insurgent group; the others, including the most violent organizations such as the Lashkar- e- Toiba, the Jaish- e- Muhammad, and the Harkat-ul- Mujahideen, are all led, manned, and financed by native Pakistanis. This reality notwithstanding— and perhaps because of it— Islamabad continued to sustain the operations of these groups against India but, in an effort to maintain the consistency of its commitments to the global war on terror, now began to emphasize that its support took only the form of moral, and not material, encouragement.

This charade was rudely interrupted by the December 13, 2001, terrorist attack on India's parliament when, in response to New Delhi's subsequent military mobilization, Pakistan was compelled by U.S. diplomacy to initiate a series of measures to restrict the activities of its terrorist clients. The implementation of these actions, however, was at best halfhearted and inconsistent.

Far from seeking to extirpate these terrorist groups permanently, Musharraf sought mainly to defang India's threats of military action and to alleviate Washington's fears of an inconvenient Indo-Pakistani war. His overarching objective consisted of protecting these terrorist assets to the extent possible because they represented national investments— a "strategic reserve"—in Islamabad's subconventional war against New Delhi. Consequently, to this day, Musharraf has not sought to eliminate the Deobandi terrorist groups operating against India in Kashmir and elsewhere; he has instead sought only to modulate their activities, depending on the extent of satisfaction he derives from the prevailing state of diplomatic relations with New Delhi and the progress secured in the ongoing Indo- Pakistani peace process.

Although the Pakistani- supported infiltration of terrorist groups into Kashmir— but not into the rest of India— appears to have abated in recent years, most observers conclude that this phenomenon is linked either to Musharraf's desire not to provide India with any excuses to abandon the generally fragile peace process or to domestic crises within Pakistan. In any event, it is agreed that Musharraf simply has not made the decisive decision to abandon or eliminate the terrorist groups operating against India in the manner witnessed, for example, in the case of the more virulent anti- national sectarian entities operating within Pakistan.

The third group relevant to the Pakistani decision to join the U.S.-led coalition against terrorism consisted of the Taliban, that is, the Pashtun remnants of the regime ejected from power in Kabul as a result of the initial success of Operation Enduring Freedom. After their defeat at the hands of the Northern Alliance, the Taliban cadres hastily returned to the regions whence they originated. Many in the rank and file withdrew to their villages in the southern Afghan provinces of Helmand, Kandahar, Oruzgan, and Zabol as well as along the border areas on the western side of the Durand Line separating Afghanistan from Pakistan, that is, in the eastern Afghan provinces of Paktika, Paktia, Khowst, Nangarhar, and Konar. Given their significance as high- value targets, the core Taliban leadership— along with those Pakistani Pashtuns who had joined their movement— crossed over the

Afghanistan-Pakistan border into the relative safety of the FATA. Because most of the Taliban's fighters originally mobilized by the Pakistani ISID were drawn from the Ghilzai confederation of Pashtuns, which dominates eastern and southeastern Afghanistan, and from the other Pashtun tribes inhabiting the FATA, their return to these ancestral lands was not surprising. In fact, all the evidence relating to the incidence of terrorist attacks since 2001 suggests strongly that the war- fighting cadres of the Taliban continue to remain bivouacked in these areas.

The exact location of the supreme leadership of the Taliban movement, however, cannot be established with any self- evident clarity. Irrespective of where the rahbari shura (leadership council) centered on Mullah Omar and his closest associates found shelter in the immediate aftermath of their defeat, Afghan military and civilian intelligence officials as well as NATO commanders today believe that this coterie eventually found refuge in Quetta, the largest city and capital of Pakistan's Baluchistan Province, from where they continue to operate to this day. As Col. Chris Vernon, NATO's chief of staff for southern Afghanistan, declared forthrightly, "The thinking piece of the Taliban [operates] out of Quetta in Pakistan. It's the major headquarters— they use it to run a series of networks in Afghanistan." These networks, in turn, are judged to be directed by four subsidiary shuras based in Quetta, Miran Shah, Peshawar, and Karachi: the first three actually control or coordinate most of the ongoing terrorist operations occurring, respectively, along the southern, central, and northern "fronts" in Afghanistan, whereas the fourth is believed to connect the Taliban with the logistics, financial, and technical assistance conduits emanating from the wider Islamic world. The pattern of terrorist attacks occurring in Afghanistan from 2002 to 2007, again corroborates this judgment.

Because the Pakistani state was most intimately involved in the creation of the Taliban before their fall, Musharraf's antiterrorism campaign after September 11, 2001, deliberately avoided any concerted targeting of this group and, in particular, its senior leadership. No other explanation is consistent with the fact that, although Pakistani military, intelligence, and paramilitary forces apprehended scores of al- Qaeda operatives, including numerous key individuals in the al- Qaeda hierarchy, the senior Taliban leaders killed or captured in southern Afghanistan or in the FATA have numbered literally a handful in comparison. This asymmetry in seizures is all the more odd because, prior to Operation Enduring Freedom, Pakistani military and ISID liaison elements were deeply intertwined with all levels of the Taliban mand structure and its war fighters in the field. In contrast, the Pakistani intelligence relationship with al- Qaeda in Afghanistan was more tenuous, yet Pakistan's military forces were able to apprehend far more al- Qaeda cadres than Taliban operatives. These successes in regard to al- Qaeda have invariably been attributed by Pakistanis, including General Musharraf, to the fact that it was always easier to identify the ethnically alien al- Qaeda elements along the frontier in comparison with the Taliban who, being ethnically Pashtun, were able to disguise their identities by assimilating into the larger tribal population.

While this explanation is only partly true— non- native fighters have lived in and become amalgamated into the social structures of the Afghan- Pakistani frontier since at least the anti-Soviet jihad of the 1980s— it is also disingenuous because the Pakistani ISID was not only deeply involved in the recruitment, training, arming, and operations of Taliban fighters at multiple bureaucratic levels, but it also maintained an intense liaison relationship with the Ghilzai tribes whose population has been disproportionately represented in the Taliban. Since protecting these relationships was deemed to be especially critical for Pakistan's national security interests in the aftermath of the Northern Alliance victory in Kabul, the large number of Taliban foot soldiers who made their way into the FATA were largely ignored by Pakistani counterterrorism operations so long as they did not engage in any untoward activities that either called attention to their presence or magnified the troubles confronting the Pakistani state. All told, then, the Taliban network, just like the Pakistani- aided terrorist groups operating in Kashmir and elsewhere in India, was deliberately permitted to escape the wrath of General Musharraf's counterterrorism operations in the initial phase of the war on terror.

Such an approach, however, could not be extended to the fourth group, al- Qaeda, which had also taken up sanctuary in the FATA, particularly in South Waziristan initially. Although al- Qaeda continued to have sympathizers within the extreme fringes of Pakistani society even after the terrible events of September 11 were conclusively attributed to its operations, the Pakistani military establishment did not enjoy the luxury of slackening its campaign against this target because of the consequences for U.S.-Pakistani relations at a time when bilateral ties were just recovering after a decade of U.S. disfavor and when Washington had just embarked on a ferocious campaign against al- Qaeda worldwide. Most senior Pakistani military officers at the corps command level were also genuinely horrified by the destruction that al- Qaeda wreaked in New York and Washington and, fearing for their country's own future in the face of the monster now present in their midst, supported Musharraf's decision to engage and destroy this terrorist organization of global reach.

Pakistan's military, accordingly, began to prosecute the war against al- Qaeda with great vigor, if not always with finesse, through multiple instruments. These included providing the United States and its military with facilities and access for the prosecution of Operation Enduring Freedom in Afghanistan, and conducting various law enforcement and internal security operations (sometimes in cooperation with their U.S. counterparts) aimed at interdicting terrorist financing and apprehending and rendering terrorist targets for prosecution abroad. Most important, however, the Pakistani military initiated Operation Al Mizan, a large- scale effort that involved moving major military formations from the Army's XI Corps and elite Special Services Group (SSG) battalions into the FATA, an area where regular army units had not ordinarily been deployed for decades. These infantry forces joined the Frontier Corps regiments— the paramilitary formations usually located in the region— as a show of force in order to both reassert the strong state presence that historically was lacking and apprehend the al-Qaeda elements that had taken shelter within the area.

This military campaign, which took the form of a gigantic cordon- and- search operation, had several consequences. First, it resulted in the capture of numerous al- Qaeda and other extremist operatives— some 700 at last count— who have since been turned over to the United States. Because these individuals are mostly foreigners— non-South Asian arrivals living in what are essentially Pashtun lands— detecting their presence, while not easy because of the local support they receive from the natives for ideological reasons and sometimes simply out of greed or fear, was certainly easier.

Second, it forced some though by no means all senior al-Qaeda operatives— for example, Khalid Sheikh Muhammad and Ramzi Binalshibh— to leave the relatively secure FATA sanctuary and disperse further inward into Pakistan, where their insertion into less ideologically congenial surroundings and their need to rely on more complex means of communication increased their susceptibility to detection and arrest.

Third, the dramatic irruption of the Pakistani state into the FATA, through a significant military presence of the kind not seen in more than a century, resulted in making conditions sufficiently inhospitable for al- Qaeda such that its senior leadership and cadres were compelled to relocate under fire from South to North Waziristan and beyond, where they operate to this day. This forced displacement, which unfortunately remains at continuous risk of reversal, nonetheless had the beneficial effect of disrupting many planned terrorist operations, but the dispersal of the organization's leadership in the northern FATA, especially in the Bajaur Agency where the terrain is inhospitable, the population is violently pro-Taliban, and the presence of the Pakistan Army is thin, has inadvertently made the task of destroying the al- Qaeda core all the more difficult.

In any event, these outcomes suggest that although Pakistan began as a reluctant entrant into the global war on terrorism, it has since become an active participant in the struggle. More than 85,000 Pakistani troops remain garrisoned along the Afghanistan-Pakistan border— a deployment that predates the initiation of the global war on terror. A significant fraction of these forces, however, is engaged today in counterterrorism operations in the border areas, and more than 600 soldiers have already sacrificed their lives in this effort. Further, Islamabad itself has now become a victim of terrorism as a variety of groups, ranging from those previously nurtured and now discarded by the Pakistani state, such as the al-Alami faction of the Harkat- ul- Mujahideen, to more distant beneficiaries of past Pakistani policies, such as al-Qaeda, seek to wreak an orgy of revenge against institutions and individuals whom they had previously counted among their sponsors and friends.

That Pakistan has made significant contributions to defeating various terrorist groups is therefore undeniable, yet its larger campaign against terrorism has also been conspicuously selective and perhaps self- serving. While it has secured major gains in eradicating some domestic anti- national sectarian terrorist groups and has contributed disproportionately to the ongoing campaign against al- Qaeda, it has been much more reluctant to conclusively eliminate those terrorist entities operating against India in Kashmir and elsewhere and against Afghanistan both in the FATA and in transit back and forth to the southern and eastern Afghan provinces. Further, the protection of the terrorist infrastructure that supports these groups has produced undesirable blowback because the actors traditionally involved in perpetrating terrorism in Kashmir increasingly either coordinate with or directly assist the Taliban and al- Qaeda in operations against not only Afghanistan but also the United States and even Pakistan itself.

Clearly, strategic and geopolitical calculations play an important part in accounting for this segmented Pakistani response. Islamabad, for example, has long viewed the terrorist groups operating in Kashmir and now in other Indian states as useful instruments for executing its policy of "strategic diversion" against New Delhi. For this reason, Pakistan has been reluctant to target and eliminate these groups conclusively, preferring instead to alternately tighten and loosen control over their operations depending on how much satisfaction it receives from India at any given moment.

The decision to avoid targeting the Taliban was born of similar calculations. Initially, it was owed simply to the inclinations of senior Pakistani military commanders who were just not prepared to add insult to injury by physically eliminating the very forces they had long invested in, especially because they had now suffered the ignominy of having to consent to their client's defeat. Over time, however, the reasons for protecting the Taliban only grew stronger: India's growing prominence in Afghan reconstruction, its increased influence and presence in Afghanistan more generally, the weakening of the Hamid Karzai government in Kabul, the progressive souring of Pakistani- Afghan relations (including those between Karzai and Musharraf personally), and the disquiet about a possible U.S. exit from Afghanistan (a prospect inferred from the mid-2005 announcement that the United States would divest full command of Afghan combat operations to NATO) once again increased Pakistan's paranoia about the prospect of a hostile western frontier. It was exactly the desire to avert this outcome that led to the initial Pakistani decision to invest in sustaining the Taliban. And with fear of the wheel turning full circle gaining strength in Islamabad since at least 2005, the temptation to hedge against potentially unfavorable outcomes in Kabul— by protecting the Taliban as some sort of a "force- in- being"—only appeared more and more attractive and reasonable to Pakistan.

Although Pakistan's discriminative approach to fighting terrorism was shaped and implemented by General Musharraf in his dual capacity as president and previously chief of army staff, it would be erroneous to conclude that this prevailing strategy is owed simply to the whim of one man. This is particularly relevant today when Musharraf's hold on power has become progressively weaker and the future of his political status and effectiveness increasingly clouded. Rather, Musharraf's decisions in regard to counterterrorism strategy since 2001, although publicly perceived as personal dicta, invariably reflected the consensus among the corps commanders of the Pakistan Army and, hence, represent the preferences of Pakistan's military- dominated state. In other words, even if Musharraf were to suddenly exit the Pakistani political scene at some point, Islamabad's currently disconsonant counterterrorism strategy would still survive so long as the men on horseback continue to be the principal guardians of national security policy making in Islamabad. Because it is unreasonable to expect that the uniformed military will give up its privileges in this regard anytime soon— even if a civilian regime were to return to the helm in the future— the internally segmented counterterrorism policy currently pursued by Pakistan will likely persist for some time to come.

Even if it could be imagined that a civilian dispensation could wrest some control of Pakistan's national security policy from the military, it is not at all certain that the current strategic direction would change dramatically: a civilian regime would probably have greater incentives to combat all sectarian terrorist groups more evenhandedly, but that too is uncertain. After all, both the Pakistan People's Party led by the late Benazir Bhutto and the Pakistan Muslim League led by Nawaz Sharif have had problematic Islamist political allies in the past and, depending on the political exigencies of the moment, could harbor incentives to give even sectarian or otherwise radical entities a breather from prosecution, although that would likely be justified as only a temporary expedient. Both civilian parties historically also permitted the Pakistani military and intelligence services to aid, abet, and arm the terrorist groups operating in Kashmir and elsewhere in India, sometimes because they were simply powerless to prevent it but at other times with their full knowledge and consent. It also ought not to be forgotten that even a radically atavistic Islamist group such as the Taliban was raised, promoted, and unleashed by the civilian government of the late Benazir Bhutto (during her second term in office from 1993 to 1996) with the full collaboration of the Pakistani military and intelligence services— and that the Taliban continued to receive complete moral and material support under her civilian successor, the then prime minister, Nawaz Sharif.

Both the principal civilian political alternatives in Pakistan would likely continue to prosecute the current antiterrorist operations against al- Qaeda because there seems to be a fragile consensus among Pakistani political elites that this group remains a grave threat to both their country and the international community. This fact, however, only underscores the continuity that is likely to persist in Pakistan's approach to counterterrorism even if a civilian government were to ascend to power in Islamabad. Although there are likely to be differences in style, nuance, and emphasis, the weaknesses of Pakistan's moderate political parties, Islamabad's enduring interests vis- à- vis Afghanistan and India, and the likely inability of any civilian government to exercise comprehensive control over the Pakistani military and intelligence services all combine to suggest that dramatic changes in attitude and performance toward the Taliban and the terrorist groups operating on Indian soil may not be forthcoming. And, although sectarian groups within Pakistan may be pursued more uniformly and hopefully just as resolutely as the war against al- Qaeda, the net deviation from Musharraf's currently segmented antiterrorism policies may be either too subtle or too insignificant to really matter.

Ironically, the Bush administration itself bears some responsibility for reinforcing Musharraf's original instincts and entrenching what has now become the enduring Pakistani calculus. Although President Bush affirmed in the aftermath of the September 11 attacks that his war on terrorism would be total and that states supporting terrorist groups would be required to divest themselves of these entanglements decisively or face America's wrath, his own government never implemented his stirring vision in regard to Pakistan. Rather, during the Indo- Pakistani crisis of 2001–2002— a key moment of truth for Pakistan and its future course in the war on terror— successive U.S. intermediaries visiting the subcontinent pursued an approach that only permitted Islamabad to conclude that the war on terrorism was in fact eminently "divisible." By not pressing Pakistan to relinquish all its terrorist clients once and for all during that crisis— as Washington had previously compelled Islamabad to forsake the Taliban on September 13, 2001[36]—the United States lost a momentous opportunity to help Pakistan rid itself of its long addiction to terror. Instead, the administration's diplomacy, by declining to hold Musharraf accountable for breaching his serial promises to end Pakistani support for terrorism, enabled Islamabad to infer that so long as operatives belonging to "terrorist groups of global reach"—meaning al- Qaeda— were being regularly apprehended by Pakistan, the ISID's links to, and protection of, other regional terrorist organizations would not become a critical liability in U.S.-Pakistan relations.

The liberties thus afforded Pakistan in regard to sustaining its ties with local Kashmiri terrorist groups during the initial phase of the global war on terror consequently reinforced Pakistan's inclination to treat the Taliban remnants similarly. This blunder had few consequences as long as the Taliban movement was in remission, but it has proved to be a most costly lapse on the part of the United States because the sanctuary afforded by Pakistan to the Taliban— and especially its leadership— since 2002 has only permitted the group to rejuvenate and, once again, to begin offensive operations in Afghanistan that, in effect, threaten to undo the gains secured by the early victories in Operation Enduring Freedom.

The U.S. neglect of the early Pakistani decision to ignore the Taliban as a target of counterterrorism operations can be explained only by the administration's single- minded concentration on the war with al- Qaeda. This obsession was no doubt justified at the time, but its inadvertent consequences have now come back to haunt the United States, NATO, Afghanistan, and the ongoing military operations associated with Operation Enduring Freedom more generally. By failing to recognize that the early immunity provided to the Taliban would eventually complicate the effort to defeat al- Qaeda— if for no other reason than that these two groups remain geographically commingled and because Taliban endurance in southern and eastern Afghanistan and in the FATA is an essential precondition for al- Qaeda's survival— the administration lost an opportunity to consolidate its political and military gains in Afghanistan while simultaneously compelling Pakistan to hasten its march away from extremism.

The Bush administration has now begun to press Musharraf to actively interdict the Taliban— an issue that did not become the subject of high- level U.S. demarches before 2005–2006—but it is not certain that, even if responsive Pakistani counterterrorism actions were to be mounted today, they would be as effective as they could have been had they been pursued in the administration's first term. This is because Pakistan's own current intelligence capabilities with respect to the Taliban are probably not as strong as they were when Mullah Omar and his associates were first ejected from Kabul.

Although it is certain that Pakistani information about the Taliban and their leadership is still better than that possessed by other intelligence agencies, including those of the United States, the probable atrophy of Islamabad's connections during the past several years of the war on terror, the strong and growing antagonism within Pakistan toward Musharraf's counterterrorism policies in the FATA, and the increasing opposition from Pakistan's fundamentalist political parties and their social bases of support toward Musharraf's domestic and foreign policies all viciously interact to increase the risk that belated Pakistani actions against the Taliban, including its leadership, may end up being far less successful than they otherwise might have been if executed a few years earlier. And that, in turn, implies not only that the challenges of defeating the Taliban are from a historical perspective rooted in fateful U.S. decisions to treat the Kashmiri terrorists differently when the administration should have done otherwise, but also that Washington ignored the Taliban until it was too late.

## TERRORISM PROBLEM IN PAKISTAN

The complex relationship between the state and the Islamists in Pakistan makes it difficult for the government to fulfil its promise of eliminating terrorism even if it had the will to stop all groups. India, in particular, argues that General Musharraf is willing to fight anti-U.S. terrorists affiliated with al-Qaeda only to the extent of securing U.S. assistance. From New Delhi's point of view, Pakistan is still unwilling to clamp down on jihadi groups that it sees as allies in its long-standing conflict with India. Pakistan became a centre for Islamic militants when it served as the staging ground for the West's war against Soviet occupation of Afghanistan beginning in 1979. During the anti-Soviet Afghan resistance, militants from all over the Muslim world passed through Pakistan to participate in the Afghan Jihad. They were, at the time, supported by the intelligence services of the West as well as Islamic nations. Some of them created covert networks within Pakistan, taking advantage of poor law enforcement and the state's sympathetic attitude toward pan-Islamic militancy.

Now that al-Qaeda and the Taliban have been uprooted from Afghanistan, they are using their former transit station as a temporary staging ground for terrorist operations. Domestic terrorist groups remain active, and at least some of them have developed tactical or strategic alliances with each other as well as with foreign groups.

Pakistan has paid a price for not confronting the terrorists in the past. They brought their battles to Pakistan, while holding out the promise of helping in Pakistan's conflict with India. Even before the current wave of attacks, al-Qaeda's ally, Egyptian Jihad, bombed and destroyed the Egyptian embassy in Islamabad on November 19, 1995. A few months earlier, on March 8, 1995, two employees of the U.S. Consulate in Karachi, Gary Durell and Jacqueline Van Landingham, were killed in a terrorist attack on a consulate van. On April 22, 1996 volatile devices were hurled on the U.S. Information Service building in Lahore. Four Americans and two Pakistanis working with the Union Texas Oil Company were killed on November 12, 1997, again in Karachi. On November 12, 1999 rocket attacks targeted offices of the United States government as well as the United Nations in Islamabad.

AT THE HEART of Pakistan's past support for Islamists is its conflict with India arising out of the dispute over Kashmir. Pakistan seeks implementation of UN resolutions for an internationally supervised plebiscite to determine the future of Muslim majority Jammu and Kashmir, which India claims as its integral part. India and Pakistan have fought twice over the territory since their independence in 1947.

Even while announcing what was billed as a break from the past, Musharraf 's January 12 speech highlighted Pakistan's preoccupation with Kashmir. "Kashmir runs in our blood," Musharraf said. "No Pakistani can afford to sever links with Kashmir.... We will continue to extend our moral, political and diplomatic support to Kashmiris. We will never budge from our principled stand on Kashmir."

By 1989, protests over a rigged state election in 1987 in Indian-controlled Kashmir had transformed into an insurgency. By all accounts, the insurrection was indigenous in its initial phase and represented Kashmiri frustration with Indian rule. India has also been held responsible for massive violations of human rights in

Kashmir, which Pakistan sees as the instigating factor in the continued militancy.

International media and human rights groups have been denied access to the disputed region by New Delhi, which limits the potential for agitating Kashmiri rights through political means. India's refusal to discuss Kashmir's future with Pakistan has been accompanied by international indifference over the issue. This in turn has led to the belief in Islamabad that militancy and violence may be the only means of internationalizing the core issue in the India-Pakistan dispute. Soon after the beginning of the uprising, Pakistan started applying the experience gained during the orchestration of anti-Soviet resistance in Afghanistan to the Kashmir insurgency. In addition to Kashmiri refugees, training was provided to Pakistani and international volunteers who sympathized with their Muslim brethren. Thus, Kashmir's indigenous struggle for self-determination became linked with the global jihad of the Islamists.

The United States has been worried by Pakistan's involvement with the Kashmir insurgency since its earliest days. In May 1992, the Bush Senior administration threatened to designate Pakistan a state sponsor of terrorism. The focus of U.S. concerns was the activities of Inter-Services Intelligence Directorate (ISID), which had been the CIA's counterpart in providing weapons and training to the anti-Soviet Afghan resistance.

U.S. Ambassador to Islamabad Nicholas Platt delivered a letter from Secretary of State James Baker to Prime Minister Nawaz Sharif saying, "we have information indicating that ISID and others intend to continue to provide material support to groups that have engaged in terrorism."

Ambassador Platt added verbally, "we are very confident of our information that your intelligence service, the Inter-Services Intelligence Directorate, and elements of the Army, are supporting Kashmiri and Sikh militants who carry out acts of terrorism."

"This support takes the form of providing weapons, training, and assistance in infiltration ... We're talking about direct, covert Government of Pakistan support. There is no doubt in our mind about this ... Our information is certain. It does not come from the Indian government. Please consider the serious consequences to our relationship if this support continues." Prime Minister Sharif responded to the U.S. demarche with assurances that any covert support to militants fighting India would be discontinued. But he also listed Pakistan's grievances with India over Kashmir and asked for an active U.S. role in resolving that dispute. The United States did not carry out its threat, though Pakistan was subjected to numerous sanctions over its nuclear program and, after Musharraf 's coup in 1999, for its lack of democracy.

Ten years later, little has changed in Pakistan's basic stance. The government denies direct involvement in supporting the militants, emphasizes the indigenous character of the Kashmiri resistance and holds private citizens and groups responsible for any support mobilized in Pakistan for the Kashmiris. Like Sharif in 1992, Musharraf, too, links the end of militancy to the resolution of the Kashmir question even after the changed circumstances since September 11.

Over the years, the connection with Kashmir has provided social respectability to the jihadi movement, which has ambitions beyond Kashmir and Pakistan. The state apparatus, particularly the Pakistani armed, looked upon the jihadis as low-cost foot soldiers who could tie down large numbers of Indian troops in Kashmir. In the process, the jihadis managed to lay the foundations of a vast infrastructure that includes newspapers and magazines, Islamic charitable trusts, and religious schools (madrassas). Tolerance and covert support of extremist groups have allowed them to spread their tentacles throughout Pakistani society and to mobilize large sums of money for their operations. Ideologically motivated religious extremists have also developed links with organized crime, especially in the city of Karachi. At times, this underworld alliance appears to command greater means than those of the country's police or intelligence services.

It is also difficult for some members of the law enforcement machinery to look upon Islamists as enemies of the state, after almost two decades of treating them as national heroes. One of the accused in the kidnapping and murder of Daniel Pearl was an employee of the Special Branch of Karachi police. A member of the paraarmed Rangers has been charged with plotting to murder Musharraf in concert with the group responsible for the car bomb attack at the U.S. Consulate in Karachi.

Pakistan has looked upon militant Islam as a strategic option for at least three decades, going back to the Bangladesh war with India in 1971. The anti-Soviet Afghan resistance fortified the relations between Islamists and the Pakistan armed, which had already been formed.

During the 1971 war against India and the people of Pakistan's then eastern wing, Pakistan's armed rulers had helped create volunteer militias of Bengali Islamists to fight the pro-Bangladesh militia and Indian troops. India had backed Bangladeshi fighters, though the trouble in then East Pakistan had started with Pakistani leaders' refusal to accept the prospect of Bengalis leading a united Pakistan after the general election of 1970. Instead of accepting political negotiations with Bengali politicians who secured a majority in that election, the West Pakistan-led armed chose to define the issue as a religious war between Islamic Pakistan and Hindu-backed Bangladesh.

The *al-Badr* and *al-Shams* Islamist militias could not help Pakistan retain control of Bangladesh. The Pakistani armed saw the bifurcation of Pakistan as the result of collaboration between secular nationalists and India. This led to the belief that Islamists were the most dependable political allies of the Pakistani state, especially in resisting Indian ascendancy in South Asia. This belief was strengthened during the anti-Soviet phase of the Afghan resistance. It also manifested itself in the form of Pakistan's support for the Taliban as well as the Kashmiri militants.

Pakistan's participation with the jihadi groups and its tolerance of armed extremist religious groups have contributed to generally ineffective law enforcement in the country. Musharraf himself has acknowledged that "Pakistan has become a soft state where law means little, if anything." Sectarian and ethnic murders as well as unexplained bombings have been a common occurrence for the last several years. At least five million small arms are in private hands in Pakistan. The most notable of these is the Kalashnikov assault rifle that served as the weapon of choice during the anti-

Soviet Afghan resistance. Even if General Musharraf decides finally to root out Islamic militancy, it will be years before the terrorist networks are completely eliminate. Resources of the police and intelligence-gathering agencies are over-stretched as the armed government uses them to stay in power and not just to keep crime and terrorism in check. The terrorists know that and take advantage of the state's weakness.

General Musharraf has clamped down on groups directly linked with al-Qaeda, and his government has helped the United States in apprehending foreign fighters, including high-ranking al-Qaeda fig-ures. But Pakistan will have to completely abandon using Islamic militants as an instrument of policy if terrorism is to be rolled back effectively.

India mistrusts Pakistani intentions, while Pakistan demands guarantees of dialogue over Kashmir before completely closing the chapter on Kashmiri militancy. India's refusal to withdraw the threat of armed force, initiated after the terrorist attack on parliament last December, was cited in Pakistan as an argument against reversal of policy. Supporters of the insurgents within Islamabad's policy-making circles said that Islamic militants would serve as an significant fifth column for Pakistani soldiers, sabotaging the much larger and better-equipped Indian army, in case of war.

More than two thousand members of Islamic militias were detained after General Musharraf announced the ban on five militant groups in his January 12 speech. Of these, 1,800 were released after signing pledges of good conduct. The government announced another crackdown in May, though it is likely that the four hundred militants detained this time around were part of the batch that had earlier been released. The government has arrested some leading militants, and several sectarian terrorists have been killed in police encounters. But Pakistan remains far from the stage of a complete break with its past covert support for Islamic militants.

The halfway move toward to tackling terrorism has left Pakistan vulnerable to pressure from both the Islamists and the international community. General Musharraf 's continuing war against domestic political rivals and the ongoing confrontation with India give the terrorists an advantage. They have nothing to protect, only targets to destroy. Musharraf, by contrast, must safeguard Pakistan's interests in addition to keeping himself, and the armed, in power.

Recent clashes between Pakistani forces with al-Qaeda fighters in the country's remote tribal areas indicate that there may be no turning back from General Pervez Musharraf 's decision to join the international coalition against terrorism. Even if Pakistan wanted to nuance its position on the issue, making distinctions between terrorists targeting the United States and Pakistan and terrorists opposed to India, neither its international friends nor the terrorists would allow such distinctions. Pakistan must now bravely complete its U-turn and end its reputation as a militant-infested nation. This can be accomplished if three conditions are met:

First, Pakistan's relations with India must move toward normalization. The tactical deployment of Islamic militancy as a means of combating Indian armed advantage was the starting point of Pakistan's involvement with the jihadis. In the absence of peaceful relations with India, it is unlikely that Pakistan will be able to completely close the option of calling upon Islamists in case of a confrontation with its traditional rival. From Pakistan's point of view, normalization of ties with India would involve the beginning of a process of dialogue about the future status of Jammu and Kashmir. The international community can encourage such a process, even without an immediate resolution of the dispute.

Second, decision making in Pakistan must revert to elected civilian leaders rather than being vested in the armed. Over the last ten years, the intelligence-armed complex in Pakistan has retained control of key decision making over matters relating to national security. As a result, conduct of diplomacy by civilians has been hampered by covert operations run by the armed. Civilian leaders have often been vilified or undermined for seeking to change the course of the country's Afghan and Kashmir policies.

Since 1999, direct armed rule has also subordinated Pakistani decision making to armed biases. Given the history of the last thirty years, in particular, it is clear that Pakistan's armed looks upon the Islamic militants as its allies against India. Mainstream civilian politicians, on the other hand, are generally secular and less strident about confrontation with India. Political and economic factors have weighed more in the calculations of civilians than have the strategic doctrines propounded by the armed.

PAKISTAN'S ISLAMISTS had never been able to do well in electoral politics until the legislative elections of October 10, 2002 when they won a significant number of seats in parliament and control of the North West Frontier Province (NWFP) provincial assembly with only 11 percent of the popular vote.

Their strength in recent years has been the direct result of covert state patronage and the armed's decision to assign them a role in its regional strategy. Even their recent election success resulted from the armed's efforts to weaken mainstream political parties. In the long run, however, a democratic political process is likely to contain Islamist influence, making it easier to isolate and eliminate extremist groups. Third, Pakistan must disarm all militias and dismantle the jihadi infrastructure. The international community should use all means at its disposal to ensure this is done with broad national consensus within Pakistan.

So far, the armed regime has not sought the cooperation of legitimate Islamic groups or mainstream political parties. Instead, it has antagonized traditional religious and political parties and allowed the war against terrorism to be cast as a U.S. war being fought with Pakistan's help.

Domestic political disputes have prevented any scheme of disarming local militias. For terrorism to be defeated, Pakistan would have to make a serious effort in re-orienting its national priorities from armed power and militancy toward modernity and development. Pakistan needs to roll back terrorism to secure its own future. But that objective cannot be attained through half-hearted measures or without a paradigm shift in the Pakistani armed's worldview. In the absence of a constitutional democratic government, Pakistan's ruling elite seeks acceptance through Islamic rhetoric and confrontation with India. Until that changes, terrorists will continue to feel emboldened to challenge the inefficient state apparatus that lacks both legitimacy and broad public support.

## PAKISTAN INTERNAL SECURITY AND TERRORISM

In the new literature on national security, internal factors are equally and sometimes more important than the traditional factors. The state of Pakistan at the moment has a stronger challenge to its security from the internal factors as compared to external. Pakistan faces multi forms of terrorism, no other country in the world is entangled in this problem as the Pakistan of today.

Ethnic terrorism which led to the dismemberment of Pakistan in 1971 resurfaced again on the question of linguistic differences in the some parts of the country but has been brought under control with the mainstreaming of ethnic political parties. Nationalist terrorism has mainly been witnessed in province of Baluchistan at regular intervals and mainly revolves around the issues of exploitation of resources and threat to the political identity and culture of minorities sub-nationalities.

Sectarianism in Pakistan was an extended version of rivalries between Northern Alliance and certain Sunni factions in Afghanistan and an aftermath of Iran & Iraq War, Jehadi terrorism which emerged in the post 9/11 scenario is by far the most serious threat to Pakistan so far because of its role as the front line state in war against terrorism. The tension between ultra conservative and moderate followers of Islam is mounting and weakening the sate structure. It is beyond the capacity of a single person or a one time effort to eradicate the deep rooted problem from the society. An institutional mechanism with wide ranging participation on regular and permanent basis is the only way to fight this menace.

No doubt for century's national security has been the basic and paramount concern of the nation states. While achieving enduring security has remained to be the most cherish able reward for states, over the years the concept of security has developed and considerably changed. Since its inception, Pakistan has been facing the challenge of national security. Traditionally, the threat to Pakistan's security has been external. However, today it can be arguably asserted that the major threat to national security in Pakistan emanates more from internal sources rather than external. The most serious threat facing Pakistan at the moment is posed by terrorism and the focus of our national efforts to ensure lasting security should be addressed to these internal factors.

***Comparative Levels of Violence in Pakistan, 2003-2007***

| Year | Civilians | Security Force Personnel | Terrorist | Total |
|---|---|---|---|---|
| 2003 | 140 | 24 | 25 | 189 |
| 2004 | 435 | 184 | 244 | 863 |
| 2005 | 430 | 81 | 137 | 648 |
| 2006 | 608 | 325 | 538 | 1471 |
| 2007 | 1523 | 597 | 1479 | 3599 |

Source: Institute for Conflict Management Database

### *Kind of Threats Faced By Pakistan*

Pakistan is facing the menace of terrorism in multiple forms. Pakistan at present is facing the most unique, difficult and gruesome faces of terrorism. No other country in the world is so deeply entangled in this problem as the Pakistan of today. All text book categories of terrorism confront Pakistan.

a. Ethnic threat. Pakistan had the first taste of ethnicity in the very early period of its being when the whole eastern wing agitated on the question of one national language – Urdu. The discontent established itself into a political movement and led ultimately to the unfortunate events of 1971 resulting in dismemberment of the state. The political struggle organized on ethnic lines gave a harrowing display of ethnic terrorism when militant organization like Mukti Bahni started eliminating West Pakistanis and specially the Punjabis. In the recent history of 'New' Pakistan, ethnicity emerged again in the wake of language riots. This time in the province of Sindh where Urdu speaking urbanites of Karachi and Hyderabad clashed with native Sindhis. The quest of Mohajirs – migrants in the wake of partition – for a parallel political identity as the fifth sub nationality along with the native Punjabi, Sindhi, Pashtuns and Balochs lead to large scale bloodshed and terrorist activities. The ethnic terrorism took hold of major urban cities for nearly a decade in late 80s and 90s but it has subsided for the time being partly due to rejuvenated economic activity and mainstreaming of the ethnic groups but mostly due to political stability giving enough economic and political space to the major players. Sub nationalists who like to call themselves nationalists have been fighting for a proper identity and recognition within the federation. Their main fears and apprehensions emanate from the pre-dominant role of Punjab in military and civil bureaucracy. They are frustrated by the prospects of facing permanently the majority of one province. They feel threatened about their value system traditions and culture. They also agitate against the use of their resources by other regions at cheaper costs. The poverty around them frustrates them and the advantaged amongst them successfully point their fingers to the other provinces to turn their gaze that way. The centre and its power corridor on the other hand take this insistence on rights as a kind of revolt against the centre and the rejection of federation. These strained relations have led the extremists amongst the nationalists/sub nationalists to take up arm against the centre quite regularly and sometimes against the state itself. The sub nationalist's terrorism has been emerging intermittently since military operations in Pakistan in 1960s.Governments of the day have been pointing at the external backing of both these types of terrorism. Pakistan on the whole has done fairly well to withstand the ethnic and sub nationalist terrorism even when fanned by external hands and the state structures have been able to work regularly and formally even in the face of these threats.

b. Sectarian Thereat. Another major form of terrorist threat facing Pakistan emanates from the sectarian terrorism. Since long, Pakistan has been a victim of the violence by sectarian motives, the recent years have witnessed a high rise in both the frequency and lethality of the sectarian violence. "Domestic terrorism in Pakistan, much of it associated with Islamist sectarianism, has become an increasingly serious problem affecting major Pakistan's cities". Sectarian terrorism in Pakistan has been an off shoot of some historical and some regional rivalries. There are four different schools of thought in Muslims of Pakistan i.e. Brailvi, Deobandi, Ahle Hadith and Shias. The first three are commonly grouped as Sunni but their thinking and its expressions are wide apart. The differences between Sunni and Shia thinking and intra Sunni faction have been historical but they have generally co-existed peacefully. The prolonged Iraq-Iran war and then post Afghan Jehad rivalries between Northern Alliance, pre-dominantly Shia and orthodox Sunni backed by Saudi Arabia and Pakistan, had adverse impact on sectarian harmony in Pakistan. The main source of recruitment for Jehad in Afghanistan had been Deo Bund and Ahle Hadith madrasas which got undue patronage from Zia govt. and finances from Saudi Arabia and some international agencies. These two groups aligned themselves with anti Shia forces in Afghanistan in late 1980s, and all along in 1990s. The battle in Afghanistan raged in the towns of Pakistan as well when there was pointless and ruthless killings of Shia's and then by Shias in large number. The country virtually had a blood bath on this account during the period 1985-1990. Sectarian terrorism has affected all parts of the country in varying degrees at different points in time. The northern areas and southern Punjab were the worst sufferers with sporadic strikes in major urban centers as well. The decade of 1990s has been the worst on this account. It did pose a serious threat to the internal security of the country but it has lost its sting due to two major reasons; one the people of Pakistan refused to get divided on sectarian lines and the fissure remained restricted to the fanatics and the extremists with the vast majority remaining detached, unsympathetic and rather antagonist to this approach. Secondly, the emergence of a far grave phenomenon of Jehadi terrorism overshadowed rather watering down the sectarian terrorism. Taking it as a national security concern the government of Pakistan need to overcome and address the genuine grievances of these sectarian groups. The groups involved in terrorist activities should be banned by the government, other groups to be brought into dialogue with government. It is the emergence of Jehadi terrorism, which is posing a real threat to the national security of Pakistan. The epicenter of Jehadi terrorism is Afghanistan. Initially, it was directed towards infidels and occupation forces but gradually it had to turn towards Pakistan, because of its alliance with the West in the War on Terrorism. The Jehad of 1980s, against the Soviet occupation of Afghanistan degenerated first into in fighting on ethnic lines and ethnic terrorism and then to sectarian terrorism with the arrival of Taliban on the scene. The Taliban took upon themselves the so called divine duty of enforcing Islamic order with the force of arms. Their narrow, myopic and ultra orthodox view of Islam is a force of regression and decadence. When the resistance moment against American occupation of Afghanistan started engulfing Pakistan also, the perpetrators of Jehadi terrorism were out to chastise the Muslims of Pakistan. The march of Jehadi terrorism towards Pakistan has refueled the sectarian terrorism as well and we have been witnessing the most lethal combination of these two evil forces. "The scene in Pakistan resembled a jungle in which every one was fighting at times everyone else. The terrorists were making money by drug trafficking and gun running, so they were heavily armed. Their operations endangered the very existence of the state, and no one put an estimate even remotely how many people were killed in this fighting". Military means cannot be the only solution to eradicate terrorism as causes of terrorism can be social, political and economic. The roots of Jehadi terrorism can also be found in social, economic and political factors. Looking at the present economic, social and political conditions in Pakistan it is inconceivable that there are going to be no Jehadi elements in the country. The Jehadi terrorism and its combination is threatening the national security of Pakistan on both the external and internal fronts. 'The acquisition of nuclear war heads by India and Pakistan threatened to make their resolved conflict over Kashmir go ballistic'. On the external front the vital freedom movement in Kashmir has been undermined. Though the freedom movement in Kashmir is essentially different from the Jehadi terrorism as it is against the occupation forces of India and not to enforce a particular doctrine, but Indians have got a golden chance to malign it by drawing analogies with the Jehadi terrorism. Resultantly forcing Pakistan to be more flexible than it is due on the issue of Kashmir.

***Sectarian Violence in Pakistan, 2007***

| Month | Incidents | Killed | Injured |
|---|---|---|---|
| January | 3 | 5 | 21 |
| February | 0 | 0 | 0 |
| March | 9 | 8 | 1 |
| April | 72 | 121 | 119 |
| May | 2 | 3 | 1 |
| June | 0 | 0 | 0 |
| July | 0 | 0 | 0 |
| August | 2 | 2 | 0 |
| September | 0 | 0 | 0 |
| October | 0 | 0 | 0 |
| November | 118 | 181 | 314 |
| December | 135 | 121 | 174 |
| Total | 341 | 441 | **630** |

Source: Institute for Conflict Management database

c. Islamic Militancy. Today the most challenging issue emanates from the Islamic militancy. Pakistan has become a hot bed of various militant organizations, resorting to violence in the name of religion. Since the Afghan jihad against the Soviet Union, the militant Islamic organizations have flourished and have been supported by the governments in Pakistan. Therefore their growth was not controlled. One of the most major damages of the 1980s United States – Afghan War was the support provided to anti modern, extremist and intolerant forces of this region. To defeat the Soviet, the US and Pakistan government provided official support to militant and fundamentalist

Islamic groups, which eventually led to religious extremism and sectarianism. This religious radicalism spread out in the other parts of the world also. Those forces became influential which rejected tolerance and secularism. With the changed regional and global environment, Pakistan drastically needs to change its approach towards the militant organizations. 'Sponsoring terrorism is like riding a tiger. Pakistan has to pay a heavy price for its support for Taliban. Even though Musharraf demonstrated wisdom by supporting US war on Terror against Taliban in neighboring Afghanistan, the country continues to be caught in a very complex web of terrorist activity, with greater radicalization of extremists groups'. The bases of this militant challenge operates in the Tribal areas of west of Pakistan and North West Frontier Province and Federally Administered Tribal Area (FATA). These areas mostly comprise of the Pushtuns and ethnic groups which are conservative, have close religious and tribal links with Pushtoon in Afghanistan and anti western. 'The Pushtun tribal areas have long been a heaven for displaced Afghans and refugees'. The hilly and difficult terrain of this region has turned out to be a heaven for militant organizations both foreign and national. The foreign militants over here mainly are Uzbek, Chechens and Pushtun Afghanis.

d. Ethno-Nationalist Threat. In Pakistan, minority and separatist movements are common. In the south west of Pakistan is the province of Balochistan which is mostly a tribal area, over there, intermittent gorilla war has been a feature since last two decades.10 This is another major form of terrorist threat to Pakistan which is of the separatist nature. The largest but the most underdeveloped area of Balochistan currently is the centre of this threat. It is the ethno-nationalist conflict between the government and the separatists for long that these separatists comprising of tribal militants have been indulged in violent acts for more political and economic authority in Balochistan. In Balochistan the various insurgents have adopted various violent tactics to sabotage the system. This problem if not resolved in time has the potential to challenge the national integrity of the state.

e. Threat To Creating State Within The State. Another new form of terrorism which has started to challenge the state is the takeover by the students, of religious seminaries in the capital city Islamabad of a children's library. The students and administration of madrasa lately took over law in their hands abducting women, police men and Chinese nationals on various charges thus creating state within the state. This brought great embarrassment to the government at both national and international level.

## EXTERNAL FACTORS FOR TERRORISM IN PAKISTAN

Identifying and dealing with internal factors are just one aspect of solving Pakistan's terrorism puzzle. External factors cannot be ignored either. It is clear that the governments of other countries, or groups from there with vested interests, have used Pakistan for their causes.

a. Indian Role

(1) While other countries did not have any ill will against Pakistan, India has been a long time sponsor of separatist movements in the country. Indian funding of Sindhi and Pashtun separatists has been an open secret in Pakistan. This author once visited a neighbor who came back injured from a fight in a Karachi college. Upon asking how students can get so many arms to fight each other, he revealed which classmates were getting the arms and support from India which were being used in those ethnic fights.

(2) India, with which it has fought three wars over the issue of Kashmir, is probably among the most active external elements to create violence and terror in Pakistan. Knowing that the country supports the Kashmiris' resurgence, India has supported and financed terrorist attacks in Pakistan, sometimes burning train stations, other times providing arms in ethnic conflicts. Or it engages in random shootings

through agent provocateurs or supports criminal elements.

(3) Sometimes it seems that Pakistanis and Indian agencies settle scores between themselves through terrorist activities. In the early 1980s, seven Pakistani train stations in Sindh were burned down. But the interesting thing was that those processions were far away from the train stations. Some Indian agents were arrested and then there was silence in the media until suddenly one day 27 Indian train stations in the state of Punjab were burned down. That was also followed by a curious silence in the Indian media about who did it.

b. Russian Factor

(1) Remember the "Hathora" (hammer) groups of the 1980s? These terrorists would attack innocent civilians as they slept, crushing their heads with hammers. After a series of these terrifying incidents, law enforcement discovered that the vicious culprits were from the Soviet bloc, teaching a lesson to Pakistan for its pro-Afghanistan policy.

(2) Another was the phenomena of shootings in Masjids, now commonly associated with the Shia-Sunni conflict in Pakistan. Curiously, this method of terrorism was not a response to particular grievances. Rather, it was very obviously an attempt to ignite violence, hatred and dissension between groups that had a potential for conflict.

(3) For instance, my son was once standing outside a Pakistani Masjid after prayers when suddenly, two terrorists on a motorcycle with their faces covered appeared. Facing the mosque's gate, one of the terrorist sprayed it with bullets and drove off. This was a well-known multi-ethnic mosque in a city that was ethnically divided. This meant that the terrorist attacker probably didn't know the ethnically diverse nature of the worshippers. The attack failed to ignite a conflict between any groups because those killed and injured

were part of all communities.

(4) On other occasions, these terrorists, however, were successful in starting ethnic or sectarian violence because they targeted one specific group. The February 26, 2002 attack on a Shia mosque in Rawalpindi which killed ten people was conducted in exactly the same manner. This attack, because it targeted a predominantly Shia mosque, could serve as an incentive to Shia gangs to retaliate against Sunni mosques. Most religious leaders believe that although now there are well-known armed groups on both sides. Initially this conflict was engineered by others.

(5) Pakistan needs to strengthen checks on diplomats in the country by not allowing them to use their position to foment internal destruction and dissension. Pakistan must take a strong stand in ensuring that they do not go beyond promoting legitimate public relations for their countries by cultivating a sectarian clientele, be it ethnic or religious.

(6) Because of the Kashmir issue, it is unlikely that India will reduce its support to dissent and subversion in Pakistan any time soon. Therefore, it is important for Pakistan to enhance its counter-intelligence operations within the country to reduce the subversive support to terrorism within its borders.

## Role of Law Enforcing Agencies In Controlling Terrorism

After 9/11 incident and also when Pakistan Govt. realized the gravity of the threat posed by the uncontrolled militant elements, the govt. decided to establish the writ of the state in these areas. Pakistan military initiated operations against these forces and had to face stiff resistance. Wana operation which was started by the military became very controversial and has brought about heavy losses to the government forces and has also resulted in heavy criticism of the government. But still the Pakistan Army Along With other law enforcing agencies is playing its role in troubled areas of Pakistan to control terrorist activities in Pakistan

## *Possible Solutions to these Internal and External Problems*

Some of the possible solution of the problems that are been faced by Pakistan are as under:-

a. Formal Education Needs to be Enhanced with the Message of Tolerance: The first effort should be on the educational front. Pakistan has made significant improvement in its literacy rate in the last ten years. There is a popular national consensus about the importance of education. It is important to develop the curricula and syllabi of the first twelve years of education and to rewrite books on Islamic studies, social studies, history, Urdu, and English for all school levels to strengthen the elements which deal with pluralism, the rights of others, tolerance, justice and love. These books need to develop a unique mix which relies on Pakistan's Islamic heritage but also benefits from the content and techniques developed for the multicultural education movement in America and inner-city educational experiments.

b. Dialog Between Shias and Sunnis: An ongoing dialog between the leaders of the two groups at a national as well as at the city level is important. Many times, culprits of the violence between the two groups have been unknown gunmen who have killed at either Sunni or Shia Masjids with no one claiming any responsibility. Most leaders from both sides are not involved in the violence. Most Masjids do not preach violence against any group. Then who starts these fights? If leaders from both sides engage each other in dialog, there is a good chance that they will be able to help save lives on both sides. If, for 1,000 years, with little exception, Shias and Sunnis have lived together peacefully, there is no reason for this extraordinary surge in violence of the last decade.

c. Regular Conference Between Ethnic Groups in Karachi: Karachi has seen the most ethnic violence and still it manifests the resilience of Pakistanis by continuing to be the most multi-ethnic city of Pakistan. At the height of ethnic violence, Dr. Akhtar Hameed Khan developed a dialog between two warring factions and was able to develop an island of peace. If the civil leadership facilitates a dialog at the city level and puts the Muhalla (neighborhood leadership) in contact with each other, many of the incidents could be averted as they work together on a common agenda in their neighborhoods.

d. Dialog between Muslims and non-Muslims: Most Pakistanis rarely meet a non-Muslim considering it is Muslim majority country. Muslim leadership in civil society needs to take the initiative to develop a positive relationship with the minorities living in their midst. Muslims must understand and properly deal with the concerns of Christians, Hindus and Qadianis in Pakistan. A dialog between people of different faiths will reduce tension and enhance the chances for peace.

e. A Drug Jihad is Needed: A major Jihad against drugs is overdue for Pakistani society. One cannot think of winning the safety and security of Pakistani citizens unless a massive educational movement is unleashed. It should accompany rehabilitation programs. Masjids and Islamic organizations can be enlisted in the fight against drugs both as instruments of mass education and centers for rehabilitation programs. Since crime and terrorism in Pakistan are linked with drug trafficking and drug abuse, it will not be possible to deal with the issue of security without dealing with the issue of drugs.

f. Education of Police: Pakistani police need better education, better training and refresher courses on an ongoing basis. So that they can come up to the standards of new era.

g. Better Arms and Equipment is Needed: Pakistan makes the type of equipment which can help the police. But equipment does not mean only weapons. It includes computers, databases, detection gear, testing equipment and DNA technologies.

h. Electronic Surveillance Equipment to Fight High-Tech Criminals: Cell phones and emails are being used by criminals along with other citizens. However, in the absence of electronic monitoring systems, the police resorts to funny things like banning all cell phone usage which has been done more than once in Karachi. This of course doesn't stop the criminals, but it hinders business and the average Pakistani who can afford it an important tool whereby he can quickly access safety in a dangerous situation. Electronic monitoring systems are very much needed in the urban terrorist culture of Pakistan.

i. A Research and Analysis Wing of the Police Academy: Pakistan needs to start learning from criminals while trying to fight crime. There should be surveys of those in prison and crime statistics. We need to learn about criminals, trends in crime statistics and criminology. This is not the traditional Pakistan. The crime's Pakistan is facing is a fairly new ball game.

j. Empowering Citizenry: While Pakistan is working on coming up with systemic change and processes which can enhance internal security for Pakistan, citizens need to be empowered to safeguard themselves.

k. Independent Security Companies: In response to the lack of adequate police protection, civil society has given birth to an enterprising private security business. Many Pakistanis have turned to these companies. This phenomenon has helped businesses and factories start operating again. It will be good if in the private sector there is an association of these companies that can work on standardization, licensing, and a defined and open relationship with police, a training program and a grievance board.

l. Better Law Schools: There is a need to enhance the criminology portion of law schools' curriculum. Bar exams should also be stricter so that the quality of law education can be improved.

m. Citizens' Task Force on Law & Order: The author proposes a task force in civil society which can study, recommend and supervise the whole law and order situation in Pakistan. It should issue its quarterly report and act as a watchdog group as well as a semi-think tank for law and order. The leading scholar/lawyer Khalid Ishaq can be requested to take the lead in this field. Other participants can also be people of insight and scholarship.

## EXPLAINING PAKISTAN'S COUNTERTERRORISM PERFORMANCE

The Afghan government's dissatisfaction and now increasingly the American polity's displeasure with Pakistan's performance in counterterrorism operations are conditioned considerably by the perception of Pakistan's unwillingness to crack down on terrorism comprehensively. This is a serious and, in actuality, complex charge. By all accounts, President Musharraf himself is strongly committed to purging both al- Qaeda and the Taliban. The imperatives of eliminating al- Qaeda are obvious: Pakistan was never directly a sponsor of this group in Afghanistan, and destroying its network remains the sine qua non of the lucrative Pakistani counterterrorism partnership with the United States. Musharraf also remains personally opposed to the political philosophy represented by the Taliban. He has repeatedly identified the "talibanization" of Pakistan as the most pressing threat facing his state, but whether this translates into a decision to physically apprehend or eradicate the Taliban cadres, and especially their leadership, is less clear. Drawing a distinction between "diehard militants and fanatics," who "reject reconciliation and peace" and accordingly must be targeted even though they are hard to find, and the larger Taliban cadres, "most of [whom] may be ignorant and misguided" but "are a part of Afghan society," Musharraf has urged Kabul, Washington, and the larger international community to begin instead a campaign of reconciliation with the Taliban focused on "winning [their] hearts and minds."

Musharraf's attitude toward the Taliban thus remains complex and multifaceted: he clearly detests their worldview, referring to talibanization as a species of extremism that "represents a state of mind and requires [a] more comprehensive, long- term strategy where military action must be combined with a political approach and socioeconomic development." He is also opposed to what he calls "terrorist elements and foreign militants" within the movement, which he acknowledges "must be dealt with a strong hand." Musharraf argues, however, for peacefully integrating the Taliban's rank and file into civil society, a judgment that is premised heavily on the belief that these elements are merely misguided miscreants rather than implacable foes.

The nucleus of military officials around Musharraf appears to reflect his own sinuosity. While all senior Pakistani military officers are agreed that the al- Qaeda presence in the FATA must be eliminated, there is a considerable diversity of views in regard to the Taliban. Although many feel that the optimal outcome for Pakistan would be simply a Taliban that progressively lose their effectiveness and support and thereby fade into obscurity— a finale that would spare Pakistanis the distasteful obligation of having to turn their guns against their old clients— others are conflicted about these reactionaries for different reasons.

To begin with, many officers are disenchanted by Washington's approach to managing the larger issues associated with Afghanistan's political reconstitution. Since the emergency loya jirga held in 2002 and the subsequent Afghan presidential election of 2004, these officials have been dismayed by what they perceive as the U.S. partiality toward the Durrani Pashtuns, who have traditionally been the privileged political elite in Afghan society (and from whose ranks, through the Popalzai tribe, emerged President Hamid Karzai). The calculated neglect of the Ghilzai Pashtuns— who are primarily rural and uneducated peasantry and who constituted a critical source of manpower for the Taliban cause— grates on many Pakistani national security managers not only because they believe that the continuing alienation of the Ghilzai feeds the Taliban ranks but also because it represents an enduring and deliberate disregard of their own clients in intra-Afghan politics. This latter consideration is significant because it has the effect of portraying Islamabad as feckless and incapable of influencing U.S. policy in directions more helpful to its friends despite Pakistan's large investments in the U.S. war on terror.

When these concerns are added to other strategic calculations about protecting the Taliban as a hedge against either the failure of the Karzai regime in Kabul or the dreaded prospect of increasing Indian influence in Afghanistan, the senior leadership of the Pakistani military— as well as President Musharraf— believe they have good enough reasons to avoid targeting the Taliban comprehensively in the manner sought by both Kabul and Washington. The dangers of a heightened and targeted anti- Ghilzai campaign leading to a political mobilization that renews the demand for an independent "Pakhtunistan" further exacerbate the fears of senior Pakistani military officials. Because the status of the Durand Line separating Afghanistan and Pakistan is still formally contested by Kabul, any provocation that results in strengthening the political dimensions of Pashtun solidarity among the tribes living on both sides of this boundary is viewed immediately as a potential threat to the territorial integrity of Pakistan. With the vivisection of 1971 indelibly emblazoned in the consciousness of the Pakistani military, senior commanders are extremely reluctant to embark on any military operations that would aggravate the local Pashtun tribes in the FATA and provoke them into making common territorial cause with their confreres on the other side of the border against the Pakistani state.

While ambivalence about the Taliban at senior levels in the Pakistani military thus has both strategic and self- interested dimensions, other more prosaic, but tactically important, considerations also play a role. Recognizing that the Taliban are essentially Ghilzai Pashtuns with deep consanguineal ties to the tribes that have dominated the FATA for centuries, many Pakistani commanders are afraid that any continued large- scale military presence in the area, especially if exemplified by massed infantry operations of the kind mounted in 2002–2004, will only further inflame tribal sensitivities and diminish cooperation between tribal leaders and the armed forces, a cooperation that is absolutely necessary if the armed forces are to successfully apprehend the "terrorist elements and foreign militants" located in their midst.

Although such embitterment has already occurred with problematic consequences for the success of antiterrorism operations, the leadership of the Pakistani military remains continually fearful that any added aggravation could lead to even greater tribal support for terrorist groups closeted in the area and a systematic denial of access to the military units tasked for operations therein. That such contingencies already appear to have materialized in the FATA suggests that the reluctance of senior Pakistani military leaders to violently engage the Taliban will be reinforced even further.

The most problematic elements within the Pakistani state, however, are probably the ISID officers in the field who were tasked with managing the liaison relationship with the Taliban over the years. Some simply feel loyalty to their old clients. Others are content to exploit their leadership's own ambivalence about the Taliban. And some others are prepared to disregard leadership directives that enjoin interdicting the Taliban for either nationalist, ideological, or personal reasons— if they believe they can get away with it. Whatever the cause, the field operatives of the ISID are widely perceived in Afghanistan and in the United States as being less than fully committed to targeting the Taliban leadership in the manner required for the success of counterterrorism operations in the FATA and beyond.

At first sight, this is indeed a curious phenomenon because nothing in the organizational structure of the ISID suggests that it is either an autonomous or a rogue entity. The reportedly 10,000-strong ISID is staffed primarily by Pakistani military officers who are assigned to the service on deputation for a fixed period of time, and its leadership reports to the chief of army staff. The pay, promotions, and operations of the directorate are also regulated by military rules and procedures, and by all accounts the Pakistan Army is a professional and bureaucratically efficient organization. Consequently, the notion that ISID officers might be undermining policies pursued by the corporate leadership of the Pakistan Army appears counterintuitive at first sight and cannot be reconciled with the image of the Pakistan Army as a tightly centralized organization unless due credit is given to three realities.

To begin with, the ISID, similar to many other intelligence organizations worldwide, has considerable operational latitude because of the nature of its activities in the covert realm: this includes access to financing "off the books," recruitment of agents from diverse sources to include those with unsavory backgrounds, and the systematic use of retired case officers who can conduct officially permitted operations while still providing the state with plausible deniability. Further, the implementation of many ISID operations is typically regulated by "directive control" as opposed to "detailed control," where field officers have the flexibility to accomplish strategic goals without having to secure prior approval of every particular from their superiors. And, finally, because ISID is simultaneously an external intelligence organization as well as a coercive instrument for implementing the preferences of military authoritarianism in Pakistan, Musharraf's management of this organization historically was manifested primarily through the promulgation of broadly defined policies, which were then implemented by a chain of subordinates who acted upon their understanding of his strategic intent and which simultaneously served to protect him from detailed knowledge of what may frequently have been highly troublesome activities.

Given these realities, the pervasive belief about ISID unreliability in the war against terror, and particularly against the Taliban, can be accounted for— despite the otherwise professional character of the Pakistan Army— only by one or more of the following hypotheses:

- That, despite their public claims, President Musharraf and his corps commanders are not yet committed to a policy of eliminating the Taliban and especially its leadership, root and branch; consequently, Musharraf and his commanders have not directed their military and intelligence services to systematically implement such a strategy.
- That, although President Musharraf and his corps commanders have settled on a strategy of eliminating the Taliban in principle, the operational predicates of this policy insofar as they apply to the leadership and other high-value targets have not yet been specified deliberately, thus permitting line- level officers to use their discretion when it comes to supporting or undermining particular counterterrorism operations.

- That, although President Musharraf and his corps commanders have settled on a strategy of eliminating the Taliban, to include its leadership and other "diehard militants," the large size and complex bureaucratic structure of the ISID permit its field officers, and especially the retired case officers still on its active payroll, to covertly ignore or violate leadership directives in many instances for nationalist, ideological, or personal reasons without fear of immediate retribution.

Whatever the real explanation for ISID recalcitrance may be—and the truth probably implicates a complex admixture of factors—the fact remains that the Pakistani campaign against the Taliban, and particularly its leadership, remains hobbled by convolution and hesitation. During the past several years, this has resulted in a deepening entrenchment of the Taliban and their sympathizers throughout the seven administrative agencies of the FATA and a growing expansion of their influence in the Tank, Dera Ismail Khan, and Swat Valley areas of the North West Frontier Province of Pakistan. Since October 2007, for instance, the idyllic mountain region of Swat, barely 90 miles from Islamabad, has been occupied by self- styled "Pakistani Taliban" forces led by Maulana Qazi Fazlullah and his Tchrik- e- Nafaz- e- Shariate- Muhammad (Movement for the Enforcement of Islamic Laws) shaheen (fighters), who may be present in the area in greater than brigade strength. This development suggests not only that the Taliban movement and its sympathizers have moved beyond the traditionally stateless regions close to the Durand Line and into more settled areas within Pakistan but also, and more ominously, that what began as localized terrorist operations now threatens to evolve into a mature insurgency with the militant opposition able to eject government forces from a given territory, hold ground against state opposition, and coerce any local opponents into cooperating in order to sustain the newly secured safe haven.

This intensifying talibanization in the sensitive areas of the North West Frontier Province has had diverse effects, including increased tensions with and between the traditional tribes resulting in both growing intertribal conflicts as well as bolder attacks on the Pakistan Army and paramilitary units in the region. In one dramatic encounter, more than three hundred Frontier Corps infantry men were taken hostage by local militants in August 2007 in South Waziristan, to be freed only after President Musharraf ignominiously released more than two dozen previously jailed Islamists, including Mullah Obaidullah Akhund, the highest-ranking Taliban official captured by the Pakistani military.

On occasion, the tribal dissatisfaction with local talibanization, and particularly with some of the groups that support it, has been all to the good as, for example, when indigenous tribes in the Azam Warsak area of South Waziristan, supported by Pakistani military forces, attacked and expelled numerous Uzbeks belonging to the Islamic Movement of Uzbekistan— a constituent of Osama bin Laden's International Islamic Front— who had settled in that locale. Unfortunately, such successful cleansing operations have been all too few.

The main consequence of talibanization in the FATA instead has been, as one observer put it, to "provide more opportunities to the ISI[D] to indirectly support some Taliban commanders sympathetic to Pakistan's objectives" in the ongoing war in Afghanistan.

The growing talibanization in the FATA and beyond has in fact resulted in the creation of a secure sanctuary for a variety of terrorist groups now conducting anticoalition military operations in Afghanistan. The evidence suggests that Taliban presence is strongest in the Helmand, Kandahar, Zabol, and Oruzgan provinces in southern Afghanistan and is either significant or conspicuous in Paktika, Khowst, Nangarhar, Konar, and Nuristan provinces in eastern Afghanistan. In these areas, the Taliban have been able to deploy and sustain a large number of armed fighters in situ, which has permitted the movement to effectively displace the Afghan state by usurping its traditional functions such as maintaining law and order; extracting resources through taxation; administering justice through various adjudicative mechanisms backed by local militias; and dispensing welfare through the maintenance of schools, provision of social services, and the oversight of economic activities.

Performing these statal functions is possible because the Taliban undoubtedly continue to derive support from the Ghilzai Pashtuns in Afghanistan; however, their record of increasingly ruthless retribution against any uncooperative tribal leaders does not hurt either. In this context, the Taliban's ability to sustain the strong coercive presence they currently have in the southern and eastern Afghan provinces is enhanced considerably by their access to the safe haven in the FATA whence they can draw a large number of fighters, procure diverse kinds of ordnance and combat equipment, and tap into different streams of financial resources (including, but not restricted to, the zakat, the Islamic tithe) for the prosecution of the ongoing jihad against the Karzai regime and the foreign forces now present in Afghanistan. As one respected analysis has noted, "using [the sanctuary provided by the FATA] to regroup, reorganize and rearm," Taliban and other foreign militants, including al- Qaeda sympathizers, "are launching increasingly severe cross- border attacks on Afghan and international military personnel, with the support and active involvement of Pakistani militants."

The fruits of this activity are witnessed in the deteriorating security situation in Afghanistan. Since the successful presidential election in October 2004—an event that received the full support of the international community and heralded hope for a new Afghanistan— the Taliban insurgency has metastasized in scale, intensity, and fury. By 2006, the level of violence had increased dramatically, and previous operations that had been centered on assassinations, ambushes, and isolated hit- and- run attacks were now supplemented by more ominous tactics involving beheadings and suicide bombings, which historically have been utterly alien to Afghan culture. Equally problematic has been the employment of ever more sophisticated improvised explosive devices, rockets, missiles, and man- portable air defense weapons, many of which continue to be fabricated in the arms foundries in the FATA but are now also increasingly supplied by al- Qaeda and foreign powers such as Iran. Even more remarkably, Taliban military operations have gradually evolved from singular covert attacks mounted by tiny groups to more complex, set- piece military operations undertaken by larger units, often involving attempts to seize and hold territory against superior forces, and employing more diverse and sophisticated crew- served weaponry, including indirect fire systems such as mortars and unguided rockets, as supplements to the traditionally ubiquitous personal firearms and direct- fire weapons.

The strategic objectives of these new modes of warfare have also become more complex. Rather than simply harassing the new Afghan government, which seemed to be the original intention, the current military activities of the Taliban are accompanied by sophisticated forms of information operations. Betraying evidence of lessons learned from their al- Qaeda accomplices, Taliban operatives use a variety of techniques ranging from sending crude low-technology "night letters" often conveying threats to specific individuals, to circulating DVDs and videotapes containing political propaganda, to exploiting more advanced technology such as radio, television, mobile and satellite telephony, and the Internet. In general, all these technologies are used to signal to the Afghan tribes that the return of the Taliban to power in Kabul is inevitable—despite whatever tactical losses might be suffered at the hands of NATO forces in the interim— and that resistance or neutrality is therefore futile. As one analysis pointed out, even if this campaign does not persuade the Afghan people, "[t]he Taliban's own hearts and minds activities are now prolonging and exacerbating an already difficult insurgency problem for the Afghan Government and the International Security Assistance Force (ISAF) in the south of the country."

Finally, and perhaps most important, both the Taliban's information and its actual war-fighting operations have moved beyond simple terrorist attacks aimed at disrupting the Afghan government toward more ambitious objectives revolving around the progressive domination of territory. Focused today primarily on NATO's Regional Command (South) for both symbolic and strategic reasons, the Taliban leadership appears intent on slowly seizing critical areas, district by district, through a strategy of covert infiltration in the Helmand, Kandahar, Oruzgan, and Zabol provinces as a prelude to wresting control of the city of Kandahar, which is intended to become the base for first dominating the

South and eventually all of Afghanistan itself. If this evolution gradually succeeds, the Taliban insurgency in southeastern Afghanistan will have successfully metamorphosed from a guerrilla operation into something resembling a more conventional civil war with grave advantages to the militants in their struggle against the Karzai government in Kabul.

Although the safe havens in the FATA and the ability to derive local Ghilzai support in the southern and eastern Afghan provinces (by providing the benefits of security, justice, and even development) have thus enabled a dramatic transformation in both the character of the ongoing Afghan war and the fortunes of the Taliban as an insurgent organization, a particularly dangerous consequence— especially from a U.S. perspective— has been the enhanced prospects for survival they have offered al- Qaeda. There is little doubt today that the survival of the Taliban sanctuary in the FATA (to include the talibanization of the wider area more generally) has been singularly responsible for the continuing regeneration of al- Qaeda as an organization because it has permitted the leadership and the operatives of this terrorist group, who are relatively smaller in number, to safely "dissolve" into a larger geosocial environment that is either hospitable to them directly or that protects them by disguising their presence amid a larger pool of Taliban adherents.

The al- Qaeda leadership, which is believed to be currently ensconced somewhere in the Bajaur Agency of the FATA, has further enhanced its immunity to interdiction by pursuing what appears to be a subtle strategy toward its Taliban hosts. Recognizing that the Taliban's Pashtun cadres remain the original denizens of the FATA and the adjacent areas in eastern and southern Afghanistan, al- Qaeda's overseers have been careful to tread lightly: despite their independent access to significant streams of foreign resources, they do not seem to have levied any excessive demands in terms of either hospitality or security, nor have they used their superior access to advanced military- technical capabilities worldwide to attempt any "takeover" of the Taliban movement. Rather, they appear to understand that an independent Pashtun insurgency that answers to no one but its own indigenous leadership stands the best chance of not only regaining control in Afghanistan but also securing the continued support of the tribal elements in the FATA, which in turn only better conduces to al-Qaeda's survival over the long term.

Al- Qaeda leaders thus have repeatedly endorsed the Pashtun leadership of the Taliban, centered on Mullah Omar's coterie, on many an occasion publicly, beginning in 2002 when Osama bin Laden conferred on Mullah Omar the title of Emir Al- Momineen (Leader of the Faithful). The increasing sophistication of the Taliban's military operations, the new integration of suicide attacks into its modus operandi, and its increasing emphasis on information operations for a group that historically despised the modern media also indicate that al- Qaeda elements continue to assist Taliban forces with at least technology and training, and possibly financial assistance, as partial recompense for the refuge they receive in the FATA as they continue to bide their time awaiting the reestablishment of Taliban control in Afghanistan.

Pakistan's failure to target the Taliban and especially its leadership since 2001 has, therefore, had several deleterious consequences. To begin with, it has resulted in the creation of a safe haven for various terrorist elements in the FATA, whence the Taliban war against the Karzai regime can be prosecuted and the al- Qaeda leadership protected and regenerated as it plans more catastrophic attacks on the West and on the United States in particular. It has also permitted the Taliban to nurture their indigenous bases of support within southern and eastern Afghanistan itself, whence they can slowly evolve into a tumorous state within a state.

Further, it has bred a cancerous nest of violent extremism inside Pakistan resulting in the rise of new Islamist militant groups, sometimes labeled the Pakistani Taliban, that are either sympathetic to or affiliated with al- Qaeda and committed to waging a holy war against the Pakistani government, the liberal elements in Pakistani politics, as well as other foreign adversaries such as India, Israel, and the United States. The invigoration of these indigenous radical outfits has in the process produced a new generation of foot soldiers available to different extremist entities throughout the country and strengthened the social bases of support for the otherwise marginal Islamist parties in Pakistani politics. Finally, it has added to the already long and intractable list of problems confronting Pakistan as it struggles to transform itself into a moderate and successful Muslim state: in particular, it has condemned the Pakistani leadership, including acknowledged moderate leaders like Musharraf, to prosecute antiterrorism operations under highly disadvantageous conditions and in an area that by history and tradition has long been lawless, has been bereft of any concentrated state penetration, and that had no regular military presence worth the name until recently, yet is dominated by those very groups that have strong ethnic and increasingly ideological ties to the same terrorist elements sought by the Pakistani state.

If the foregoing discussion amplifies how Pakistan's counterterrorism performance has been structurally compromised by motivational and institutional problems, this is by no means the whole story. An equally important source of inadequacy has been the operational complexity of the counterterrorism operations themselves and Pakistan's myriad weaknesses in coping with these challenges. These difficulties— three of which are illustrated in the discussion that follows— only complicate the challenges caused by the larger problem of whether Pakistan believes eliminating the Taliban decisively is in its national interest.

First, Pakistan's inability to secure the tactical intelligence required for successful counterterrorism operations against key Taliban and al- Qaeda elements in the FATA has now become painfully obvious. Although the ISID and the army's director general of military intelligence have primary responsibility for the collection of targeting intelligence in the FATA, their ability to carry out these tasks has been severely hampered in recent times. In part, this is undoubtedly because many Pakistani intelligence officers are simply sympathetic to radical Islamist elements who have been their clients for many years. Even when this is not the case, however, state intelligence activities have been hindered by the peculiarities of the political structures in the FATA and the corrosive changes that have been occurring therein.

It is often insufficiently recognized that, although the tribal areas are physically located within Pakistani territory, they are not governed by either Pakistani laws and regulations or the political institutions normally associated with national politics. In fact, the relationship between these tribal areas and the Pakistani state is regulated not by any common laws but by formal treaties between the resident tribes and the federal government in Islamabad. The existence of such treaties exemplifies what two analysts have rightly labeled "the anomaly of [the] FATA": it signifies that the link between the tribes and the Pakistani government resembles one that exists between coordinate, and not superordinate and subordinate, political entities. This is further corroborated by the fact that these treaties not only guarantee the tribes' immunity to the codified laws and regulations that govern political life in the rest of Pakistan but also bestow on them exclusive responsibility for the management of their own internal affairs. With the exception of the Frontier Crimes Regulation, a written document more than a century old that elaborates the principle of settling disputes through arbitration by tribal jirgas, most of the governing rules in the FATA are essentially unwritten, being based on a combination of rewaj (tribal customs) and Sharia (Islamic law).

The foundation of maintaining order and authority in such a system, which is anchored in custom, tradition, and legal practices going back to the British Raj, lay in the inculcation of harmonious relations between the political agent— a mid- level civil servant with sweeping powers who, although deputed by the governor of the North West Frontier Province as the highest- ranking official representative in each tribal agency, was ultimately responsible to the federal government in Islamabad— and the tribal maliks, or elders, who managed tribal affairs day to day and who until 1996 were the only individuals permitted to vote in elections for Pakistan's National Assembly. The ties between the agents and the maliks were critical to the production of good intelligence: the agents disbursed the resources provided by Islamabad to acquire the information required to keep the government up to date about developments along the frontier, and the maliks used the subventions provided to buttress their own influence, access, and standing with the tribes they supervised.

Although it was possible to alter this traditional structure of management in the FATA, successive authoritarian regimes in Islamabad eschewed that alternative because the system of direct control through the political agent invariably appeared more attractive to Pakistan Army leaders who were innately uncomfortable with the idea of democratic alternatives involving the introduction of universal adult suffrage, the development of representative institutions, and the presence of civilian political parties in local politics. As a result, the traditional governing mechanisms, centered on the interactions between agents and maliks against the backdrop of the privileges encoded in the old treaties, were only reinforced by Islamabad despite the fact that the bonds between these agents and maliks had became increasingly discredited because of the widespread corruption and politicization that came to characterize their relationship. As a result over time, the tribes along the frontier no longer looked up to their own maliks as selfless leaders or to the political agents as fair representatives of a federal government that sought to advance their welfare.

By the time the 1980s set in, the anti- Soviet jihad brought about a further— and deadlier— acceleration of this crisis. Egged on by the initiatives of Pakistan's Islamist president, Zia ul- Haq, the FATA witnessed a steady social transformation that resulted in the traditional authorities— the political agents and the maliks— being slowly supplanted by new religious leaders, the maulvis, who viewed issues of political loyalty primarily through religious or ideological lenses. The progressive demise of the old social order thus made the long- standing Pakistani human intelligence collection apparatus dramatically ineffective as the radicalized maulvis, viewing the protection of the Taliban and al- Qaeda cadres in the FATA as a politico- religious obligation, appear determined to deny the Pakistani state the necessary information required to apprehend these targets. The widespread outcry in the frontier areas against the U.S. war in Iraq, coupled with the growing perception that Musharraf's prosecution of counterterrorism operations represents illegitimate support for a U.S. administration involved in a global anti- Muslim crusade, has only strengthened the determination of the maulvis and the new Islamists, who have filled the "power vacuum" caused by the demise of the agent-malik relationship in the FATA, to protect the terrorist targets sought by Pakistan and the United States.

The limitations of Pakistani technical intelligence capabilities in the context of counter terrorism operations also do not help matters any. As a matter of fact, Pakistan does have an impressive array of national intelligence collection capabilities. These systems, which are focused primarily on gathering signals and communications intelligence (SIGINT and COMINT), are largely under ISID control although the actual intercept operations are conducted by inter- services signals units that employ technical personnel drawn from the army's Corps of Signals, the air force, and the navy. For the most part, however, strategic SIGINT and COMINT collection in Pakistan— the intercept, analysis, and dissemination of electronic signatures and communications waveforms— is disproportionately oriented toward targeting India. Islamabad's most sophisticated assets, accordingly, focus on the detection, direction finding, surveillance, and intercept of the high frequency (HF), very high frequency (VHF), ultra high frequency (UHF), and satellite bandwidths used by Indian diplomatic and military communications. These resources, together with the tactical SIGINT and COMINT systems possessed at the corps level in the Pakistan Army, make Islamabad certainly capable of monitoring the communication devices used by the Taliban and al- Qaeda, because these in fact most likely resemble those supplied by the ISID to various Kashmiri terrorist groups and recovered over the years by the Indian military. The insurgency in Kashmir revealed that Pakistani-supported terrorist groups in South Asia, including those operating in Afghanistan, generally use HF radio, satellite telephony, and cellular phones for long- range connectivity, with commercially available line- of- sight VHF and UHF radios produced by companies such as Yeasu, Kenwood, and I- Com for their operational and tactical communications.

Targeting the communications traffic generated through these systems, however, requires Pakistan's national and tactical collection assets to be systematically tasked for this purpose, but both Indian and Afghan military intelligence officials believe that New Delhi continues to remain a higher- priority target for Pakistani technical collection in comparison with either the Taliban or al- Qaeda. Even when this is not the case, however, Pakistani surveillance systems may continue to be ineffective in the counterterrorism mission for many reasons. If Taliban and al- Qaeda operatives use low- power devices sporadically for tactical communications, the short range and random nature of these transmissions may defeat even a technically competent operator if no surveillance devices are in proximity to the threat. Further, sophisticated technologies such as frequency hopping, portable encrypted, or digital burst radios, many of which are available commercially, can be used to elude even skilled surveillance especially if the monitoring systems are not available or are not dedicated full- time to the mission.

Finally, the increased use of the Internet by Taliban and al-Qaeda operatives, including their growing use of encryption software, makes it hard for the ISID to monitor such communications systematically because, in the absence of prior cueing, high- speed computation married to sophisticated search algorithms would be required if the relatively large volume of Internet traffic, even within an otherwise relatively low tele- density state like Pakistan, is to be successfully monitored. It is simply not clear whether Pakistan possesses such capabilities.

In principle, U.S. advantages here could serve to compensate, but the growing appreciation of the capabilities of U.S. assets has resulted in these opposition forces— both Taliban and al- Qaeda—increasingly relying on more primitive but more secure means of communication, such as "snail mail" and human couriers, for their operational planning. This workaround, in turn, denies both Pakistan and the United States the kind of targeting data that might otherwise have become available through technical intelligence.

Recognizing these problems, Pakistan has begun the arduous task of rebuilding both its technical and its human intelligence collection assets in the FATA. The latter capabilities are indeed the most critical, but these also take the longest to mature and to yield their fruit. A long- term Pakistan Army presence in the FATA amid conditions of relative peace is, therefore, an essential precondition for Islamabad to be able to develop and consolidate an effective human intelligence network. The $750 million U.S. assistance program to the FATA, if properly directed, could help considerably in advancing this goal of local stability; but the complicated and time- consuming nature of this endeavor, the uncertainty about the program's effective implementation, and Washington's failure to condition the availability of these funds on Islamabad's implementation of political reforms in the tribal regions— to include, inter alia, the drastic revision of the Frontier Crimes Regulation; the elimination of the political agent as part of the larger process of integrating the FATA into Pakistan's North West Frontier Province under the full jurisdiction of the provincial and national legislatures and the judicial system; and the withdrawal of restrictions on political parties operating in the FATA with an eye to introducing conventional political institutions— imply that neither the United States nor Pakistan ought to expect quick breakthroughs in their efforts "to build confidence and trust between the Government of Pakistan (GOP) and [the] FATA tribal communities" leading to the demolition of the al- Qaeda and Taliban networks that have regenerated in this area over the last few years.

Second, the arrival of the Pakistan Army in strength in the FATA has resulted in social disruptions that have undermined its counterterrorism effectiveness. Although the insertion of the Army's XI Corps and the SSG battalions into the autonomous areas was a brave and necessary decision of the part of General Musharraf, it has nonetheless eroded the delicate compact that previously existed between the FATA and the Pakistani state. The resulting alienation and resentment on the part of the indigenous population have been reflected in significant counterterrorism problems. The Pakistan Army— which draws its cadres largely from outside the FATA and is primarily non- Pashtun in composition— is a highly professional force, but its maneuver units have often been stymied by their inability to secure the cooperation of the local populace, which views it today as an unwelcome intruder. The army's SSG is very effective in tactical counterterrorism operations but, being an elite unit, is far too diminutive to make a difference at the theater level.

The Frontier Corps, which is composed primarily of tribal levies and is the resident paramilitary force, could be potentially the most effective element, but it is often compromised by its close ties with the local inhabitants. Riddled with sympathizers, inadequately motivated, suspicious of both Islamabad's and Washington's intentions, poorly trained and equipped for counterterrorism operations, yet present in strength throughout the FATA, the Frontier Corps (along with its other local siblings such as the Frontier Constabulary, the tribal police [khassadars], and tribal militias [lashkars]) represents the perfect exemplar of the structural challenge facing Pakistan's counterterrorism effort: its best local units, the ones that share affinities with the tribes they patrol and consequently the forces likely to secure potentially the most useful intelligence, are also the fighting elements least able or willing to cope with the battle-hardened terrorists they are deployed against.

Unfortunately, the infantry elements of the Pakistan Army that have been pressed into the fight have their own problems as well. Unlike the Indian Army, which thanks to two decades of combating Pakistani- supported subconventional conflict now has considerable counter terrorism skills, the infantry battalions of Pakistan's XI Corps are configured primarily as strategic reserves for possible conventional warfare against India. Counterterrorism operations are not their forte, and, while they have done a decent job of learning by doing, they still betray a proclivity for operational responses that while sensible against a conventional adversary are less than effective (and, perhaps, even counterproductive) when dealing with irregular forces: large unit deployments, intense (and sometimes indiscriminate) employment of fire, and sledgehammer cordon- and- search tactics.

While the attrition strategies of the Pakistani military have been criticized by many for their detrimental consequences, it must be recognized that these are not always attributable to the "self- proclaimed invincibility of the [Pakistani] armed forces." Rather, the hostile terrain in which counterterrorism operations are conducted and the unexpectedly heavy firepower that Taliban and al- Qaeda terrorists have mustered in the past have been the two factors most responsible for the military's recourse to the relatively coarse counterterrorism tactics that are invariably derided. It is not difficult to sympathize with Islamabad's predicament. For starters, the topography of the FATA is incredibly inhospitable as far as counterterrorism operations are concerned. The general geography of the area is characterized by harsh, rugged, and inaccessible mountainous terrain with steep slopes being the rule rather than the exception. The crest elevations in the region vary from 3,600 meters to 4,700 meters in the Khyber, Kurram, and Orakzai agencies of the central FATA, dropping somewhat to between 1,500 meters and 3,400 meters in the southern agencies of North and South Waziristan. These mountain ranges running roughly from northeast to southwest function as a complex barrier that breaks up the terrain into numerous tiny basins or valleys that are dotted with minuscule settlements surviving either through livestock grazing, subsistence agriculture, or petty trade. The size of these settlements is generally very small, ranging from literally a few dozen people in some instances to a few thousand at most in the largest hamlets.

The lines of communication between these outposts are invariably tenuous, extending along the ridgelines of the adjacent mountains or traversing them through numerous passes, tracks, and trails, many of which support only pedestrian traffic or pack animals. Because many of these routes are intestinal and insignificant, they are often known only to the locals who, along with smugglers, drug runners, and arms peddlers, have exploited these conduits in the natural terrain to carry out their business undisturbed for centuries.

These terrain features produce three significant operational consequences that have great impact on the conduct of military operations. First, the isolation of the hamlets amid craggy geophysical features and the small sizes of the populations sheltered within them make it virtually impossible for outsiders to monitor any personnel movement to or from these locations, especially if the transit occurs on foot, by animal, or by isolated vehicular traffic (where possible). This is especially true if the movement concerned occurs in adverse weather or at night. Second, the consanguineal character of the tribal populations living in these areas implies that strangers cannot travel within the area without being readily detected, and safe passage in such circumstances usually occurs only when the local inhabitants are persuaded about the alien's peaceful intentions through some form of attestation by individuals known to the resident tribes. Third, the distances between the populated outposts can be significant given the absence of paved or metaled roads and, consequently, quick movement across the terrain invariably requires either strenuous marches on foot on or off established paths (depending on circumstances) or the use of animals, accompanied by guides in most cases. In several locations vehicular traffic is in fact possible, but, because such movement invariably hews to well- established roads and pathways, covert entry and exit through such access routes is generally difficult.

This concatenation of features abundantly explains why Pakistani counterterrorism operations have often run into tactical difficulties requiring recourse to "excessive" force. The isolated setting of many FATA settlements where terrorist cadres find refuge essentially prevents the Pakistani pursuers of the terrorists from being able to approach these locales clandestincly. Even small commando units operating on foot are susceptible to premature detection by the locals, and the munitions and weapons required to be carried over the harsh terrain and along the great distances within the region often tax the abilities of even the fittest infantry units, which must conserve their strength for the arduous military action at the end of their insertion. This consideration invariably mandates traveling on established tracks and paths, but even off- track approaches do not provide any assurance that the attacking force will be able to close in on its target undetected.

Because the risk of compromise is consistently high, many terrorist refugees have been able to simply escape at the first warning of military units moving en route to their hideouts. Early engagements with the Taliban and al- Qaeda cadres who chose to remain bivouacked also revealed— often to the surprise of their attackers— just how heavily armed they were; in fact, the character of their military equipment could often make the difference in whether they chose to escape or stand their ground and fight. Whenever they settled upon fighting, their employment of heavy weapons was invariably made doubly effective by the natural advantages accruing to the defense especially in mountainous terrain— gains that were further magnified by the clever use of stealthy tactics, the cunning utilization of the surrounding topography, the erection of effective positional defenses, and the exploitation of the timely warning provided by the local inhabitants.

The persistence of such challenges compelled the Pakistani military to seek operational work- arounds that offered some chance of success. The solution that proved most attractive in many circumstances was to forgo tactical surprise, which might have ensued from the exclusive use of small units relying entirely on covert foot penetration, in favor of larger operations that sought to exploit tactical superiority through the employment of heliborne elements for both the transportation of substantial strike teams to some location in proximity to their designated target and for the firepower required in support of the actual assault. Because the final engagement in such situations usually involved a heavily armed and a partially or fully alerted adversary— if the latter had not already escaped— the attacking Pakistani combat teams were often forced to employ even heavier weapons than might have been originally intended, including mortars, antitank recoilless rifles and guided missiles, field artillery, helicopter- and aircraft-fired cannon and unguided rockets, and occasionally even general-purpose bombs delivered by tactical aircraft. The lessons offered by such engagements since 2002 are stark and clear: unless the tribal populations residing in the FATA are sympathetic to the government and are willing to either warn the army of the militants' presence in their midst or desist from alerting the terrorists to the military's anticipated arrival in their hamlets, counterterrorism missions will either fail or be condemned to rely on even greater applications of brute force for their success.

The inevitable, but unintended, consequence of implementing such solutions has been significant collateral damage among civilians in the tribal areas. The residents, in response, have reacted to these losses by mounting violent attacks on, and repeated seizures of, Pakistani troops and paramilitary forces deployed in the area. The more extremist outfits, to include al-Qaeda elements, have sought to exact their revenge by undertaking lethal suicide attacks against Pakistani military and intelligence personnel both within the FATA and deep inside the nation's heartland in an effort to compel President Musharraf to terminate his counterterrorism operations conclusively. These continuing attacks on Pakistani military personnel have, by many anecdotal accounts, lowered morale within the frontline units now operating inside the FATA and caused increased desertions, suicides, and frequent discharge applications. Not surprisingly then, these developments have induced deepened soul- searching on the part of local commanders who wonder about the strategic wisdom of the ongoing war on terror and question the benefits specifically accruing to Pakistan. The growing antagonism caused by the collateral damage associated with U.S. military strikes from the Afghan side of the FATA has not helped make the Pakistan Army's problems any easier in this regard.

Throughout Pakistani society in general, there is a growing weariness with the counterterrorism operations presently being waged on the country's soil. Recent polling, for example, suggests only weak support for using force against Islamic militants operating within Pakistan, and most respondents overwhelmingly oppose allowing outside forces to combat al-Qaeda on their national territory. A survey recently conducted by the Program on International Policy Attitudes at the University of Maryland in collaboration with the U.S. Institute of Peace found that just 44 percent of urban Pakistanis favored sending the Pakistan Army to the tribal areas to "pursue and capture al Qaeda fighters," and only 48 percent would allow the Pakistan Army to act against "Taliban insurgents who have crossed over from Afghanistan." In general, the survey concludes that "Pakistanis reject overwhelmingly the idea of permitting foreign troops to attack al-Qaeda on Pakistani territory. Four out of five (80 percent) say their government should not allow U.S. or other foreign troops to enter Pakistan to pursue and capture al Qaeda fighters," and three out of four (77 percent) oppose allowing foreign troops to attack

Taliban insurgents based in Pakistan. Other polls reveal similar levels of disenchantment with the U.S.-supported campaign against terrorism. One report summarized it: ... despite their own concerns about terrorism, Pakistanis overwhelmingly oppose U.S.led efforts to fight terrorism— six- in- ten (59%) oppose America's anti- terror campaign, while only 13% back it. Like many other Muslim publics throughout Asia, the Middle East, and elsewhere, Pakistanis also oppose other key facets of U.S. foreign policy. Three- quarters (76%) say the U.S. should remove its troops from Iraq, and a similar proportion (75%) believe the U.S. and NATO should withdraw from Afghanistan, which shares a 1,500 mile border with Pakistan.

But Pakistanis are not just worried about the use of U.S. force in neighboring countries. They also fear they could become a target. More than seven- in- ten (72%) are very or somewhat worried that the U.S. could become a military threat to their country. And 64% name the U.S. as one of the countries posing the greatest potential threat to Pakistan, more than even long-standing arch- rival India (45%), with whom Pakistan has fought three major wars in the last sixty years.

Musharraf has attempted to cope with this increasing national weariness and to circumvent the problems caused by his army's operations, minimize its casualties, and soothe the roiling political environment in the tribal areas by episodic strategies of appeasement built around so- called peace accords with the pro-Taliban locals in South and North Waziristan. Under these accords, the indigenous residents were tasked with preventing cross- border movements of terrorists into Afghanistan and further attacks on Pakistani civilian and military targets. They were also to ensure either the ejection or the surrender of all foreigners, meaning the non–South Asian cadres loyal to al- Qaeda, from the FATA in exchange for which the Pakistan Army would withdraw to its barracks, suspend its combat operations against the terrorists, and defer to the tribes in regard to resolving disputes relating to the status of particular individuals.

Musharraf's understandable objective in pursuing such a solution was to restore the status quo ante— hold the tribes responsible for maintaining peace and security as they had done traditionally— but it was a strategy that was doomed to failure because it did not appreciate the extent of radicalization in the FATA and the tribes' new determination to protect their al-Qaeda and Taliban cortege against the Pakistani government and the United States, which were viewed as the greater threats. Thus, although several tribal groups have sought to cooperate with the government in rooting out the radicals in their midst, the more extremist entities, not surprisingly, used the breathing space provided by the accords to recruit, train, and rearm the terrorists in anticipation of a heightened and continuing campaign in Afghanistan. The Pakistan Army's attack on the Lal Masjid in Islamabad proved to be the proverbial straw that finally destroyed the charade embodied by the peace accords in the FATA, but the failure of these agreements has left Musharraf in an unenviable limbo where neither peace nor war seems able to deliver the counterterrorism goals pursued by the Pakistani state.

Third, the operational context surrounding the counterterrorism effort in the tribal areas and in Afghanistan has changed considerably— to the disadvantage of the Western coalition— since Operation Enduring Freedom began in 2001. To begin with, the Taliban movement, which was never a tight and cohesive political entity in any case, has become an even looser network of affiliated individuals and groups since it was forced from power in Kabul. Today, the Taliban "alliance" can be characterized as a disparate congeries of several elements united only by a common religious ideology, a desire to regain power in either Afghanistan or their local areas of operation, and a deep antagonism toward the United States and its regional allies. Several distinct elements can be identified in the current Taliban coalition:

- The leadership shura centered around Mullah Omar and his cohort in Quetta and the subsidiary war councils in Quetta, Miran Shah, Peshawar, and Karachi;
- The Taliban cadres who survived the defeat in Afghanistan, which are loosely controlled by the regional shuras and continue to draw on the madaris in the FATA and the refugee camps in Pakistan for their continuing recruitment;

- The tribal networks of former mujahideen commanders like Jalaluddin Haqqani who operates in Paktika, Paktia, and Khowst provinces and provides a key bridge between al-Qaeda and the Taliban; Gulbuddin Hekmatyar who leads the Hezb-i-Islami and operates in Nangarhar, Konar, and Nuristan provinces; Anwar- ul- Haq who leads the Hezb-i-Islami (Khalis) also operates in the Nangarhar area and is believed to lead the Tora Bora Military Front; and Saifullah Mansoor, a veteran field commander who is known to be active in the eastern areas;
- The Pakistani Taliban commanders like Baitullah Mahsud, the chieftain of the Mahsud tribe in South Waziristan; Maulana Faqir Muhammad who is associated with the Tehrike- Nafaz- e- Shariat- e- Muhammad and who operates in the Bajaur Agency; Maulana Qazi Fazlullah, also affiliated with the same group but operating out of Swat; Mangal Bagh Afridi, who leads the Lashkar- e- Islami in the Khyber Agency and is believed to be part of a larger local opposition network led by Mufti Munir Shakir; and Sharif Khan and Nur Islam, tribal leaders who have demonstrated considerable operational effectiveness in South Waziristan;
- The drug lords in eastern and southern Afghanistan, especially in Helmand and Kandahar provinces, who are either taxed or willingly contribute revenues that are indispensable for the Taliban war against Kabul;
- The sundry former anti- Soviet commanders who control small groups of fighters and are engaged primarily in criminal activities such as bank robberies, kidnappings for ransom, and assassination of local officials while they simultaneously offer their services as guns for hire;
- The disaffected Afghan Pashtun tribes, most conspicuously the rural Ghilzai, who, feeling disenfranchised in the current governing arrangements, continue to support the Taliban with manpower and sanctuary within Afghanistan; and, finally,
- Al- Qaeda, which, while distinct from all the foregoing groups in that its focus of operations remains the global

jihad, nonetheless collaborates with the Taliban in order to assist the Taliban in recovering control of Kabul while it continues to preserve its sanctuary in the FATA in the interim.

The implication of such a diverse target set is that destroying the Taliban today has become much more difficult because its previously weak hierarchical structure has become even more diffuse, with truly diverse entities coordinating as necessary but with each also carrying out its own local agenda.

This reality, in turn, implies that while some specific nodes in this network will have to be defeated "kinetically" if the Taliban threat is to be erased, these tactical successes will have to be procured despite the political hesitation in parts of the Pakistani state and the real operational limitations of the Pakistani military. The complexity of Islamabad's relations with many of the constituent elements in the Taliban coalition does not help either: although Islamabad may readily cooperate in targeting some of the Pakistani Taliban commanders, drug lords, petty former anti-Soviet captains, and al- Qaeda elements, the ties nurtured by Pakistan's military and intelligence services with the Taliban leadership and the tribal networks of key former mujahideen commanders make these targets relatively inviolate, at least in the near term. For understandable sociopolitical reasons, Pakistani leaders are also likely to find it very difficult to conduct any large-scale interdiction operations aimed at the Taliban foot soldiers and the disaffected tribes— even if only in the FATA— partly because of the unmanageable chaos that would ensue in a very sensitive area of great importance to the Pakistani state and partly because of the fact that the insurgents drawn from these groups today are truly protean, capable of participating in military operations when required but at other times fluidly mutating into ordinary tribals.

There is no doubt, therefore, that winning the war on terror in Afghanistan will require dealing with the sanctuary enjoyed by various militant groups inside Pakistan. But it is probably an exaggeration to conclude "that the solution lies not in Afghanistan, but across the Khyber Pass in Pakistan."80 What happens in Afghanistan itself is critically important—not only in regard to ongoing military operations but, more fundamentally, in respect to reconstruction, economic development, nation building, and political reconstitution—because the counterterrorism campaign will not be won until the political environment in Afghanistan improves to the point where these insurgent forces are denied the conditions that allow them to survive and flourish. As General James L. Jones succinctly stated in his testimony before the Senate Foreign Relations Committee, "I am convinced that the solution in Afghanistan is not a military one."

It is in this context that Afghanistan's— and not just Pakistan's— political failures are particularly galling. Despite the advances in developing a constitutional government in Kabul with strong international support, the Karzai regime has turned out to be conspicuously ineffective. The inability of the government to deliver basic services, education, justice, and economic development, even in those areas not directly threatened by the insurgency, has fueled great frustration with President Karzai throughout the country. The growing corruption witnessed at all levels of government only exacerbates this resentment. And the runaway upsurge in poppy cultivation, which in 2006 yielded an all- time- high output of 6,100 metric tons, has resulted in a situation where "militia commanders, criminal organizations, and corrupt officials have exploited narcotics as a reliable source of revenue and patronage, which has perpetuated the threat these groups pose to the country's fragile internal security and the legitimacy of its embryonic democratic government." The complexities of intra- Afghan politics only compound the situation further: many Pashtun groups, for example, stung by the government's inability or unwillingness to address their specific grievances, often view the local insurgents as more effective instruments for achieving their immediate security or developmental goals. Any efforts made by the government to assuage Pashtun bitterness directly, however, complicates its relations with the non- Pashtun groups, who are apt to see most initiatives aimed at bolstering central authority, reinvigorating the traditional Pashtun tribal structures, and negotiating with Pakistan as evidence of a surreptitious attempt to reassert Pashtun hegemony over the rest of Afghanistan.

The Karzai government has thus far not succeeded in steering clear of these competing pressures, and its sharply alternating policies have not helped its standing either. Its most recent stab at neutralizing the growing insurgency by implementing a reconciliation program involving the "moderate Taliban" is a good example. After resisting such an idea for a long time, in part because of opposition from former Northern Alliance figures supportive of the government, President Karzai changed course and embarked on an effort to reintegrate the less extreme Taliban members into the national mainstream. The idea is indeed sensible in principle but difficult to implement successfully in practice. That President Musharraf is its most ardent advocate has not raised the credibility of the program particularly, because it is often viewed in Afghanistan as a Pakistani stratagem to evade fulfilling its obligations to erase the insurgent sanctuaries in the tribal areas. In any event, the notion of reconciling moderate Taliban into Afghan society, while certainly commendable if it is understood to mean coopting the poor and disenfranchised confederations such as the Ghilzai, is invariably tricky and possibly even counterproductive because of the difficulties of distinguishing genuinely alienated individuals, who might be desirous of integration, from their more diehard and utterly intractable counterparts. One very thoughtful analysis concluded:

While more efforts should have gone into reconciliation in the early days, seeking to quell the insurgency now by rewarding criminal behavior would only perpetuate a culture of impunity and betray the trust of those who have backed the new, democratic, participatory institutions. It appears that the concept of reconciliation is being used interchangeably with amnesty. While such compromise may bring some measure of short- term relief, it would ultimately do nothing to break the cycle of violence.

Not surprisingly then, this Program Takhim- e Solh, which translates roughly into the Strengthening Peace program, has not been a noteworthy success. It does not appear to have made any significant dent in the manpower available to the insurgency, even as it has increased the fissures between Karzai and his non- Pashtun allies, has created new political threats to his 2009 presidential ambitions, and has failed to undermine the Taliban's social base of support in the interim.

One news report summarized the current crisis within Afghanistan laconically by declaring: "Government corruption and poppy cultivation are rampant and public services remain a wreck; food prices are soaring, unemployment remains high and resurgent Taliban forces in the south are pressing toward th[e] capital."86 Defeating this last threat obviously represents a classic chicken- and- egg dilemma: Taliban resurgence prevents the Karzai regime from effectively extending central control in the east, south, and southeast of the country, while the lack of effective state presence in these areas is precisely what makes the Taliban's return possible in the first place. Unfortunately, the three critical elements that could help Afghanistan break out of this cruel trap are constrained for different reasons.

To begin with, and as the foregoing discussion has elaborated, Pakistan is hobbled by political hesitancy and myriad operational limitations. To make things worse, NATO forces in Afghanistan are constrained by various "national caveats," that is, operational restrictions that prevent the alliance's International Security Assistance Force (ISAF) from undertaking the necessary combat operations required to prevent the Taliban from consolidating their foothold in southern and southeastern Afghanistan. Although ISAF is formally charged with the provision of security throughout Afghanistan, the main thrust of its effort revolves around supporting the approximately thirty- four provincial reconstruction teams (PRTs) operating throughout the country.

The PRTs are joint military- civilian units of between sixty and one thousand personnel engaged in reconstruction activities aimed at enhancing local security in order to permit the larger nation-building exercise to succeed. This essentially humanitarian mission, however, presumes the consent of local residents for its success and requires the PRT to be neutral and impartial with respect to any overarching political rivalries that may otherwise characterize its operating environment. The PRT is supposed to be robust enough to defend itself against attack, but it is emphatically not intended to be the spear point of change through offensive military action. Although the vision underlying the PRT is defensible, the fact that the social change it engenders has consequences for the local balance of power within Afghanistan implies that its activities are entirely unwelcome to those who oppose the larger nation-building project. Consequently, the PRTs specifically and the international community's reconstruction activities more generally have become the target of concerted attacks by Taliban and al-Qaeda forces, especially in southern and eastern Afghanistan. It is in this context that the national caveats handicapping ISAF— some seventy- one at last count— become relevant because they prevent the various contingents that compose the 38,000-strong force from effectively engaging the adversary as required in accordance with tactical necessity.

Thus, although ISAF's area of operations has now extended to all of Afghanistan thanks to its stage 3 expansion to the South and its stage 4 expansion to the East, the differential rules of engagement under which each national contingent now operates ensures that its full combat power cannot be brought to bear uniformly over the entire battlefield— to the obvious advantage of its Taliban and al- Qaeda adversaries. To make things worse, although ISAF is declared to be NATO's highest- priority mission, the alliance has had enormous difficulty convincing its member states to make the requisite contributions of manpower, equipment, and finance to secure victory in the combat operations in Afghanistan. As things stand today, NATO fields some 1.2 soldiers per thousand Afghan inhabitants. Even if the 85,000 Afghan security personnel and the 12,000-odd U.S. forces dedicated to Operation Enduring Freedom are added to the number, the ratio of security forces to population hovers at about 4 soldiers per thousand inhabitants. This level of force presence is abysmal, given that a considerable body of research suggests that successful nation-building operations require at least 10 soldiers per thousand inhabitants, and preferably 20 soldiers per thousand inhabitants if there is an active conflict.

NATO thus far has simply not been able to contemplate, let alone provide, combat forces at anything approximating these levels required for success in Afghanistan. The British, the

Canadians, and the Dutch have supplied the largest contingents actually involved in combat operations; although the Germans and the Italians have a significant presence, they are not involved in active combat. The French, too, while politically supportive of the ISAF mission in Afghanistan have declined to support the effort through either enhanced contributions or a restructuring of their current force posture. Although French forces remain among the most capable units within ISAF, the thousand- odd troops currently present in Afghanistan are deployed in the relatively secure areas in and around Kabul, with Paris continuing to resist NATO entreaties to dispatch these forces to the eastern and southern areas of Afghanistan where the Taliban opposition is most active.

The NATO presence in Afghanistan is thus characterized by a curious paradox: the most capable European states, largely those in western Europe, have simply declined to make the robust contributions required to win what is universally acknowledged as the "good war," while the alliance's newest entrants from eastern Europe appear far more willing to contribute to the ISAF effort even though they lack the depth of national and military resources possessed by their western European counterparts. Although the early U.S. disinclination to involve NATO in Afghan peace operations played some role in sustaining this paradox, the later European disenchantment with the U.S. war in Iraq, Washington's treatment of terrorist detainees, and the U.S. emphasis on attacking the adversary as opposed to protecting the population all appear to have contributed toward the western European inclination to stay aloof from any war- fighting entanglements.

This reluctance to contribute on the part of the stronger European allies is also reinforced partly by the presence of competing security priorities and the remarkably weak domestic support for any foreign military operations. Above all else, however, it is owed to the alliance's failure to create a consensus on the implications of a failure in Afghanistan for European security; the lack of a clarifying continental debate on the goals, strategy, and tactics associated with winning the war against al- Qaeda and the Taliban; and the stunning unwillingness on the part of the wealthier "post- heroic" European states to actually fight a war that would require them to expend blood and treasure by remaining ensconced, deployed, and operating with their full panoply of military capabilities in southern and eastern Afghanistan until the adversary is eventually routed.

Finally, the principal combatant elements conducting Operation Enduring Freedom, through war- fighting actions against the al-Qaeda and Taliban forces in Afghanistan, are also handicapped by several limitations. Among the most important of these is the availability of deployable troops. The 10,000-odd soldiers that the United States contributes to this combat operation, supplemented by token forces provided by the United Kingdom, Canada, and a few others, are increasingly insufficient given the growing scale and intensity of the Afghan insurgency. Although coalition forces are superbly trained and equipped and have proved themselves devastatingly effective in combat with their Taliban adversaries, they are simply insufficient to maintain the large- scale presence that is now required to win the war in southern and eastern Afghanistan, given the virulence of the challenge.

In the initial phase of Operation Enduring Freedom, when military operations essentially consisted of search- and- destroy operations that targeted roving bands of terrorists, the current force size was probably appropriate because the superior mobility, firepower, and training of U.S. forces permitted them to sanitize large areas of territory despite their relatively small numbers. With the Taliban insurgency now nourished by local roots particularly in the Nimruz, Helmand, Kandahar, Oruzgan, and Zabol provinces, simply defeating the insurgents in battle is insufficient because they appear able to replenish their numbers relatively easily using both local recruits and imports from across the border, and, more important, they are able to return covertly to the contested districts after their tactically victorious U.S. adversaries withdraw to their rear bases. Defeating this strategy requires a long- term presence of military forces in situ, which the division- sized U.S. combatant elements simply cannot provide. NATO's inability— and reluctance— to fulfill this role and to include combat operations whenever required merely compounds the problem with the result that the local inhabitants, especially those opposed to the Taliban, are compelled to make their peace with the insurgents merely as a means of preserving their security. The surreptitious return of the Taliban in this fashion to any given district invariably results then in the ejection of the nongovernmental organizations working therein, the interruption of state- organized developmental assistance, and a crisis in local governance— all of which exacerbate the vicious circle that further undermines security. Given this dynamic, there is good reason to fear that, just as in Vietnam several decades earlier, U.S. and allied military forces could win every tactical engagement with the Taliban and yet lose the general war for Afghanistan.

Attempting to defeat this problem with the small number of combatant forces available only ends up overusing them. The Fort Drum, New York–based U.S. 10th Mountain Division, for example, has already deployed to Afghanistan thrice in five years, and when deployed in the field it is invariably overextended operationally because of the need to cover those alliance contingents that are unable to engage in combat operations when required because of their nationally constrained rules of engagement. The only solution to this problem will be to beef up the U.S. military presence in southern Afghanistan: this may necessitate deploying more troops and equipment but, more importantly, entails creating a dedicated U.S. command operating under NATO aegis with full and exclusive authority to conduct the war as required without being hampered by the need to support the less able allied contingents.

The slow progress in raising the indigenous Afghan security forces has not helped either in the interim. Most NATO officials interviewed on this subject declared flatly that the Afghan National Police is currently incapable of satisfactorily performing even basic law enforcement functions and, further, that it would be a long time before the Afghan National Army would be capable of operating as a tactical partner with allied units in counterinsurgency operations and even longer before it could do so independently. Last, and despite many recent improvements, the coordination among the multiple national militaries engaged in reconstruction, counternarcotics, and counterterrorism in Afghanistan has simply not been as effective as it could be. In fact, problems of command and control among various coalition elements remain a serious and continuing impediment to the success of the Afghan stabilization effort. The vicious interaction of these many problems implies that the chicken- and- egg dilemmas confronting Afghanistan in regard to security and state presence are unlikely to be resolved any time soon.

On balance, therefore, the failure to eliminate the al- Qaeda and Taliban cadres in Afghanistan is owed to a complex cluster of causes. Pakistan's initial reluctance to interdict the Taliban stragglers who settled in the FATA and the leadership shuras that found homes in Quetta and elsewhere in Pakistan played an important role in permitting this organization to regenerate. This process has been aided, however, by Afghanistan's own missteps in governance, including the failure to deliver security and economic and social development as well as to limit the runaway expansion in the cultivation of poppy in southern Afghanistan. The Pakistani effort to systematically interdict al- Qaeda while simultaneously going easy on the Taliban is riddled with inescapable contradictions. Although this strategy provided some early and important fruit, its tensions are now exploited by both the Taliban and al- Qaeda as well as by the vitally important tribal constituencies that are increasingly less bystanders than full participants on the wrong side in the ongoing war on terror in the FATA. The operational, technical, and organizational limitations of the Pakistani counterterrorism forces deployed in some of the most inhospitable terrain in the world provides the final component of the explanation for why Islamabad has not done better. There is thus no doubt that Pakistan's reluctance to prosecute counterterrorism operations indivisibly has played an essential role in the failures along the Afghanistan- Pakistan border, but it is by no means the whole story, and any political posturing that suggests otherwise contributes neither to our understanding of the problem nor to its resolution.

## CONCLUSION

President Musharaf has on a number of occasions reteriated that serious efforts are required to 'combat this modern day evil, which threatens to destabilize our societies'. Unlike terrorist groups in other countries, the groups in Pakistan involved in terrorist activities and violence are also active in political arena in Pakistan. Internally, the latest ultra orthodox combine preaches a distorted, tri ballistic, ritualistic and dark version of Islam with no light of tolerance, peaceful co-existence, human rights and finer things of life. This deadly combine seeks to impose their version with the use of arms. The most dangerous part is that they can allure the law, befool the young, hoodwink the questioner, and over the skeptic in the garb of divine authority. They are against every institution and manifesto of modern age. Their special focus and victims are the women. They want them to be frightened within home: good only for domestic chores and child rearing. They are moving forward as they see a real chance of seizing power in this country and with their march the whole process of development, all institutions of the country, the way of life, religious beliefs and the state structure are under threat, forcing us to think what else constitutes the national security.

# 7

# Pakistan's Proxy Wars, Islamic Jihad and the Taliban

## EFFECTS OF PAKISTAN'S ROLE IN THE WAR

### *On the International Stage*

Pakistan's role in war against terrorism significantly improved her international status. Scholars argue that, US would leave Pakistan after gaining her objectives in war against terrorism. After joining the war on terror Pakistan gained billions of dollars of economic and military aid and also made some gains diplomatically but has lost its control over Afghan affairs.

### *Within Pakistan*

After September 11 and US invasion in Afghanistan there has been a dramatic rise in domestic terrorism, extremism and sectarianism in Pakistan. Pakistan is in the grip of regular suicide bombings, and has suffered high levels of civilian and military casualties as a result. Baluchistan and Tribal area issues are other implications for Pakistan, with US drones attacks in tribal areas being a real source of concern for Pakistani citizens. The US so far has carried out number of attacks in Pakistani territory. These attacks have led to deterioration of the security situation in tribal areas and the rest of the North-West Frontier Province. In Pakistan there is a growing resentment among people against these attacks on Pakistani soil.

## Western Involvement in Terrorism Inside Pakistan

On July 8, 2010, Pasha categorically stated that foreign powers are involved in terrorist activities inside Pakistan. He said, ""The foreign powers are involved in terrorism and destabilization of the country." During a briefing in the National Security Committee session headed by Senator Raza Rabbani, DG ISI Ahmed Shuja Pasha said that the western powers are involved in the terror activities inside the country.

"The US policy against terrorism is under consideration and the changes will be brought with time in accordance with the national interest," he said. This is not new claim inside Pakistan, many Pakistani political commentators have been speaking publicly about this phenomenon. It is alleged that terrorist activities inside Pakistan were actively carried out by the CIA, the RAW and the MOSSAD for different purposes. Chief among those, is changing the public perception of the War on Terror in the favor of the United States. There are confirmed reports that to achieve its objectives the CIA hired the services of at least a dozen Afghan warlords inside Afghanistan and provided through them arms and finances to militants in FATA and Swat to carry out murders and devastation in the country. It was like a double-edged sword not only to get the Army launch attacks against Taliban on Pakistani side of the border but also to give a message to the ISI that the CIA can use the Pakistani Taliban against their own security forces. Thousands of people have been killed in Pakistan due to terror attacks since the beginning of war on terror.

## Future Concerns

There is no doubt that a military campaign is necessary against extremists in the country but it must be supported by social, economic and political change with political reforms being at the top of agenda. The future of Pakistan's role in the war against terrorism is dependent on its political and economic ties with the US. Pakistan is a part of global war on terrorism and was not only defending itself, but also protecting the entire world form the catastrophe of terrorism and extremism, therefore, needs strategic partnership with the rest of the world to foster peace and stability in the region, promote economic stability and address energy needs.

## WAR IN NORTH-WEST PAKISTAN

The War in North-West Pakistan is an armed conflict between the Pakistan Armed Forces and armed religious groups such as the Tehrik-i-Taliban Pakistan (TTP), Lashkar-e-Islam, TSNM, Arab and Central Asian militants including Al-Qaeda, regional armed movements and elements of organized crime. The armed conflict began in 2004 when tensions, rooted in the Pakistan Army's search for Al Qaeda fighters in Pakistan's mountainous Waziristan area (in the Federally Administered Tribal Areas), escalated into armed resistance. Pakistan's actions were presented as Pakistan's role in the War on Terror in the international War on Terrorism. Clashes erupted between Pakistani army troops and Arab and Central Asian militia forces. The foreign militants were joined by Pakistani non-military veterans of the War in Afghanistan (2001–present) which subsequently established the Tehrik-i-Taliban Pakistan and other militia organizations such as Lashkar-e-Islam. The Tehreek-e-Nafaz-e-Shariat-e-Mohammadi (TSNM) established in 1992 allied with the Tehrik-i-Taliban Pakistan and Lashkar-e-Islam.

### *Background*

December 2003: Waziri attempts on President Musharraf's life

In December 2003, two assassination attempts against President Pervez Musharraf were traced to Waziristan. The government responded by intensifying military pressure on the area, however the fighting was costly and government forces would sustain heavy casualties throughout 2004 and into early 2005 when the government switched to a tactic of negotiation instead of direct conflict.

### *2004: Fighting Breaks Out*

On March 16, 2004, the bloody mountainous battle between Pakistan Army and the combined Taliban and Al-Qaeda fighters was insued. Both the International and National media speculated that Pakistan Armed Forces had surrounded the *"High Value Target"* in the mountainous region, possibly Al-Qaeda's Second-in-

Command Ayman al-Zawahiri. The battle was concluded as the Army had captured the entire mountainous region, and captured hundreds of Al-Qaeda fighters. However, the Army was failed to captured Ayman al-Zawahiri as he was either later escaped or he was never among the fighters.

## *Peace Deals*

In April 2004, the Government of Pakistan signed the first of three peace agreements with militants in South Waziristan. It was signed with militia commander Nek Muhammad Wazir, but was immediately abrogated once Nek Muhammad was killed by American Hellfire missile in June 2004. The second was signed in February 2005 with Nek's successor Baitullah Mehsud, which brought relative calm in the South Waziristan region. This deal will be later mimicked in the neighboring North Waziristan territory in September 2006 as the third and final truce between the government and the militants. However, all of these truces would not have a substantial effect in reducing bloodshed. The later two deals were officially broken in August 2007 with the Lal Masjid siege, which raised the suicide attacks on Pakistani forces tenfold throughout the country.

## *2005-2006*

On May 4, 2005, Pakistani commandos captured Abu Faraj al-Libbi after a raid outside the town of Mardan, 30 miles northeast of Peshawar. Abu Farraj al-Libbi was a high ranking al-Qaeda official, rumored to be third after Osama bin Laden and Ayman al-Zawahiri. Al-Libbi replaced Khalid Shaikh Mohammed after his arrest in March 2003 in connection with the September 11th attacks. The Pakistani government arrested al-Libbi and held him on charges in relation to being a chief planner in two assassination attempts on the life of President Pervez Musharraf in December 2003.

On January 13, 2006, the U.S. launched an airstrike on the village of Damadola. The attack occurred in the Bajaur tribal area, about 7 km (4.3 mi) from the Afghan border, and killed at least 18 people. The attack again targeted Ayman al-Zawahiri, but later evidence suggests he was not there.

## *June 2006: Ceasefire*

On June 21, 2006, pro-Tehrik-i-Taliban Pakistan militants in the Bannu region of North Waziristan stated they shot down a Bell military helicopter that was reported to have crashed. The government denied missile fire as the cause, stating it was due to technical faults. The helicopter had taken off from a base camp in Bannu at around 7am for Miramshah and crashed 15 minutes later into the Baran Dam in the Mohmandkhel area on Wednesday morning. Four soldiers were killed including Captain Shams (pilot), Captain Faisal (co-pilot), Lance Naik Ikram and sepoy Altaf, while three other, Sardar Ali, Waseem Abbas and Mohammad Arshad, were rescued. On the same day militants killed an inspector and two constables on a road connecting Bannu and the main town of Miranshah. On June 21, 2006, Afghan Taliban leader Sirajuddin Haqqani issued a decree that it was not (Afghan) Taliban policy to fight the Pakistan Army. However, the Tehrik-i-Taliban Pakistan intentionally did not circulate the decree in North Waziristan thereby keeping pressure on the government.

## *September 2006: Waziristan Peace Accord Signed*

On September 5, 2006, the Waziristan Accord, an agreement between tribal leaders and the Pakistani government was signed in Miranshah, North Waziristan. to end all fighting. The agreement includes the following provisions:

- The Pakistani Army will help reconstruct infrastructure in tribal areas of North and South Waziristan.
- The Pakistani Military will not tolerate any assistance to intruders in North Waziristan, and will monitor actions in the region.
- The Pakistan government is to compensate tribal leaders for the loss of life and property of innocent tribesmen.
- "Foreigners" (informally understood to be foreign jihadists) are not allowed to use Pakistani territory for any terrorist activity anywhere in the world.
- 2,500 foreigners who were originally held on suspicion of having links to the Taliban were to be detained for necessary action against them.

The agreement, dubbed the Waziristan accord, has been viewed by some political commentators as a success for Pakistan. Further details of the agreement, as well as comments on the agreement made by US, Pakistani, and Taliban spokesmen is available in the Waziristan accord article.

## October 2006: The Madrassa Air Strike

On October 30, 2006, the Pakistani army conducted an air strike against a madrassa in the Bajaur region bordering Afghanistan. The madrassa was destroyed killing 70 to 80 people. In retaliation for the attack the militants conducted a suicide bombing on an army camp on November 8, 2006, killing 42 Pakistani soldiers and wounding 20.

## 2007

In March, Pakistan signed a peace treaty with Faqir Mohammed, the main militant leader in Bajaur. Militant groups now held three districts in the Federally Administered Tribal Areas: South Waziristan, North Waziristan and Bajaur Agency.

## Waziri-Uzbek Tensions

Reportedly, the fighting sparked by the killing of Saiful Adil, an al-Qaeda-linked Arab, blamed on the Uzbeks by Maulavi Nazir, described as a top pro-Taliban militant commander in the region. According to the other version, fighting started after Mullah Nazir, whom the government says has come over to its side, ordered the Uzbek followers of Tohir Yo'ldosh, formerly a close confidant of Osama bin Laden, to disarm. It was also preceded by the clashes between the IMU and a pro-government tribal leader in Azam Warsak, in which 17 to 19 people died before a ceasefire was announced.

## Defeat of the Islamic Movement of Uzbekistan

Local militants allied to the tribesmen were reported attacking and seizing the IMU's private jail in Azam Warsak. The Pakistan Army said it did not intend to step in, but witnesses say government artillery fired on the Uzbek bunkers they set up to fight the tribesmen. Heavy fighting resumed on March 29, ending a week-long ceasefire between tribal fighters and foreign militants. According to initial reports, tribesmen attacked a checkpoint manned by Uzbek militants and captured two of them. The clashes also left one tribal fighter dead and three wounded.

The following day, a senior Pakistani official announced that 52 people were killed during the past two days, 45 of them Uzbeks and the rest tribesmen. One of Maulvi Nazir's aides put the death toll at 35 Uzbeks and 10 tribal fighters.

However, residents in the area said that the death toll on both sides was inflated. The conflict further escalated on April 2 when a council of elders declared jihad against foreign militants and started to raise an army of tribesmen. According to Pakistani security officials, heavy fighting concentrated in the village of Doza Ghundai left more than 60 people dead, including 50 foreigners, 10 tribal fighters and one Pakistani soldier. He also said that "dozens" of Uzbeks had surrendered to tribal forces and that many bunkers used by militants were seized or destroyed. On April 12, 2007 the army general in charge of South Waziristan said that tribal fighters had cleared the Uzbeks out of the valleys surrounding Wana and the foreign militants had been pushed back into the mountains on the Afghan border. Four days later, the local tribesmen has urged Islamabad to resume control of law and order in the area.

## Lal Masjid siege

On July 3, 2007, the militant supporters of Lal Masjid and Pakistani security forces clashed in Islamabad after the students from the mosque attacked a nearby government ministry building with stones. Their resultant faceoff with the military escalated, despite the intervention of then-ruling Pakistan Muslim League (Q) leaders Chaudhry Shujaat Hussain and Muhammad Ijaz-ul-Haq. The Pakistani security forces immediately put up a siege around the mosque complex which lasted until July 11 and resulted in 108 deaths. This represented the main catalyst for the conflict and eventual breakdown of the truce that existed between Pakistan and the Pakistani Taliban groups. Already during the siege there were several attacks in Waziristan in retaliation for the siege.

### Truce in Waziristan Broken

As the siege in Islamabad ensued, several attacks on Pakistani troops in Waziristan were reported. On July 14, 2007, a suicide bomber attacked a Pakistani Army convoy killing 25 soldiers and wounding 54. On July 15, 2007, two suicide bombers attacked another Pakistani Army convoy killing 16 soldiers and 5 civilians and wounding another 47 people. And in a separate incident a fourth suicide bomber attacked a police headquarters killing 28 police officers and recruits and wounding 35 people. The assault on the Red Mosque prompted rebels along the border with Afghanistan to scrap the controversial Waziristan Accord with the government.

### The New War in Waziristan

The Army moved large concentration of troops into Waziristan and engaged in fierce clashes with militants in which at least 100 militants were killed including wanted terrorist and former Guantanamo Bay detainee, Abdullah Mehsud. The militants also struck back by attacking Army convoys, security check points and sending suicide bombers killing dozens of soldiers and police and over 100 civilians. In one month of fighting during the period from July 24 to August 24, 2007, 250 militants and 60 soldiers were killed. On September 2, 2007, just a few dozen militants led by Baitullah Mehsud managed to ambush a 17-vehicle army convoy and captured an estimated 247 soldiers without a shot being fired, an event that shocked the nation. Several officers were among the captured.

After the army returned to Waziristan, they garrisoned the areas and set up check-points, but the militants hit hard. In mid-September the Tehrik-i-Taliban Pakistan and other forces attacked a number of Pakistani army outposts all across North and South Waziristan. This resulted in some of the heaviest fighting of the war. Following the Lal Masjid Siege, On September 12, 2007, the first outpost was attacked and overrun by the militants resulting in the capture of 12 Pakistani soldiers.

The next day on September 13, 2007, a suicide bomber in Tarbela Ghazi attacked a Pakistani army base, destroying the main mess hall and killing 20 members of the Karrar commando group; Pakistan's most elite army unit. A series of attacks ensued and by September 20, 2007 a total of five Pakistani Army military outposts had been overrun and more than 25 soldiers captured. More than 65 soldiers were either killed or captured and almost 100 wounded. A little over two weeks later, the Army responded with helicopter gunships, jet fighters and ground troops. They hit militant positions near the town of Mir Ali. In heavy fighting over four days, 257 people were killed, including 175 militants, 47 soldiers and 35 civilians.

## Battle of Swat Valley

By the end of October fighting erupted in the Swat district of the Khyber Pakhtunkhwa province, with a large Tehreek-e-Nafaz-e-Shariat-e-Mohammadi force, under the command of Maulana Fazlullah, trying to impose Sharia law. Around 3,000 paramilitary soldiers were sent to confront them. After almost a week of heavy fighting the battle came to a standstill with both sides suffering heavy casualties. Then on November 1 and November 3, 220 paramilitary soldiers and policemen surrendered or deserted after a military position on a hill-top and two police stations were overrun.

This left the Tehreek-e-Nafaz-e-Shariat-e-Mohammadi (TNSM) in control of most of the Swat district. The fighting in Swat is the first serious insurgent threat from militia forces in what is known as a settled area of Pakistan. Forces loyal to Maulana Fazlullah, including some foreign fighters, after taking control of a series of small towns and villages, tried to implement strict Islamic law in November 2007. In mid-November the regular army was deployed with the help of helicopter gunships to crush the uprising. The Pakistan Army deployed over 2,500 men. By the beginning of December the fighting had ended and the Army recaptured Swat. Almost 400 of Maulana Fazlullah's fighters were dead along with 15 Pakistani soldiers and 20 civilians in the military offensive. Despite the victory by the Pakistani army, TNSM militants slowly re-entered Swat over the coming months and started engaging security forces in battles that lasted throughout 2008. By early February 2009, the whole district was in Pakistan Army Control.

## The Rawalpindi Attacks

On September 3, two suicide bombers targeted a military intelligence (ISI) bus and a line of cars carrying ISI officers. The bus attack killed a large number of Defence Ministry workers and the other attack killed an Army colonel. In all 31 people, 19 soldiers and 12 civilians, were killed. Over two months later on November 24, one of the targets was a military intelligence bus. Almost everyone on the bus was killed. The other bomber blew up at a military checkpoint. 35 people were killed, almost all military.

## State of Emergency

The 2007 Pakistani state of emergency was declared by Pervez Musharraf on 2007-11-03 and lasted until 2007-12-15. During this time the constitution of the country was suspended. This action and its responses are generally related to the controversies surrounding the re-election of Musharraf during the presidential election that had occurred on 2007-10-06, and also was claimed by the government to be the reaction to the actions by militants in Waziristan.

## Benazir Bhutto's Assassination

On December 27, 2007, Pakistani opposition leader Benazir Bhutto was killed upon leaving a political rally for the Pakistan Peoples Party (PPP) in Rawalpindi, Pakistan. A suicidal assassin reportedly fired shots in Bhutto's direction just prior to detonating an explosive pellet-laden vest, killing approximately 24 people and wounding many more. Musharraf and the army blamed the attack on Al-Qaida, but the following day a statement by Baitullah Mehsud was sent to the media saying that he and Al-Qaida had no involvement in the murder of the former Prime Minister, he briefed that these were the crimes of Musharraf and the army.

The killing was followed by a wave of violence across the country that left 58 people dead, including four police officers. Most of the violence was directed at Musharraf and the pro-Musharraf political party, Pakistan Muslim League (Q). The public chanted slogans against the army and Musharraf: "Musharraf Dog", "General is a murderer", "uniform (army) wearing murderers", etc. Bhutto had previously survived an assassination attempt made on her life during her homecoming which left 139 people dead and hundreds wounded.

## 2008: More fighting in South Waziristan

In January 2008, militants overran Sararogha Fort, and may have overrun a fort in Ladah as well. Both forts are in South Waziristan, and were held by the Pakistani army. On February 25, 2008, a suicide bomber struck in the garrison-town of Rawalpindi killing Pakistani Lt. Gen. Mushtaq Baig along with two more soldiers and five civilians. Baig was the highest-level military official to be assassinated since Pakistan joined the war on terror.

## Operation Zalzala

A full-fledged security operation called 'Zalzala' (*earthquake*) by Pakistan Army's 14th Infantry Division in January to flush out Baitullah Mehsud's Tehrik-i-Taliban Pakistan militants from the area. Until then the area was infested with militants, with some villagers providing them support and shelter. Many militants were killed during the operation, and within three days the security forces were in full control of the area. The army later captured a few other villages and small towns to put the squeeze on Baitullah Mehsud. However, the operation led to a huge displacement of local population. According to 14 Division GOC Maj Gen Tariq Khan, about 200,000 people, including men, women and children, were displaced. Khalid Aziz, former NWFP chief secretary and expert on tribal affairs, said the displacement was "one of the biggest in tribal history" adding that human cost of the conflict in Waziristan "has gone unrecorded."

## Peace agreement

On February 7, 2008, the Tehrik-i-Taliban Pakistan (TTP) led by Baitullah Mehsud offered a truce and peace negotiations resulting in a suspension of violence. On May 21, 2008 Pakistan signed a peace agreement with the Tehrik-i-Taliban Pakistan (TTP). Despite the agreement sporadic fighting continued until late June and escalated with the takeover of the town of Jandola on June 24, by the militants. 22 pro-government tribal fighters were captured and executed by the TTP at that time. On June 28, 2008, Pakistan's Army started an offensive against militia fighters in Khyber, codenamed *Operation Sirat-e-Mustaqeem*. The military took control of a key town and demolished an insurgent group's building. 1 militant was reportedly killed while 2 soldiers died in Swat valley. The operation was halted in early July.

On July 19, 2008, clashes erupted between the Tehrik-i-Taliban Pakistan and a faction of pro-government Taliban militants. 10-15 of the pro-government fighters were killed and another 120 were captured.

Among the captured were two commanders who were tried under "Islamic" law by the Taliban and then executed. On July 21, 2008, heavy fighting in Baluchistan killed 32 militants, 9 soldiers and 2 civilians. More than two dozen militants were captured and a large weapons cache was found. Between July 28 and August 4, 2008, heavy fighting flared up in the northwestern Swat valley leaving 94 militants and 22 soldiers and policemen dead. Another 28 civilians were also killed.

## Bajaur Offensive Starts

Heavy fighting erupted on August 6, 2008, in the Loisam area of Bajaur district. Loisam lies on the strategically important road leading towards the main northwestern city of Peshawar. The fighting started when hundreds of militants poured into the area attacking government forces. After four days of fighting on August 10 the military withdrew from the area. 100 militants and 9 soldiers were confirmed killed and another 55 soldiers were missing, at least three dozen of them captured by the militants. While the fighting was going on in Bajaur, in the Buner area of Khyber-Pakhtunkhwa militants killed at least nine policemen in an attack on a check post. The checkpoint was then abandoned, and the local Pakistani forces withdrew to Khar, the main town of Bajaur Agency. There were reports that the town of Khar was then besieged by tribal militants. On August 21, 2008, in response to the military offensive in Bajaur, two suicide bombers attacked the Pakistan Ordnance Factories in Wah while workers were changing shifts. The attack killed at least 70 people.

## Tribesmen Declare War Against the Militants

By the beginning of September 2008, Pakistani tribal elders began organising a private army of approximately 30,000 tribesmen to fight the militias. A lashkar, or private army, composed of Pakistani tribesmen, began torching the houses of militia commanders in Bajaur, near the Afghan border, vowing to fight them until they are expelled. This included the house of a local militant commander named Naimatullah, who had occupied several government schools and converted them into seminaries. A tribal elder named Malik Munsib Khan, who heads the lashkar, said that tribesmen would continue their struggle until the militants were expelled from the area, adding that anyone found sheltering militants would be fined one million rupees and their houses will be torched. The tribesmen also torched two important centres of the militants in the area and gained control of most of the tehsil.

The main reasons for this was that the operations that were taking place in the Federally Administered Tribal Areas had displaced some 300,000 people while dozens of citizens have been killed in clashes between the militants and military. Since the start of Pakistan's war against the militants some 150,000 tribesmen have sided with them.

## US Support and Aid for Pakistani Tribesmen

Recent American military proposals outlines an intensified effort to enlist tribal leaders in the frontier areas of Pakistan in the fight against Al Qaeda, the Afghan Taliban and Pakistani militia groups, as part of a broader effort to bolster Pakistani forces against militancy in the region. The proposal is modeled in part on a similar effort by American forces in Iraq that has been hailed as a great success in fighting foreign insurgents there. But it raises the question of whether such partnerships can be forged without a significant American military presence in Pakistan. And it is unclear whether enough support can be found among the tribes. Small numbers of United States military personnel have served as advisers to the Pakistani Army in the tribal areas, giving planning advice and helping to integrate American intelligence. Under this new approach, the number of advisers would increase. American officials said these security improvements complemented a package of assistance from the Agency for International Development and the State Department for the seven districts of the tribal areas that amounted to $750 million over five years, and would involve work in education, health and other sectors. The State Department's Bureau of International Narcotics and Law Enforcement Affairs is also assisting the Frontier Corps with financing for counternarcotics work.

### Islamabad Marriott Hotel Bombing

On September 23, 2008, the Pakistani Army, backed by helicopter gunships and artillery killed more than 60 insurgents in northwest Pakistan in offensives as the response to the Islamabad Marriott Hotel bombing over the weekend at the Marriott hotel in the capital Islamabad that killed 53 people. In the nearby Bajur tribal region, the Army killed at least 10 militants, according to government officials. The Bajur operations, which the army says has left more than 700 suspected militants dead, has won praise from U.S. officials.

### Renewed Bajaur Offensive

Pakistani President Asif Ali Zardari publicly vowed revenge in response to the Islamabad Marriott Hotel bombing. By September 26, 2008, Pakistani troops had successfully conducted and completed a major offensive in the Bajaur and the Tang Khata regions of the Federally Administered Tribal Areas, codenamed *Operation Sherdil*. Pakistani troops had killed over 1,000 militants in a huge offensive, a day after President Asif Ali Zardari lashed out at US forces over a clash on the Afghan border.

Tariq Khan, Inspector General of the Paramilitary Frontier Corps, mentioned to journalists that since the beginning of the Bajaur operations, there were up to 2,000 militant fighters including hundreds of foreigners who were fighting with the soldiers and the security forces. The overall death toll was over 1,000 militants and also adding that 27 Pakistani soldiers had also been killed with 111 soldiers seriously wounded. Five top Al-Qaeda and militia commanders were among those killed in a month-long operation in Bajaur. Of the five militant commanders killed, four appeared to be foreigners: Egyptian Abu Saeed Al-Masri; Abu Suleiman, an Arab; an Uzbek commander named Mullah Mansoor; and an Afghan commander called Manaras. The fifth was a Pakistani commander named only Abdullah, a son of ageing hardline leader Maulvi Faqir Mohammad who is based in Bajaur and has close ties to Al-Qaeda second-in-command Ayman al-Zawahiri.

Between October 22 and October 24, security forces engaged in another push against militants in the restive Bajaur and Khyber tribal regions. Air strikes were carried out in the Nawagai and Mamond sub-districts of Bajaur Agency. The troops destroyed several centres of militants at Charmang, Chinar and Zorbandar and had inflicted heavy losses on them. Gunship helicopters shelled in Charming, Cheenar, Kohiand Babarha areas of Nawagai and Mamund Tehsil of Bajaur agency, destroying various underground hideouts and bunkers of militants. The security forces had also taken control of different areas of Loisam, a militant headquarters, and advanced towards other areas for complete control..

## BENAZIR BHUTTO'S ISLAMIC FUNDAMENTALISATION OF PAKISTAN

Benazir Bhutto's first advent as Prime Minister coincided roughly with the disintegration of the Soviet Union and the Soviet withdrawal from Afghanistan where Pakistan was spearheading the American effort. Since strategic aims had been met, it would have been logical for the self-proclaimed Pakistani democrat Prime Minister to wind up the Islamic fundamentalist Mujahideen bases in Pakistan and their nurseries. No such thing happened. On the contrary "Benazir Bhutto, who became the Prime Minister in 1989 had a profoundly different perception of the role and utility of Islamist terrorism. Convinced that Pakistan's destiny lay in strategic alliances with such countries as Syria, Iran, China (PRC) and North Korea, Benazir Bhutto's Islamabad re-examined all aspects of Pakistan's involvement in Afghanistan and the world of State-sponsored terrorism became an instrument of crucial significance for Pakistani policy. Islamabad now committed to furthering Islamism in the heart of Asia . . . Islamabad recognized the growing specter of confrontation with the United States over strategic posture in the region. Still Islamabad shifted to active support for militant Islamism."

As a follow-up of Benazir Bhutto's policy of exploiting Islamic fundamentalist terrorism as a state-sponsored tool, Pakistan was flooded with about 16000-20000 Islamist militants from over 20 countries all freely given visas for Pakistan. The Soviets had withdrawn from Afghanistan and surely they had not come for Afghanistan's liberation. They had come for training in Pakistan and to fight for Pakistani state-sponsored Jehads from Kashmir to Central Asia. General Zia as military ruler of Pakistan for eleven years preceding Prime Minister Bhutto could not achieve what she achieved in terms of Islamic fundamentalisation of Pakistan: " In the quest for Islamic violence the camps of the Islamist Afghan resistance in Pakistan became to Sunni Islamist terrorism what Lebanon had been for radical leftist terrorism. Pakistan became a place of pilgrimage for aspiring Islamist radicals." Benazir Bhutto on return to power in 1993 had not lost her zeal for Islamic fundamentalisation : "By the end of 1993, after her round of visits to Beijing, Pyongyang and Tehran, Bhutto clearly demonstrated her determination to implement these policies (Islamic terrorism as state-sponsored foreign policy tool) and realise this strategic posture as soon as possible. Markedly increasing Pakistan's participation in the Islamist international terrorist system was an integral part of Bhutto's new strategy."

Benazir's active linkages with Pan-Islamic fundamentalist terrorist organisations stands adequately exposed in the book referred: "In mid-December 1993, Turabi (Sudanese Islamic fundamentalist leader) organised another "Popular Arab and Islamic Conference (PAIC) in Khartoum to discuss the next phase of the Islamist struggle . . . The PAIC conference focussed on the role of Pakistan . . . in particular Pakistan's future active support for Islamist armed struggles and international terrorism. The official Pakistan delegation was led by two other Bhutto confidants (the other was a close Bhutto adviser from her party PPP) General Mirza Aslam Beg, the former Chief of Staff of Pakistani Armed Forces and Lt. General Hamid Gul, the former chief of ISI (Pakistani intelligence) . . . Their participation in the Khartoum conference and leading role in the formulation of Pakistan's relations with the PAIC and the Islamist (read Islamic fundamentalist) world was proof that Bhutto's Islamabad would continue to pursue Islamist policies."

## THE TALIBAN'S CREATION DURING PREMIERSHIP OF BHUTTO

Pakistan figures prominently in any discussions related to the Taliban in terms of creating this medieval monster in Afghanistan and the subsequent inhuman repression that the Taliban has imposed on the Afghans themselves. ISI also figures prominently in relation to provision of Pak Army cadres, military advisers and military hardware. However what does not figure is Benazir Bhutto's role in its creation. The Taliban emerged forcefully on the Afghan scene in the period 1993-94 and captured the whole of Afghanistan, less the Northern Provinces by September 1996. It requires to be noted that all these developments took place during Benazir Bhutto's second tenure as Prime Minister, i.e., 1993- 1996. As one author puts it: "Furthermore, there was considerable evidence to suggest that the Taliban were being strongly supported by the Pakistani government led by Benazir Bhutto, ironically a woman educated at Oxford and Harvard."

Initially, more than the ISI, it was the Bhutto party machine both at Islamabad and in the provincial capitals at Peshawar (NWFP) and Quetta (Baluchistan) which were active in the reinforcement and furtherance of Taliban operations. It is indicated that: "When the Taliban captured Kandahar, the ISI was initially more sceptical than the Government about the chances of further success. While General Babar( Bhutto's Interior Minister) and the Jamiat-e Ulema-i Islam pushed for support to the Taliban, the ISI took a back seat. Thus Babar had a free hand in "civilianising" the initial support to the Taliban."

Benazir's newly created Taliban ensured that they had the right connections in Pakistan to enable continued support as this would suggest: "And the Taliban soon developed close relations with several businessmen close to Asaf Ali Zardari- the husband of Benazir Bhutto, who in turn were given the highly lucrative permits to export fuel to Afghanistan. As the Taliban's war machine expanded, permits for fuel supplies from Pakistan became a major money earner for Pakistani politicians" . . . The linkages and implications are self evident.

## Conclusion

Benazir's pretentious pronouncements are avidly lapped up in Washington and New Delhi as emanating from a committed democrat, a Pakistani politician of moderate hues and above all a Muslim with western educated secular values, in short someone New Delhi could trust in political dealings. The above record of Benazir Bhutto however does not match up with what she would like us to believe about her.

Bodansky states that: " Pakistan's ascent in the Islamist terrorist system is particularly important in a strategic context. Pakistan's growing involvement resulted in both escalation of the war by proxy in Kashmir and the rise of Taliban in Afghanistan, two movements that still provide shelter and closely cooperate with Osama bin Laden."

What Bodansky has not added to complete this summation is that in terms of contextual time-spans both these developments emerged during the two tenures of Benazir Bhutto as Prime Minister of Pakistan. Benazir's duplicity against the United States of America of forming a Trans-Asian anti- US alliance while mouthing platitudes on democracy during Washington visits indicates a fatal flaw in her political credibility. Comparatively speaking, former PM Nawaz Sharif appears far superior to Benazir's Bhutto. He had at least the courage to fight an election in Pakistan on the agenda of improvement of Indo-Pak relations and won on this issue with an overwhelming majority.

Regrettably, Benazir Bhutto's record on Islamic fundamentalism of Pakistan, escalation of the proxy war in Kashmir and the creation of the Taliban leads one to the conclusion that Washington's assessments of Pakistani politicians and Pakistan's political scene tend to be faulty and unreliable as inputs for any Track II diplomacy. Both these conclusions are pertinent presently for those advising and espousing the continuation of India's cease fire in Kashmir.

## PAKISTAN, TALIBAN-STYLE?

The war between India and Pakistan over the fate of Kashmir is as old as both states. When Pakistan was formally created in 1947, the rulers of Muslim-majority states that had existed within British India were given the option of joining India or Pakistan. The Hindu monarch of the predominantly Muslim state of Jammu and Kashmir chose India, prompted partly by a tribal rebellion in the state. Pakistan responded by sending in troops. The resultant fighting ended with a 1949 cease-fire, but the Pakistani government continued covertly to support volunteer guerrilla fighters in Kashmir. Islamabad argued then, as it does now, that it could not control the volunteers, who as individuals were not bound by the cease-fire agreement. (On the other hand, Maulana Abul A'la Maududi, the late founder of the Islamist party Jamaat-e-Islami, argued that as individuals, these "mujahideen" could not legitimately declare jihad, either.)

Pakistani officials admit to having tried repeatedly to foment separatism in Kashmir in the decades following the 1948 cease-fire. These attempts were largely unsuccessful; when separatist violence broke out in the late 1980s, the movement was largely indigenous. For their part, Indian officials admit their own culpability in creating an intolerable situation in the region. They ignored Kashmir's significant economic troubles, rampant corruption, and rigged elections, and they intervened in Kashmiri politics in ways that contradicted India's own constitution. As American scholar Sumit Ganguly explains, the rigged 1987 state-assembly elections were the final straw in a series of insults, igniting, by 1989, widespread violent opposition. By 1992, Pakistani nationals and other graduates of the Afghan war were joining the fight in Kashmir.

What began as an indigenous, secular movement for independence has become an increasingly Islamist crusade to bring all of Kashmir under Pakistani control. Pakistan-based Islamist groups (along with Hizb-ul-Mujahideen, a Kashmir-based group created by Jamaat-e-Islami and partly funded by Pakistan) are now significantly more important than the secular Kashmir-based ones. The Indian government estimates that about 40 percent of the militants in Kashmir today are Pakistani or Afghan, and some 80 percent are teenagers. Although the exact size of the movement is unknown, the Indian government estimates that 3,000 to 4,000 "mujahideen" are in Kashmir at any given time.

Whatever their exact numbers, these Pakistani militant groups — among them, Lashkar-i-Taiba and Harkat-ul-Mujahideen — pose a long-term danger to international security, regional stability, and especially Pakistan itself. Although their current agenda is limited to "liberating" Kashmir, which they believe was annexed by India illegally, their next objective is to turn Pakistan into a truly Islamic state. Islamabad supports these volunteers as a cheap way to keep India off balance. In the process, however, it is creating a monster that threatens to devour Pakistani society.

## Schools of Hate

In Pakistan, as in many developing countries, education is not mandatory. The World Bank estimates that only 40 percent of Pakistanis are literate, and many rural areas lack public schools. Islamic religious schools — madrasahs — on the other hand, are located all over the country and provide not only free education, but also free food, housing, and clothing. In the poor areas of southern Punjab, madrasahs funded by the Sunni sectarian political party Sipah-e-Sahaba Pakistan (SSP) reportedly even pay parents for sending them their children. In the 1980s, Pakistani dictator General Mohammad Zia-ul-Haq promoted the madrasahs as a way to garner the religious parties' support for his rule and to recruit troops for the anti-Soviet war in Afghanistan. At the time, many madrasahs were financed by the zakat (the Islamic tithe collected by the state), giving the government at least a modicum of control. But now, more and more religious schools are funded privately — by wealthy Pakistani industrialists at home or abroad, by private and government-funded nongovernmental organizations in the Persian Gulf states and Saudi Arabia, and by Iran. Without state supervision, these madrasahs are free to preach a narrow and violent version of Islam.

Most madrasahs offer only religious instruction, ignoring math, science, and other secular subjects important for functioning in modern society. As Maududi warned in his 1960 book, First Principles of the Islamic State, "those who choose the theological branch of learning generally keep themselves utterly ignorant of [secular subjects, thereby remaining] incapable of giving any lead to the people regarding modern political problems." Even worse, some extremist madrasahs preach jihad without understanding the concept: They equate jihad — which most Islamic scholars interpret as the striving for justice (and principally an inner striving to purify the self) — with guerrilla warfare. These schools encourage their graduates, who often cannot find work because of their lack of practical education, to fulfil their "spiritual obligations" by fighting against Hindus in Kashmir or against Muslims of other sects in Pakistan. Pakistani officials estimate that 10 to 15 percent of the country's tens of thousands of madrasahs espouse such extremist ideologies.

Pakistan's interior minister Moinuddin Haider, for one, recognizes these problems. "The brand of Islam they are teaching is not good for Pakistan," he says. "Some, in the garb of religious training, are busy fanning sectarian violence, poisoning people's minds." In June, Haider announced a reform plan that would require all madrasahs to register with the government, expand their curricula, disclose their financial resources, seek permission for admitting foreign students, and stop sending students to militant training camps.

This is not the first time the Pakistani government has announced such plans. And Haider's reforms so far seem to have failed, whether because of the regime's negligence or the madrasahs' refusal to be regulated, or both. Only about 4,350 of the estimated 40,000 to 50,000 madrasahs in Pakistan have registered with the government. Some are still sending students to training camps despite parents' instructions not to do so. Moreover, some chancellors are unwilling to expand their curricula, arguing that madrasahs are older than Pakistan itself — having been "designed 1,200 years ago in Iraq," according to the chancellor of the Khudamudeen madrasah. The chancellor of Darul Uloom Haqqania objects to what he calls the government's attempt to "destroy the spirit of the madrasahs under the cover of broadening their curriculum." Mujibur Rehman Inqalabi, the SSP's second in command, told me that Haider's reform plan is "against Islam" and complains that where states have taken control of madrasahs, such as in Jordan and Egypt, "the engine of jihad is extinguished." America is right, he said: "Madrasahs are the supply line for jihad."

## PAKISTAN AND JIHADIST VERSES

While Pakistan Army and civilian government are engaged with the US and other nations in fighting terrorism within their country as well as in Afghanistan, the volatile country is leaning more towards becoming a radical State than before. This is a dangerous trend particularly when the New York Times and Washington Post have reported that Pakistan is beefing up its nuclear arsenal at a breakneck speed and has already overtaken India in terms of the number of nuclear bombs at its disposal. Pakistan now has 110 nukes as compared to an estimated 60 to 80 nuclear bombs India is currently believed to have. Already Pakistan has emerged as the world's fastest growing nuclear arsenal power and is poised to displace the United Kingdom as the world's fifth largest nuclear weapon power.

India needs to take appropriate steps to deal with the national security threat the growing number of Pakistani nukes poses. The unpredictable, mercurial nation that India's Islamic neighbour is adds to New Delhi's problems. Unlike India, Pakistan does not subscribe to the no-first-use doctrine with regard to nuclear weapons. In fact, Pakistan had considered nuking India during the 1999 Kargil war. Therefore, it is all the more important for India in particular and the international community in general for Pakistan to behave responsibly and maturely. Unfortunately this is not happening and there are signs that Pakistan is hurtling headlong into the jihadist matrix. Two recent incidents are telling pointers to this grave development. In November 2010, for instance, Al-Rehmat Trust organised a series of courses on "jihadist verses' in Koran in more than 18 cities of Pakistan. The Trust is a front for Jaish-e-Mohammand, one of the most notorious terrorist groups operating from Pakistan with base in Bahawalpur and Peshawar.

Jaish is headed by Maulana Masood Azhar, a former Harkat-ul Ansar rabble rouser, wanted in the 1999 Indian Airlines hijacking and several other terrorist attacks in India. According to the US Treasury Department, Jaish began using Al-Rehmat as a front organisation in 2002 after the former was banned by the US following the December 13 2001 attack on the Indian Parliament. The trust was used to recruit new set of terrorists for fighting the US forces in Afghanistan early 2009.

Another incident relates to October 2010 about the Taliban setting up schools on the outskirts of Karachi. These schools are outrightly terrorist schools where young students are taught bomb making and suicide bombings. One of the students, arrested by the police before he could blow himself up, said students were told that the Muslims in the world were being subjected to brutality and it was their duty to take revenge. It is not known how many schools and students are in these Taliban run schools. These are not the only Taliban schools. In fact, pro-Taliban madrasas have been in existence across Pakistan, including Islamabad, for quite some time. Lal Masjid in Islamabad was in fact one of the biggest of such madrasas claiming to work for turning Pakistan into an Islamic state and to establish Caliphate across the world through jihad. A survey conducted in Islamabad at that time showed Lal Masjid was not the only jihadi madrasa in the capital but at least 25 per cent of all mosques and madrasas either taught jihad or propagated extremist views.

These developments must be read with the support the Taliban has among the people, the army and the political leadership. One of the staunchest supporters of the Taliban is Pakistan's Tourism Minister Maulana Attaur Rehman. A Pashtun from Jamat Ulema-e-Islam-Fazlur Rehman party, Attaur said early this month at a public meeting that the Taliban were the true believers of Islamic ideology. He said it was the US which was the "biggest terrorist". There are others with equally strong views on the Taliban. These civilian leaders compliment the views held by terrorist leaders like Hafiz Saeed and Masood Azhar who leave no opportunity to propagate violence as a means to achieve whatever goals they have imagined for the Muslim world. Saeed has a much more powerful platform to propagate his terrorist views and objectives; he runs over 150 schools and more than 85 madrasas where hatred and violence are an integral part of the curriculum.

The school textbooks, published by his group, espouse a violent cause among the impressionable young students. His group also runs a powerful students body in Punjab University where its members promote extremist views among the student community and strongly oppose any attempt to project liberal views and opinions. It is not surprising that a large number of students from various colleges in Punjab find their way to terrorist training camps run by Lashkar-e-Toiba (LeT). In fact, a November 2010 report said several hundred students from Punjab were undergoing training at LeT camps in Pakistan Occupied Kashmir. Their agenda is to carry out terrorist attacks in India and to help the Taliban to fight the US-led forces in Afghanistan. With so many extremist forces brainwashing, indoctrinating and training the young students in Pakistan, its transformation into a radical state is not far. A deeply concerned India has to take pro-active measures to insulate it in case the Pakistani nukes fall into the hands of the jihadists by accident or by design of ever obliging elements in the Pakistani military and intelligence establishment. The increasing number of Pakistani nukes means more headaches for the Pakistani security establishment in safekeeping. It also means a higher success quotient for the terrorists in trying to steal the nuclear bombs.

## PAKISTAN'S UNHOLY ALLIANCE THE MILITANTS

The heavily guarded, high-walled concrete structure right in the heart of Islamabad has no signboard. But everyone in the capital knows that the sprawling compound surrounded by barbed wire houses the Directorate for Inter-Services Intelligence (ISI). The spy agency has been the country's big brother. It is powerful, ubiquitous and has functioned with so much autonomy from the central government that it has almost become a state within a state. It is not only responsible for intelligence gathering, but also acts as a determinant of Pakistan's foreign policy and a vehicle for its implementation. For every civilian and military government, control of the ISI was seen as crucial to maintaining a firm grip on power. The agency had been so powerful for so long that it played by its own rules. Its various heads had contrasting profiles, but emerged among the most powerful figures in the country's establishment. For years they ran semi-independent operations in Afghanistan and Kashmir and helped to form and topple civilian governments.

For more than two decades the ISI had sponsored Islamic militancy to carry out its secret wars. It was a crucial partner in the CIA's biggest covert operation ever, one that forced the Soviet Union to pull out of Afghanistan and served as a catalyst to the disintegration of the communist superpower. In Afghanistan, as well as Kashmir, the agency discovered the effectiveness of covert warfare as a method of bleeding a stronger adversary, while maintaining the element of plausible deniability. The ISI falls directly within Pakistan's military chain of command and had also served as an instrument for promoting the military's domestic political agenda and the guardian of its self-professed 'ideological frontiers' of the country. Almost all ISI officers are regular military personnel, who are rotated in and out for a fixed tenure. However, there have been some exceptions. The export of jihad sponsored by the ISI had its blowback. It had allowed the Islamists a huge space for their activities. State patronage, in the form of an 'unholy alliance' between the military and the mullahs, resulted in an unprecedented rise of radical Islam. The ISI had helped to create much of the Islamic militancy and religious extremism that Musharraf was confronted with. That unholy alliance had been a major factor in the country's drift to Islamic fundamentalism. Founded in 1948 by a British army officer, Major-General R. Cawthome, then Deputy Chief of Army Staff in Pakistan, the agency was initially charged with performing all intelligence tasks at home and abroad. Its scope of operation extended to all areas related to national security. Until the 1960s, the ISI largely remained an obscure organization that confined itself to playing its specified role. But in the mid 1970s its scope was expanded to domestic politics. Ironically, it was a civilian leader, Zulfikar Ali Bhutto who created the ISI's internal wing which played a critical role in the ousting of his government a few years later. It was to cast its heavy shadow over the country's politics in later years.

A charismatic and populist leader, Bhutto took over a humiliated military and a brutally truncated Pakistan in search of a new identity, following the Indian-supported secession of East Pakistan (now Bangladesh), in 1971. The country had been dismembered by civil war and Indian military action. It was no longer the country created by Mohammed Ali Jinnah. The Pakistan that emerged from the ashes of defeat required a different geopolitical orientation. A revolt by young Turks in the army in the aftermath of a humiliating defeat in the war had forced the military ruler, General Yahya Khan, 3 to hand over power to Bhutto. His legitimacy was rooted in the country's first democratically held elections in 1970. Bhutto's socialist Pakistan People's Party had swept the fateful polls in the western wing of then-united Pakistan, trouncing the right-wing Islamic parties.

The scion of a feudal family of Sindh and a former foreign minister, Bhutto was seen as the savior of the new Pakistan. He successfully negotiated with India the release of 90,000 troops taken prisoner by Indian forces. He had come to power with the largest support base of any Pakistani leader since the inception of the country in 1947.

But he failed to sustain the confidence of the nation. Bhutto was ideally placed to put into practice the objective of social democracy and develop secular ideas and institutions. But it did not happen. Bhutto's strategy was to bring the disparate elements of this divided society together through a kind of Islamic nationalism, which was then supposed to create the cohesion and stability necessary for socialist economic reforms, but unfortunately all Bhutto succeeded in doing was to rehabilitate religious extremism. Under pressure from the religious parties whose cooperation they were courting, Bhutto's government increased the religious content in school syllabuses and, succumbing to pressure from Saudi Arabia as well as to the demands of religious parties, declared the Ahmedis, an Islamic sect, to be non-Muslim. This apparently minor action had long-term implications for the country as it fuelled Islamic zealotry and sharpened the sectarian divide. Bhutto's attempt to co-opt religious elements merely emboldened them, and eventually the clergy joined hands with their traditional ally, the military, to plot the overthrow of his government. Bhutto's attempt to establish an authoritarian rule led him to rely more and more on the coercive apparatus of the state and the intelligence agencies.

Bhutto did little to strengthen democratic institutions and to make the process of democratic reform irreversible. Instead, his entire effort was aimed at promoting a personalized rule. He did not trust anyone. Given his overwhelming paranoia and insecurity, Bhutto geared up the ISI to keep surveillance not only on his opponents, but also on his own party men and cabinet ministers. The agency kept dossiers on politicians, bureaucrats, judges and anyone else considered important. The collapse of democratic institutions and the Constitution's loss of sanctity created a vacuum of authority that provided a favourable condition for the Bonapartist generals. Bhutto's use of the army to crush the uprising in Pakistan's western province of Balochistan provided an opportunity to the military to reassert itself in the country's politics. Bhutto's politics of expediency and attempts to appease the country's religious lobby allowed the Islamists, who were routed in the 1971 elections, to revive themselves. A nationwide agitation, led by right wing Islamic parties in the aftermath of the controversial elections in 1977, shook his government. In a desperate attempt to appease the Islamists, Bhutto prohibited the sale and use of alcoholic beverages, banned gambling and closed down nightclubs. But the die had already been cast.

Bhutto had handpicked General Zia ul-Haq, a lesser-known officer, for the post of army chief in 1976 over the heads of half a dozen senior officers, believing he did not have any personal ambitions. General Zia was a devout Muslim and Bhutto thought he would never betray his trust. Once elevated to the top position, the General did not take much time to develop secret contacts with hardline religious groups and conspired with them to overthrow his benefactor. On 5 July 1977, a bloodless military coup brought an end to Bhutto's six-and-a-half-year civilian rule. There was a complete convergence of interests between the Islamists and the military leadership which had ousted the Bhutto government. Several accounts of Bhutto's last days in power revealed that

Major-General Ghulam Jilani, Bhutto's handpicked chief of the ISI, played a key role in the coup plan. Two years later, in April 1979, Bhutto was hanged after a dubious trial on charges of murdering a political rival. A secularist, elected with an overwhelming mandate in 1970, Bhutto probably had the best chance of any leader of taking on the Islamists and winning. His inglorious demise can only fill Pakistan's current leader, attempting a similar task, with foreboding.

Bhutto's usurper, General Zia, came from a humble lowermiddle-class background. His father, a religious man, held a clerical government post during British rule in India. Despite his poverty, he provided his son with a decent education. Zia was educated at Delhi's most prestigious St Stephen's College before getting a commission in the Royal Indian Army in 1942. He was a captain at the time of the creation of Pakistan in 1947. He was a hard-working officer, but lacked brilliance. Many of his colleagues believed he was lucky to be promoted beyond Colonel. From a young age, Zia was actively involved with the popular religious movement, Tablighi Jamaat, 6 one of the most influential grassroots Islamic movements in the South Asian subcontinent, which had hardline traditionalist views on the role of Islam in modern society.

A short man with a thick moustache, Zia bore a strong resemblance to the British comedian, Terry-Thomas. But he was by no means a fool. He was shrewd enough to know how to make his way up. He convinced Bhutto of his absolute loyalty and more importantly of his incapacity to be otherwise. Zia was not only an authoritarian; he also aspired to turn Pakistan into an ideological state ruled by strict Islamic sharia laws. He was an unpopular and controversial leader, whose survival in power largely owed to the external factors that emerged after the invasion by Soviet forces of Pakistan's northern neighbour, Afghanistan, in 1979. Pakistan became a frontline state and a bulwark in the West's war against communism.

General Zia brought in his close confidant, Lt.-General Akhter Abdur Rehman, to head the ISI in 1979, as the spy agency became a crucial cog in the resistance against the Soviet forces. Its tentacles started to spread far and wide. An artillery officer, General Rehman 'had a cold, reserved personality, almost inscrutable, always secretive, with no intimates except his family.' His officers remembered him as a hard man to serve due to his brusque manner and reputation as a strict disciplinarian. 'That made him an ideal man for the job,' said Brigadier Mohammed Yousuf, a former ISI officer who served under him. General Rehman ran the organization until 1987. He was not a radical Islamist, but a staunch Muslim nationalist. Under General Rehman, the ISI, in partnership with the CIA, conducted the biggest covert operation in modern history. The two organizations had secretly collaborated for years, yet General Zia was not prepared to give a free hand to the CIA. He laid down strict rules to ensure that the ISI would maintain control over contacts with Afghan mujahidin groups. No CIA operatives would be allowed to cross the border into Afghanistan. Distribution of weapons to the Afghan commanders would be handled only by the ISI. All training of mujahidin would be the sole responsibility of the ISI. While the CIA supplied money and weapons, it was the ISI that moved them into Afghanistan. The Americans relied almost entirely on the Pakistani service to allocate weapons to the mujahidin groups. The framework provided the Pakistani spy agency with almost total control over the covert operation inside Afghanistan. The decade-long secret war raised the organization's profile and gave it huge clout. With the active help of the CIA and Saudi Arabia, the ISI turned the Afghan resistance into Islam's holy war.

The decade-long conflict in Afghanistan gave the Islamic extremists a rallying point and a training field. Young Muslims around the world flocked to Afghanistan to fight against a foreign invader. Some 35,000 holy warriors joined the Afghan war from 1979 to 1989. The largest number came from the Middle East. Some were Saudis, among whom was a young man called Osama bin Laden.

The 23-year-old son of a wealthy construction magnate said he arrived in Peshawar for the first time in 1980. He was a very shy person who had no experience of war and, as a fresh graduate from the King Abdul Aziz University, bin Laden had left the luxury of his home to help the mujahidin fighting jihad in

Afghanistan. It was the beginning of his long association with Afghan and Pakistani Islamic radicals. By 1984 he was spending most of his time in Peshawar, sometimes with Abdullah Azzam, a Palestinian Islamic scholar and an ideologue who inspired the rush of foreign Muslims to fight in Afghanistan. It was also during this period that he developed links with the ISI, which had become the main conduit for arms and training for the Islamic warriors. The Afghan war placed enormous resources at the agency's disposal. Weapons provided by the CIA were channelled to Afghan fighters through the ISI. By the mid 1980s, every dollar given by the CIA was matched by another from Saudi Arabia. The funds, running into several million dollars a year, were transferred by the CIA to the ISI's special accounts in Pakistan. The backing of the CIA and the funnelling of massive amounts of US military aid helped the ISI develop into 'a parallel structure wielding enormous power over all aspects of government.' It became all-pervasive and there was an unprecedented expansion in the surveillance of political opponents.

Even those in the army were not spared. According to a former senior intelligence officer, part of the ISI's function was to keep a careful watch on the generals and ensure their loyalty to the regime. In the words of Brigadier Yousaf, 'So powerful had the ISI become that apprehension, even fear, of what the ISI could do, was real.' The Afghan war provided the agency with the public profile that it did not have before. Former ISI officials point out that the general expansion the agency underwent as a consequence of its Afghan role had a bearing on its overall functioning. While its role in supervising a successful covert operation in Afghanistan won the ISI international acclaim, at home it was a dreaded name.

The Afghan resistance was projected as part of the global jihad against communism. The ISI's training of guerrillas was integrated with the teaching of Islam. The prominent theme was that Islam was a complete socio-political ideology under threat from atheistic communists. The Afghan war produced a new radical Islamic movement. Besides the holy warriors from Islamic countries, thousands more joined madrasas set up with funding from Saudi Arabia and some other Muslim countries. More than 100,000 foreign

Muslim radicals were directly influenced by the Afghan jihad. The military's involvement in the politics of religion, however, had started long before the Afghan jihad. General Zia not only ushered Pakistan into its longest period of military rule, but also tried to turn the country into an ideological state. He extended the army's role in domestic politics much further than defined by earlier military rulers. Previously, the military was seen as the ultimate guarantor of the country's territorial integrity and internal security. But Zia expanded its role as the defender of Pakistan's ideological frontiers as well.

Addressing army officers, Zia argued that, as Pakistan was created on the basis of the two-nation theory and Islamic ideology, it was the duty of the 'soldiers of Islam to safeguard its security, integrity and sovereignty at all costs, both from internal turmoil and external aggression'. He claimed the state was created exclusively to provide its people with the opportunity to follow 'the Islamic way of life.' Preservation of the country's Islamic character was seen to be as important as the security of the country's geographical frontiers. Zia's military rule differed by its very serious attempt to create an ideological basis for all areas of activities of the state and society. General Zia cleverly used Islam to consolidate his power and legitimize his military rule. The Islamization process became the most important feature of his eleven- year rule and its raison d'e^tre. For General Zia, Pakistan was an Islamic ideological state and therefore politics could not be separated from religion. He believed that he had a divine obligation to establish an Islamic society ruled in accordance with the Qur'an and sharia. Afraid to face a free electorate and having no mandate to govern, the General turned to Allah. He introduced a rigid interpretation of Islamic sharia, thus empowering the clergy. The move to Islamize the state found ready allies among the religious parties, many of which already had close ties with the military. The Jamaat-i-Islami and other Islamic groups were co-opted by the government. For the first time in Pakistan's history, the Islamists occupied important government positions. Being in power helped Jamaat-i-Islami, the most influential and organized mainstream religious party, penetrate state institutions. Thousands of party activists and sympathizers were given jobs in the judiciary, the civil service and educational institutions. These appointments strengthened the hold of the Islamists on crucial state apparatuses for many years to come.

The process of the Islamization of the state and society took place on two levels. Firstly, changes were instituted in the legal system. Sharia courts were established to try cases under Islamic laws. For the first time, the government assumed the role of the collector of religious taxes. Secondly, Islamization was promoted through the print media, radio, television and mosques. Through a series of religious decrees, the government moved to Islamize the civil service, the armed forces and the education system. School textbooks were overhauled to ensure their ideological purity. Books deemed un-Islamic were removed from syllabuses and university libraries. It was made compulsory for civil servants to pray five times a day. Confidential reports of government officials included a section in which the staff were given marks for regularly attending prayers and for having a good knowledge of Islam. General Zia's move to Islamize the army carried the most critical implications. Pakistan's army, carved out of the British Indian army, inherited British traditions and remained a secular organization until General Zia tried to give it a new Islamic orientation. Islam was incorporated into the army's organizational fabric. For the first time Islamic teachings were introduced into the Pakistan Military Academy.

Islamic training and philosophy were made a part of the curriculum at the Command and Staff College. A Directorate of Religious Instruction was instituted to educate the officer corps on Islam. Islamic education also became a part of the promotion exams. The officers were required to read The Quranic Concept of War, a book written by a serving officer, Brigadier S. K. Malik. The officers were taught to be not just professional soldiers, but also soldiers of Islam. In his foreword to the book, General Zia wrote: 'The professional soldier in a Muslim army, pursuing the goals of a Muslim State, cannot become "professional" if in all his activities he does not take on "the colour of Allah".' To gain promotion an officer was required to be a devout Muslim. Scores of highly professional and secular officers were sidelined for not meeting the criterion of a 'good Muslim'. As a consequence of this policy, many conservative officers reached the senior command level. Radical Islamist ideology permeated the army with the free flow of religious political literature in the armed forces training institutions. Friday prayers at regimental mosques, a matter of individual choice in the past, became obligatory. Mullahs belonging to the Deobandi sect were appointed to work among the troops.

They were supposed to be the bridge for officers between the westernized profession and the faith. Units were required to take noncombatant mullahs with them to the front line. Soldiers were encouraged to attend 'Tablighi' gatherings. The purpose was to indoctrinate cadets and young officers with an obscurantist interpretation of Islam. Many of those cadets later rose to positions of power and took control of sensitive institutions, including the ISI. The change in the social composition of the officer corps also led to the ideological reorientation of Pakistan's army in the 1980s. The army officer corps, till the 1970s, was elitist in character and composition. But the trend changed. In the past, members of the upper class or the rural aristocracy had largely dominated the army ranks; now the new officers mostly came from the lower and middle social strata. The rank and file of junior officers since the 1970s had come, not from prosperous central Punjab, but from the impoverished and relatively backward northern districts where a fundamentalist religious ethos prevailed. Unlike their predecessors, the new officers did not come from elite English-language schools, but were the product of modest state-run educational institutions. The spirit of liberalism, common in the 'old' army, was practically unknown to them. They were products of a social class that, by its very nature, was conservative and easily influenced by Islamic fundamentalism. They were distinctively less westernized.

Their narrow nationalist orientation and education, professional training and culture made them very receptive to the influence of Islamic groups, particularly to the Jamaat-i-Islami (JI), which freely carried out propaganda work among the officers and circulated Islamic literature. Most importantly, the JI's propaganda among vast numbers of troops was officially sanctioned by commanding officers on the battalion level and above. That led to the evolution of a long-lasting alliance between the military and the mosque. The main objective of the JI was to penetrate the army and use it to seize state power. The practice introduced by General Zia of sending combat officers to universities in Pakistan, in which the JI often had pervasive influence, facilitated the party's objective. The influence of the JI was particularly visible among officers from rural and semi-urban backgrounds. They had a high level of religious intolerance and held extremist views regarding 'external enemies' and the threat to Islam.

The number of officers sporting beards for religious reasons had visibly risen. These young officers constituted the main base for General Zia's regime. According to a retired general, 25 to 30 per cent of the officers had Islamic fundamentalist leanings. Many of them regularly attended 'Tablighi' groups that propagated the faith. They would take time off to join missionary bands preaching a return to purist Islamic values and recruiting other Muslim men to join them. Thousands of soldiers and army officers would join the annual gathering of the TJ at Raiwind on the outskirts of Lahore. More than one million faithful from across the country and abroad attend this Muslim congregation, the largest after the Haj in Mecca. Even the liberals adopted the philosophy on issues like jihad and support for militancy in Kashmir. The humiliating military defeat by the Indian army in the 1971 war, coupled with the disintegration of the country, also had a very deep impact on the psyche of army officers. Many young officers turned to religion for solace and became born-again Muslims. Given this situation, it was not surprising that radical Islamic officers made unsuccessful coup attempts in the mid 1980s. They wanted to bring about an Islamic revolution and establish a theocratic state. The fact that the attempts were crushed and the rebel officers were charged with treason indicated that, notwithstanding its Islamization, the state was not prepared to tolerate a theocratic rule.

The situation in Afghanistan provided inspiration to a whole generation of Pakistani Islamic radicals who considered it their religious duty to fight the oppression of Muslims anywhere in the world. It gave a new dimension to the idea of jihad, which till then had only been employed by the Pakistani state in the context of mobilizing the population against the arch rival – India. The Afghan war saw the privatization of the concept of jihad. Militant groups emerged from the ranks of traditional religious movements, who took the path of an armed struggle for the cause of Islam. The ISI's active role in the Afghan jihad brought Pakistani army officers into direct contact with the radical Islamists.

The handling of jihad also indoctrinated the military and intelligence officers. At least two former ISI chiefs – General Hamid Gul and General Javed Nasir – remained actively involved with Islamic radical movements. Both promoted pan-Islamism and strove for an Islamic revolution that would free Pakistan from perceived western, and particularly American, cultural and political influences. General Gul, who liked to call himself a 'Muslim visionary', succeeded General Rehman in 1987 when the Afghan resistance had entered its most critical juncture. The most charismatic of the ISI chiefs, he openly aligned himself with the hardline Afghan mujahidin leader, Gulbuddin Hekmatyar, and right-wing Pakistani Islamic parties. He would later take credit for dismantling the Soviet Union. General Gul had worked closely with the CIA, but turned anti-American after the Geneva Accord in 1987, which paved the way for the withdrawal of Soviet forces from Afghanistan. The Accord was signed by the Pakistani civilian government led by Prime Minister Mohammed Khan Junejo against the wishes of President Zia, who believed it deprived the Afghan mujahidin of the opportunity to take over Kabul. Resentment among the military and ISI officers deepened in 1990, just one year after the Soviets pulled out of Afghanistan and the US administration imposed sanctions on Pakistan for its nuclear programme. The CIA ended its support for the Afghan rebels and its links with the ISI went cold. It was a sudden end to the strong link between the two agencies. The military leadership accused the United States of dumping Pakistan after the collapse of the Soviet Union. Long before the Afghan war was over, General Gul had started organizing a new jihad front in Kashmir. 'It is the years of our work that has realized the armed uprising against the Indian forces in Kashmir,' he told me in early 1990 when he was commanding the country's elite armoured corps.

The death of General Zia ul-Haq in a mysterious air crash in August 1988 brought an end to Pakistan's longest-serving military government. It left the generals with the choice of either imposing martial law again or holding elections and transferring power to a democratically elected civilian government. They went for the second option, realizing that a perpetuation of military rule might provoke public resistance and exacerbate the turmoil in an already highly polarised society. However, the generals were not prepared to pull out completely and leave the political field solely to the politicians, particularly to the daughter of Zulfikar Ali Bhutto, Benazir Bhutto, who now led the Pakistan People's Party, which was certain to sweep the polls. To contain Benazir, the military cobbled together the Islamic Democratic Alliance (IDA), uniting all the right-wing parties under the leadership of Nawaz Sharif. General Aslam Beg, then Chief of Army Staff, and General Gul justified the move by saying it was necessary for the viable functioning of a democratic system.

The main objective, however, was to ensure the military's continued role in the new system, overseen by the generals. By creating a counterbalance in the form of the IDA, the generals constrained the new government of a political party that had led the resistance against military hegemony for ten years. The military-sponsored alliance comprised a mix of traditional power brokers, religious parties and politicians who had emerged on the scene during the 1980s under military patronage. General Zia's regime, needing a measure of legitimacy and a social base of support, had co-opted segments of Punjab's dominant socio-economic strata: influential landlords, industrialists and emerging commercial groups. The new leadership of the Pakistan Muslim League thus largely consisted of politicians who owed their political rise to the military's backing. The other important components of the alliance were the right-wing Islamic groups, including the Jamaat-i-Islami, which had been involved in the Afghan jihad against the Soviet forces and the separatist war in Indian-controlled Kashmir.

While the IDA, which carried General Zia's legacy, could not achieve any significant electoral gains in the 1988 elections in the three smaller provinces, it did relatively well in Punjab and prevented the PPP from winning an absolute majority in the National Assembly. The military reluctantly handed over power to Benazir at the centre, but prevented her party from forming the government in Punjab, the biggest and most important of Pakistan's four provinces, which was being ruled by Nawaz Sharif. Political manipulation by the ISI helped Sharif retain power in the province with the support of independent members. Benazir Bhutto's assumption of power, touted at the time as the dawn of a new democratic era, was in fact a transition from direct to indirect military rule. The formal restoration of civilian rule in 1988 did not reduce the ISI's clout. A return to the barracks did not mean that the military's structure of control and manipulation had been dismantled. The ISI still kept a close watch on civilian rulers. The strains in civil and military relationships remained the biggest obstacle to democracy taking root in Pakistan.

# Bibliography


Ahmed, Akbar S.: *Jinnah, Pakistan, and Islamic Identity: The Search for Saladin,* 1997.

Akbar S.: *Jinnah, Pakistan, and Islamic Identity: The Search for Saladin,* 1997.

Allison, Graham, *Nuclear Terrorism: The Ultimate Preventable Catastrophe,* New York: Times Books, 2004.

Azad, Maulana Abul Kalam: *India Wins Freedom,* New Delhi, Orient Longman, 1959.

Barbara D. Metcalf : *Islamic Revival in British India: 1860-1900,* Princeton, New Jersey: Princeton University Press, 1982.

Behera, Navnita : *State, identity and violence : Jammu, Kashmir and Laddakh,* New Delhi: Manohar, 2000.

Bhalla, Alok: *Stories about the Partition of India,* New Delhi: HarperCollins, 1994.

Chitkara, M.G. : *Indo-Pak Relations Challenges Before New Millennium,* APH, Delhi, 2001.

Choueiri, Y.M. : *Islamic Fundamentalism,* London: Pinter Publishers; Delhi, 1990.

Das. P.K.: *Jihad : Terrorist Strategies Against the West,* Sumit Enterprises, Delhi, 2009.

Dekmejian, R. Hrair : *Islamic Revolution: Fundamentalism in the Arab World* Syracuse, New York: Syracuse University Press, 1995.

Noorani, A.G.: *Islam and Jihad,* Leftword, Delhi, 2002.

Riedel, Bruce: *Deadly Embrace : Pakistan America and the Future of the Global Jihad,* HarperCollins, Delhi, 2011.

Seyyed Vali Reza Nasr: *The Vanguard of the Islamic Revolution: The Jama'at i-Islami of Pakistan,* Berkeley and Los Angeles, California: University of California Press, 1994.

Sharma, Rajeev: *Global Jihad : Current Patterns and Future Trends,* Kaveri Books, Delhi, 2006.

# Index

❑❑❑